MY HOUSE SHALL BE A HOUSE OF PRAYER

Lessons from the School of Prayer

Lance Lambert

First Printing May 2011
Second Printing July 2011
Third Printing September 2013
Fourth Printing June 2014

Available from:

Christian Testimony Ministry
4424 Huguenot Road
Richmond, Virginia 23235

www.christiantestimonyministry.com

ISBN 978-0-9895326-1-7

Printed in USA

CONTENTS

INTRODUCTION

The Lord Jesus described the conditions which would exist before His return, when He prophesied: *There shall be signs in sun and moon and stars; and upon the earth distress of nations, in perplexity for the roaring of the sea and the billows; men fainting for fear, and for expectation of the things which are coming on the world: for the powers of the heavens shall be shaken. And then shall they see the Son of man coming in a cloud with power and great glory. But when these things begin to come to pass, look up, lift up your heads; because your redemption draweth nigh* (Luke 21:25-28).

If we consider the Lord's description of the end of the age with a sober and a sound mind, we have to recognise that in all probability we are at the beginning of this period. In another prophecy He referred to the upheavals, the turmoil, the conflict, and the physical disasters, as the birth pangs of the coming Kingdom. In the previous prophecy above He declared: *When these things begin to come to pass, look up, lift up your heads; because your redemption draweth nigh.*

If that is true, then there has never been a time when effective prayer and intercession could be more strategic, more necessary, and more essential than now. In relation to the return of the Lord and the events that would precede it, He told us emphatically to **watch and pray**, and to make supplication to Him. The sad fact is that the Church in the Western nations is by and large complacent; it is lukewarm and in a Laodicean condition. At this time of crisis and confusion, when even more than normal genuine intercession is required, the Church is impotent. Corporate intercession is almost a lost art—and that when we most need it!

For those who have an ear to hear the Lord, we hear His heart cry: *I sought for a man among them, that should build up the wall, and stand in the gap before me for the land, that I should not destroy it; but I found none* (Ezekiel 22:30). It is the call and challenge of the Lord. Will anyone respond to His call and challenge?

This is the reason for this book. It has grown out of a series of messages given some years ago at the fellowship in Halford House, Richmond, Surrey, England, in what was termed a "School of Prayer." In a number of places in different parts of the world I led similar Schools of Prayer. In all these times we emphasised the necessity of corporate prayer and intercession, which is so little understood, and so little taught.

The greatest danger in this book is that it will be used as a blueprint, as a "methods" book for prayer, a methodology for prayer and intercession, or a kind of prayer "pattern" book. To start such groups of corporate intercession and prayer is excellent, but to set them up in a legalistic manner, based on this book, will lead to lifelessness. In fact, I always refused to lead a School of Prayer unless the people of God in that place were already praying together. In such groups there was already some experience of corporate prayer and intercession, however poor the experience may have been. Then what was said became a pruning of what was unnecessary, a pinpointing of what was wrong, an encouragement of what was right, and a challenge to go further in corporate prayer and intercession.

In all the worldwide shaking that is taking place on every level, may the people of God hear His call to corporate prayer and intercession, and accept His challenge. May the Lord bless and use this book to the fulfilment of such a purpose.

I wish to thank those who have helped in the producing of this book. Nathan Gosling who typed this manuscript and made suggestions helpful and otherwise! Richard Briggs, and Benjamin Chase, who took care of all the practical matters to do with the house, the cooking and the garden, in Naxos, Greece. Finally I wish to thank Joshua Fiddy, and Ernesto Schintu, who took care of the Jerusalem home whilst we were writing the book.

Lance Lambert
Jerusalem March 2011

1
THE CHARACTER OF CORPORATE PRAYER

I Timothy 2:1-4—I exhort therefore, first of all, that supplications, prayers, intercessions, thanksgivings, be made for all men; for kings and all that are in high place; that we may lead a tranquil and quiet life in all godliness and gravity. This is good and acceptable in the sight of God our Savior; who would have all men to be saved, and come to the knowledge of the truth.

This book is not dealing with private or personal prayer but rather with corporate prayer; and although I shall make references now and again to private prayer, they will be few. I will confine myself to the subject of corporate prayer which is so little understood and so little taught. Indeed, it seems that it is almost a lost art. For example, there are hardly any books written on corporate prayer. There are a multitude of books written on personal prayer and private devotions, but I know of only three books on corporate prayer. One is Arthur Wallis's *Prayer in the Spirit*, and even that is dealing more with personal prayer than corporate. The second is Stephen Kaung's book entitled, *Teach us to Pray* which is extremely valuable. The third is Watchman Nee's book entitled, *The Prayer Ministry of the Church*. This is a simple but clear book on the necessity of corporate prayer, and I strongly recommend it.

Another most valuable and helpful book on corporate intercession is Pat Hughes and Gay Hyde's book, *Helps to Intercession and Spiritual Warfare*. Another valuable book which illustrates the principles of corporate prayer is Norman Grubb's biography of Rees Howells entitled, *Rees Howells, Intercessor*. It is a living illustration of corporate prayer, and particularly of corporate intercession, drawn from that one life and the community of God's people that came together in Derwen Fawr, in Wales.

It would be helpful at the beginning of this book to define what is meant by the term *corporate prayer* and *intercession.* It is obvious from the use of the word "corporate" that it is the prayer and intercession of the body of Christ, the Church. The members of His body are in living touch with the Head, the Lord Jesus, under the direction of the Spirit of God in prayer and intercession. It requires a minimum of at least two people. It may be ten, or twenty, or fifty, or more, who are engaged in such corporate prayer or intercession. It cannot be corporate if it is one child of God alone.

It is a very sad fact that one can count on the fingers of one hand the groups, including charismatics, who really know how to pray. Of course, there must be companies of which I am unaware, but I think it is sad evidence for the lost art of corporate prayer. There are many prayer meetings, but there are very few companies of believers who really know how to move together in prayer under the leadership of the Holy Spirit, and how to pray a matter through to Divine fulfilment.

The powers of darkness have worked so insidiously and powerfully that many prayer meetings are anything but *prayer* meetings. In many of them prayer is tacked on to the end of a Bible study. (Alan Redpath used to say years ago, that if you have the Bible study and the prayer meeting on the same night, you have neither a proper Bible study nor a proper prayer meeting.) Sometimes, it is just ten minutes at the end of an evening. Other times, a tremendous amount of information is given at a prayer meeting, and the time for prayer is wasted, leaving only ten or fifteen minutes for prayer. There are also weeks when believers from different denominations come together for corporate prayer. In the end, forty-five to fifty minutes of ministry on prayer is given, leaving only fifteen to thirty minutes for prayer.

WE WRESTLE NOT AGAINST FLESH OR BLOOD

Whole companies of God's people are paralyzed or blockaded by the powers of darkness, and the work of God is rendered very largely ineffective. For whether we like it or not, God's Word tells us: *Our wrestling is not against flesh and blood, but against the principalities, against the powers, against the world-rulers of this darkness, against the spiritual hosts of wickedness in the heavenly places* (see Ephesians 6:12). We are told to take the whole armour of God and having done all to stand. And we are to take the sword of the Spirit and pray at all seasons with all prayer and supplication in the Spirit.

So often, we think we are only up against flesh and blood. We see the apathy of our neighbourhood; we see the indifference of the people around us; we see some kind of hardness against all evangelistic outreach. Sometimes, there are difficult Christians in key positions who appear to block everything. Then we often come to the conclusion that it is *flesh and blood* which is the blockage. Sometimes, we believe that it is either the pastor, some other leader in the congregation, or some child of God who has gone wrong in some way. Our mentality is that it is always flesh and blood which is the root cause of the problem. Of course, the enemy uses flesh and blood, but the Word of God says: *We wrestle not against flesh and blood,* **but** *against principalities, against powers, against the world-rulers of this darkness, against the spiritual hosts of wickedness in the heavenly places.*

PRINCIPALITIES, POWERS AND WORLD-RULERS

What are *principalities* and *powers*? Principalities are princes or rulers, who are not physical but spiritual beings. Powers are authorities. What are *world-rulers of this darkness*? It means that behind flesh and blood, behind ideologies, behind new philosophies, behind new current ideas, there are spiritual powers that are ruling the present spiritual darkness and holding in their captivity thousands of people. It can be false religion or false philosophy. Whole civic communities, even nations, can be kept in bondage to darkness by these spiritual forces. Even new current ideas which contradict the Word of God can be the result of spiritual authorities or spiritual world rulers. Local churches can be subjected to a blockade and finally paralyzed and crushed by the enemy. If God's dear children do not wake up, the enemy will sit on them and smother any spiritual life or power. These princes, these powers, these world rulers of darkness, are the great spiritual beings with whom we wrestle. Even if we take this matter at the minimal, the true Church of God and the true believer is wrestling with spiritual forces of wickedness, hosts of wicked spirits in the heavenlies. Is this a fairy tale belonging to the distant past when people believed in hobgoblins and demons? Or is it the Word of God revealing the real nature of our warfare? As the redeemed people of God in the twenty-first century, if we do not wake up to the real nature of the battle, we are destined to fail in all our endeavours and become, finally, spiritual casualties.

After all, the apostle Paul did not say, "We are playing in a tennis championship with Satan;" but he said, *Our **wrestling**... is against principalities, against powers, against the world-rulers of this darkness*. Wrestling is an impolite sport. It is not just some polite and sophisticated tennis match where one hits the ball back and forth, back and forth, and marks up the points, saying: "We have done well today; the enemy is beaten." Through the apostle Paul the Holy Spirit uses this illustration of a more violent and impolite contact sport—wrestling. That involves much sweat and at times even blood. It means that one may have his arm twisted up his back by his opponent, or his leg nearly torn off, or he may be flung to the other side of the ring and the next moment have some heavyweight sitting on him.

SPIRITUAL SOLDIERS IN A SPIRITUAL BATTLE

Many Christians, however, do not seem to think in this way. They believe that the Christian life should be one long joy ride, and we should have a wonderful and bubbly experience continuously. If there is any sense of the enemy's presence, then something must be wrong. Now we must thank the Lord for those wonderful and ecstatic experiences of Him, those spiritual blessings with which we are blessed in our Lord Jesus, and which are normal to Christian life and work. Nevertheless, we are spiritual soldiers in a spiritual battle and the fact that there are times when spiritual beings come against us and the work of the Lord, it is no evidence that we are in the wrong place or in the wrong way. Indeed, it may be evidence that we are in the centre of His will. There are times when those powers of darkness will seek to blockade us or lay siege to us, when they will sit on us or seemingly hold us in a vice-like grip. If, however, you have ever watched a wrestling match, you will know that just because some heavyweight is sitting on another heavyweight, it does not mean that he has won the match. The one underneath may rise up and proceed to win the whole match.

INTERCESSION IS THE KEY TO PARALYSING THE ENEMY AND ADVANCING GOD'S KINGDOM

So what does it mean to wrestle with these powers? Surely it means that somewhere there has to be a ministry of intercession. Before we can see a civil community broken open to the power and working of God, some believers have to go behind the scenes and paralyse the enemy. Our Lord Jesus said: *Or how can anyone enter the strong man's house and carry off his property, unless he first binds the strong man? And then he will plunder his house* (Matthew 12:29 NASB). We tend to think that as long as we have good preaching or a well organised evangelistic crusade, people will automatically be set free and saved. But one can have all of that and discover that one is up against an insurmountable and impassable wall. The more spiritually vital a work is, the more likely it will be that the enemy will seek to come in, sit on it, and paralyse it. He will not stand back and let you have a good time if

9

there is any chance that there will be a permanent and powerful breakthrough. The many great moves of the Spirit of God in the history of nations is evidence enough of this.

Therefore we have to understand this very simple fact: there can be no matter more strategically vital to the true Church of God and the work of the Lord than this matter of corporate prayer. In the days that lie ahead, during the last phase of world history, we shall need to know how to pray together. Furthermore, should real persecution come in the decades that lie ahead and should we lose our liberty, then we need to know how we can break through together, and see the fulfilment of God's purpose even in times of enormous difficulty.

LEARNING THE LESSONS OF CORPORATE PRAYER

We need to learn the lessons of corporate prayer and intercession now whilst we have time. Unless the Spirit of God has burnt into us these lessons, we shall be found lacking in the day of crisis. It is as necessary therefore for new Christians, as well as for those of us who are older in the Lord, to learn these lessons, however hard or costly they may be. Some of us who are older have learnt such bad habits in prayer that they have become second nature to us. If we feel that we are in this condition, we often think it is impossible to learn the right way to pray together. Nevertheless, the Lord can keep all that is best and most valuable in our background and can overcome all the bad habits, if we will only trust Him and be open to the correction of the Holy Spirit. The basis of all learning is to be meek. The moment a believer says I do not need that correction or realignment, that person ceases to learn.

It is not that I desire for you to swallow everything I write, but I want you to take it all back to the Lord and ask Him. Let Him sort it out in our hearts. My desire is simple! We need to learn how to use this colossally effective weapon which God has placed in the hands of His Church.

FOUR KINDS OF PRAYER

In I Timothy 2:1 the apostle Paul defines four kinds of prayer which cover all aspects of prayer. It is interesting that each of these four words is used in the plural—supplications, prayers, intercessions, thanksgivings. Furthermore, the apostle Paul by the Holy Spirit is so burdened about the importance of this matter that he urges and exhorts the people of God to pray. He sees such prayer and intercession as being of paramount importance to the health of the Church and the progress of the work of God.

Supplications

The first aspect of prayer is the word translated by the English word *supplications*. It primarily means "a need." The Authorized Version, the Revised Version, the American Standard Version, and the Revised Standard Version all use the word *supplications*. The New American Standard Bible uses the word *entreaties*. The reason is that the word primarily means a need, and then an asking, an entreaty or a beseeching concerning that need. This is not just asking something of God; it is something more. It is an earnest appeal, or entreaty, or beseeching of the Lord that we might understand His mind and will. This is the best way we can understand the word *supplications*. It is because of a need that there is an enquiry of the Lord, an earnest beseeching of Him that He would reveal His mind concerning that need.

Why is so much prayer ineffectual? Why is it that so often when we go into a prayer meeting and come out of it, we have to pull ourselves together and declare: "God does hear prayer"? It is because there is a witness within our Spirit that testifies that most of that prayer did not go beyond the ceiling. The problem is that we never stopped to enquire of the Lord, not even for a single moment. Instead we plunged into prayer matters without any direction from the Spirit of God. For this reason supplication is the first aspect of prayer because, obviously, it is the most fundamental. Unless we earnestly enquire of the Lord on the basis of the urgent needs which confront us, we shall never know His mind about them. Therefore, because we do not know His mind, we shall be threshing around in prayer, using many words and getting nowhere.

Enquiry of the Lord is fundamental to all prayer. We cannot pray aright or use the provided weapons of our warfare unless we first know the Lord's mind on the matter. Then the Spirit of God will lead us to the Scriptures we should use. When we have enquired of the Lord, and He has given us the sword of the Spirit which is the Word of God, we do not have to play around. We do not have to spend half an hour making noises or saying all sorts of lovely scriptural phrases which have no application to the need in hand.

Sometimes the Lord will give that word to one person and we only need to arise and take up that word once it has come. The Holy Spirit will then give us all insight into that word. We will be able to pray through that whole situation with that Word from God. It is the Sword of the Spirit given to us to cut right through the problem.

The fact is that you cannot just take any Scripture and batter its fulfilment into being. You have to enquire of the Lord; and when you enquire of the Lord, and clearly hear in your spirit (and not your soul), God's "Yes," then living faith is born in us of the Spirit. Only then can we go ahead. Your mind may be assailed with doubts implanted by the enemy, but in your heart there is no doubt. You have heard the Lord's "Yes." We have therefore to enquire of the Lord and know the Lord's mind and will on all kinds of matters. This is the reason why this matter of supplication is absolutely fundamental. I do not think there is anything more that could be said to underline this matter of the necessity of supplication. It is sadly the missing link in so much corporate prayer ministry.

The Lord will not keep us endlessly waiting. He only waits for us to come to Him with an enquiring attitude, and then He will say "here is the answer." It may be a clearer understanding of the need and the Word of God which He would have us use concerning it. We have the idea that the Lord is like us, and He has to be cajoled and humoured and nursed into a nice mood. Once He is in that sweet mood, we can get out of Him all that we desire. The Lord, however, is not like that; He is more interested in certain situations than we are. He only awaits a spirit of enquiry, and then, sometimes, almost immediately, He will give clearly the direction. We should not handle prayer like a bull in a china shop or like a tank mowing everything down. We need to be still and wait on Him and for Him. We need simply to ask what His mind is on this matter. How are we to pray? What is the word that God would give us? What is the right weapon to use?

An Example Of Supplication In Action

I remember many years ago when the elders at Halford House used to meet together for prayer every Monday evening to seek the Lord. The time was open to anyone in the fellowship to come with their needs or problems or criticism. On one particular Monday a very dear sister phoned and said, "I know that this time is really for people who are a part of the fellowship, but I have a friend here who is in very great need. Do you think that she could come and see you?" We said that she should come.

This dear sister had a close walk with the Lord and was a blessing to others. She had decided, in order to reach people in very great need, to move into a very run down part of the city in which she lived. She then told us how she had been through Bible school and had felt very strongly that the Lord had called her to this task of devoting herself to reaching the needy people in that city, and He had blessed her in this work. Then suddenly she found that God was no longer speaking to her through the Bible. In fact, she felt the Lord had ceased to speak to her at all; and even when she went to a good fellowship, she found that everything that was said just went through one ear and out the other. She became more and more distressed and felt that she had committed the unpardonable sin against the Holy Spirit. It was so bad that she was tempted to take her life. It was at this point that she came to stay for a few days with her close friend. We listened to the whole story and wondered what kind of demonic activity could be involved. Why was this happening to her? Our sister could not put her finger on anything that she had done wrong or any sin which she had committed.

Now it was always our habit to begin by asking the Lord for wisdom, and we sought Him with an earnest enquiry about this sister's need. We felt that her condition was desperate in that she had nearly committed suicide. She felt that she had committed this unpardonable sin, and that this was the reason why God did not speak to her. We then felt that we should cut her off from any satanic influence and tampering with her circumstances. As we got up to pray over her, one of our very dear brothers said: "The Lord is saying something to me and I cannot understand it. Water, water, water; it is the water." I thought maybe he had taken leave of his senses, because I could not see anything about our sister's circumstances which had anything to do with water. However, I asked her as a result of this word: "Why are you wearing tinted glasses?" She replied that it was because of the headaches she received from bright light. She said: "If you want me to throw them away I will do so." But I told her: "No, keep them for now." We went on then and in the Name of Jesus cut her off from demonic influences, praying for her deliverance and healing. She was obviously touched by the Lord and went back after a few days to the city in which she lived, much relieved and joyful. It seemed that the Lord had delivered her.

She had not been back in that city for more than a week or two, when all the old problems reared their head again, and once more she was tempted to take her life. She felt that coming to us at Halford House was almost her last resort and that there was now no hope at all. Then into her head came the word of our brother: "Water, water, water; it is in the water." And she decided to take a bottle of the water from her apartment to a laboratory to have it tested. Within hours they were seeking her. Apparently there was an unbelievably high lead content in the water. She was suffering from acute lead poisoning which had completely disoriented her mind and well-being. The moment the social authorities took her out of the place in which she was living into a new place, she immediately began to recover. This is a very dramatic illustration of the need of supplication or of earnest enquiry concerning a desperate need. If we had not enquired of the Lord we would never have had the word about the "water." Then, when her health took a dive again, she could well have committed suicide. Instead the Lord intervened and delivered her.

Prayers

The second aspect is translated by the English word *prayers*. Literally, it means "a pouring out." It is the most frequently used word in the New Testament for prayer. One pours out all the need one has, all the hurt which one feels, all one's feeling. It is a simple petitioning of God. The Lord Jesus said: *You have not because you ask not*. This is the most basic comprehensive word and covers all kinds of prayer—from a pouring out of one's soul's troubles to an asking of God to meet one's needs. This can also mean a request to God for very great matters to do with His purpose, and with his will. C.T. Studd used to say: "Why ask the Lord for an egg if you can ask Him for an elephant?" In other words, ask for great things according to the faith that you have. The Lord can always say, "No!"

Prayer is basically "a hit and miss operation." You may not know what the will of the Lord is or what His purpose is, but you pour out your heart. Amy Carmichael used to say, "He can say, "Yes" or He can say, "No" or He can say, "Wait." When she was a little girl growing up in a believing home, she disliked the colour of her brown eyes. She heard from her parents that the Lord Jesus could do anything, that with Him nothing was impossible. So she asked repeatedly that He would change her eyes to blue. He never did. Many years later when she went into temples to rescue little girls from temple prostitution, she realised why the Lord never answered her prayer for blue eyes. In her sari, with her brown eyes, she blended with the Indian crowd.

This word covers the kind of prayer that is generally found amongst believers. One does not have to know what the will of the Lord is, but you can just pour out your heart and ask of Him. It is not however that the Lord despises this kind of prayer. When Hannah was in her barren state, full of emotion and feeling, she poured out her heart to the Lord. Her emotions so possessed her that Eli thought she was drunk. The Lord however heard her and touched her barrenness. She produced one of the great prophets of Israel—Samuel, who stood at one of the pivotal turning points in Divine history. Hannah even called him Samuel, "asked of God."

It may appear to some people that I have been very harsh in what I have said about prayer meetings and the general understanding of prayer in Christian circles today. It is not that the Lord writes off the kind of corporate prayer we have become accustomed to; it is simply that so often it is at a kindergarten level. In His grace He sees the heart and answers accordingly. On the other hand, it is very often a religious ritual and exercise to which the Holy Spirit is a total stranger.

Intercessions

The third aspect is translated by the English word *intercessions*. The word used here has the idea of petitioning a superior, a king, a magistrate, or a prince; someone with authority. Originally, the idea was that you petitioned a superior. That is probably why the New American Standard Bible uses the word *petitions* instead of *intercessions*. The idea is to petition someone who has authority to accomplish matters. We are seeking the presence of God on behalf of others or for situations in which we are all involved. However, to use the word *petitions* instead of *intercessions* I think devalues the original meaning.

Intercession is the deepest aspect of prayer and the least experienced. There are few companies of God's people who know much about corporate intercession. Why? The reason is that intercession is not merely a few words mouthed on behalf of a situation, even if it is with great feeling and passion. In fact, our whole being has to be involved—spirit, soul, and body. It requires that the intercessor be a living sacrifice. If you would be an intercessor, God will require every single thing that belongs to you—your whole being, your time, your energy, your health, and even your possessions. God will take everything. Never devalue the word *intercessor*. It is not that one gives a half hour or an hour a week or even daily, as if that is all the Lord requires. To be an intercessor the Lord requires you, and all that you have. For this reason Daniel is the greatest illustration of this in the Old Testament. He did pray daily and gave time to intercession in his very busy life at the top level of government. However, the real key to his intercession was the fact that he was a living sacrifice and wholly committed to the Lord.

Intercession can only begin when we know the mind and will of God in any situation which we face. When the Lord revealed to Moses that He was about to destroy the nation of Israel, it became the cause for the intercession of Moses for the nation. When the Lord had decided to destroy Sodom and Gomorrah and shared it with Abraham, it became the cause for the intercession of Abraham for Lot and his family. If we understand this, then we begin to realise how important supplication or enquiry of the Lord is to intercession. We can only intercede when we know what the will of the Lord is concerning any situation.

It is possible that in writing this, many will give up all hope of ever being an intercessor or being involved in corporate intercession. Do not faint or give up on this matter. The Lord has to start, and he starts with a person who is ready to offer themselves willingly and wholly. There is a Chinese proverb which states, "A journey of a thousand miles begins with one step." We have to take the first step in faith. Once a believer is prepared to be an intercessor and offers his or her whole being to the Lord, He will lead you step by step. He will lead you firmly and strongly just as you are able. It will be first from the kindergarten of prayer into the kindergarten of intercession, then into the preparatory school, on into the high school, and finally, into the university of intercession. Intercession requires some degree of spiritual maturity. That kind of spiritual maturity comes only with spiritual growth and experience, and develops in a person whose self-life has been laid down.

Thanksgivings

The fourth aspect is translated by the English word *thanksgivings*. Thanksgiving is the giving of thanks, not only for answered prayer, but for the Lord Himself. Most people think immediately of thanksgiving as thanking the Lord for the prayers we asked of Him last week which have been answered in between. We always think of thanksgiving this way. It says, *With thanksgiving let your requests be made known unto God* (Philippians 4:6). Most believers understand this as making a request, and when you get the answer, you thank the Lord. Other believers understand it as making the request and thanking God for the answer already before it comes to pass. I think this devalues the word *thanksgiving*. But when you make the request you are to do it with thanksgiving. It is not only that we should thank God for answering our prayers; that is obvious! However, primarily we need to thank the Lord for who He is and what He is; for His so great salvation and for the finished work of the Lord Jesus upon which basis He gives us everything. We give thanks for His grace, His love, His mercy, His truth, His throne, His Kingdom. In other words, this thanksgiving is all to do with worship which is such a vital and strategic part of corporate prayer.

Many of us are so self-centred that the enemy twists us around his little finger. He comes to us and says: "Now it is no good for you to worship the Lord because you have been in a bad mood all day, or the children have been behaving badly, or the office was awful because the boss gave you too much to do, or you have had a terrible journey home from work and are in a ratty mood. It is no good you thanking the Lord, because you have nothing to thank Him for." And so often this is the way we respond: "I want to be real; I do not want to be a hypocrite. I will not open my mouth to praise and thank the Lord when it is hypocritical." The enemy has now got us into a position where we can only praise the Lord when we feel good. The Devil's whole machine will now be geared up to making sure you feel bad, because he wants to destroy any thanksgiving and worship to the Lord. He knows that worship, thanksgiving and praise are tremendous weapons in the battle that we are in. We so often fall for this tactic of the enemy. Sometimes people will go for years without opening their mouth and praising the Lord. They cannot even bring themselves to tell Him how great and wonderful and praiseworthy He is.

We must realise that we can be honest with God. We can say: "Lord, I feel awful. I had a dreadful day today, but I thank and worship You, Lord, that Your throne is unshakable." The fact that I have had an awful day has not brought about the abdication of the Lord Jesus. The idea seems to be that if we get out of bed on the wrong side, there has been a crisis in Heaven. If we have eaten something the night before that did not agree with us and we wake up with a jaundiced view of things, the Lord has stepped down from His throne. That, however, is nonsense! When you are down, you can praise the Lord, and when you are up, you can praise the Lord. When you are down you can say: "Lord, I feel dreadful but I want to thank You for who You are. You are wonderful, all Your works are wonderful, and Your truth lasts forever."

What then will the Devil say to this? "This person is talking truth now, what shall I do? I cannot do anything to stop this believer from worshipping God!" So he says to his whole hierarchy: "Leave So-and-So alone for a while; more value comes out of him when he is having a bad time than when he is having a good time." Some of us are helping the enemy to keep us in a permanent bad time because we have not learned this lesson. *Bless the Lord, oh my soul; and all that is within me, bless his holy name* (Psalm 103:1). And again: *I will bless the Lord at all times: His praise shall continually be in my mouth* (Psalm 34:1). One can bless the Lord whether one is up or whether one is down. The praise of the Lord—His greatness, His majesty, His beauty, His power, His total victory over the forces of darkness—is the kind of praise that can be continually in one's mouth.

As supplication is fundamental to all prayer, so is thanksgiving. It is the worship of our hearts for who He is, for what He is, for the salvation He has wrought, and for the way He has led us into that salvation. As human beings, we were created to worship, and we only come to an inner fulfilment when we learn how to worship. Worship is not tied to answers to prayer, but to the very being of God. When we worship the Lord, we fulfil a function for which we were created. But even further to this, we experience the fulfilment of the promise: *Let the high praises of God be in their mouth, and a two-edged sword in their hand* (Psalm 149:6). Blessed are those who have such experience.

2
A FUNDAMENTAL PRINCIPLE
IN CORPORATE PRAYER

Matthew 18:19-20—Again I say unto you, that if two of you shall agree on earth as touching anything that they shall ask, it shall be done for them of my Father who is in heaven. For where two or three are gathered together in my name, there am I in the midst of them.

Matthew 6:5-15—And when ye pray, ye shall not be as the hypocrites: for they love to stand and pray in the synagogues and in the corners of the streets, that they may be seen of men. Verily I say unto you, They have received their reward. But thou, when thou prayest, enter into thine inner chamber, and having shut thy door, pray to thy Father who is in secret, and thy Father who seeth in secret shall recompense thee. And in praying use not vain repetitions, as the Gentiles do: for they think that they shall be heard for their much speaking. Be not therefore like unto them: for your Father knoweth what things ye have need of, before ye ask him. After this manner therefore pray ye. Our Father who art in heaven, Hallowed be thy name. Thy kingdom come. Thy will be done, as in heaven, so on earth. Give us this day our daily bread. And forgive us our debts, as we also have forgiven our debtors. And bring us not into temptation, but deliver us from the evil one. For if ye forgive men their trespasses, your heavenly Father will also forgive you. But if ye forgive not men their trespasses, neither will your Father forgive your trespasses.

In this chapter we will consider one of the most important principles in corporate prayer. It is the lack of recognition of this truth that has rendered so much corporate prayer ineffective. It is the principle of harmonisation, of togetherness, of mutuality. Dear reader, these words may not seem, at a first reading, to have much to do with corporate prayer, but in fact they go right to the heart of the matter.

THE SPIRIT OF GOD HARMONISING BELIEVERS IN PRAYER

The Lord Jesus said: *Again I say unto you, that if two of you shall agree on earth as touching anything that they shall ask, it shall be done for them of my Father who is in heaven.*

This word *agree* is the Greek word *sumphoneo,* from which we get the English word "symphony" or "symphonise." Literally, it means "to sound together," "to voice together, "to speak together," "a consenting together." The simplest way we can understand it is to say that we are in harmony with one another. We have this word in the story of the prodigal son when he came home and heard the sound of music. He heard a *sumphoneo.* He heard the sound of musical instruments blending and harmonising together. It is also the word which occurs in II Corinthians 6: 16: *What agreement (or concord) hath a temple of God with idols?*

This verse in Matthew 18:19 is so often understood as "agreeing to agree." It is not that we are harmonised by the Holy Spirit, but rather that we have agreed to agree. The concept is that if some believers decide to agree on a matter, we can twist the arm of God and make Him do what he is basically unwilling to do. He does not really want to do it, but if you and I agree, He has to conform to our agenda. That may be putting this matter in a rather crude manner, but it is exactly the idea that is so prevalent about this verse.

24

The key, however, to this declaration of our Lord Jesus is found in the little preposition "for." It is not two unrelated matters that we have in these two verses, but one single matter. In my life I have heard many wonderful messages on Matthew 18:20 about the Lord being in the midst of two or three believers. I have also heard many messages on Matthew 18:19, that if a miracle takes place and believers agree to agree with one another on any matter, it will surely come to pass. I have even heard some preachers say from the pulpit or platform, "Is there anyone here who will agree with me?" Someone will put up their hand and yell: "Hallelujah, now God has to do it."

In fact, the second part of this single sentence qualifies the first. The whole first sentence has to be understood in the light of the second sentence. What does that mean? It means simply that where two or three are gathered together in the Name of our Lord Jesus, He is there; and because He is in their midst, He gives expression to His mind and will, and harmonises the believers. When they are harmonised by the Holy Spirit, it is the evidence that the mind and will of the Lord Jesus, the Head, will be done.

GATHERED IN THE NAME OF JESUS

What is the significance of being gathered in the Name of our Lord Jesus? Is His Name merely a kind of charm with which we end our prayers? Of course, it is not wrong to conclude your prayer in the Name of Jesus; but what is the meaning of it? Are we using it as a kind of magic formula for getting things done? The glorious meaning of being gathered in the Name of the Lord Jesus is that we have been made one with God in our Lord Jesus. We are joined to the Messiah. He is the Head and we are the body. The Father has positioned us in His Son by the Holy Spirit. That is our position! The Lord Jesus said: *Abide in Him, and He in us.* We have

25

no need to struggle to reach that position. By a new birth we are already there and only have to remain where God has placed us.

When we are gathered in His Name, it is the Name of the Head. As members of the body we are speaking in the Name of our Head. When this truth dawns upon us, we discover something very wonderful! Christ's presence is in the midst of us, and the Spirit of God is leading, directing, prompting, and enabling. Thus, the prayer time becomes an expression of the body of Christ, an expression of our oneness with Christ, and our oneness in Christ.

So often when believers meet together, the prayers that are offered are totally individualistic. There is no harmonising by the Spirit of God. One would almost think that the person praying has not heard anyone who has prayed before, and will not hear anyone who prays afterwards. It is totally unrelated, an individualistic type of prayer. There is nothing wrong with that kind of prayer when we are on our own, but when we are together, it is a denial and contradiction of the very principle of corporate prayer, as contained in these words: *For where two or three are gathered together in my name, there I am in the midst of them.* He is there, and because He is there He gives expression to His mind and will, and it results in our being harmonised and agreed.

When we gather together in the Name of our Lord Jesus, when we take our position in Him as His body, as we wait on Him and enquire of Him, into our midst by the Spirit of God comes the mind of the Lord. It does not need long waiting or long prayer. Sometimes it comes as someone prays because it kindles something in one's heart and one knows it is from the Lord. When a burden is thus conceived in one's heart, it is terrible when someone else prays too long. Genuine corporate prayer is when the Holy Spirit moves from one to another. If someone prays too long that prompting in the heart of another may be lost.

UNDER THE GOVERNMENT OF THE HOLY SPIRIT

Why is this harmonising so necessary? It seems that it is a matter being established in the mouth of two or three witnesses. Sometimes, one person has prayed for something and that is enough. However, on important and vital matters we need to learn the lesson of "being agreed by the Spirit of God." At times the anointing of the Holy Spirit will stay on a matter, and thirty people or more will pray on the same topic. It is like tramping around the walls of Jericho—until at the end of six days tramping around once a day and seven times on the seventh—the walls finally came down. Other times it only needs two or three people harmonised together, and the matter is done, and the Anointing moves on.

Under the Old Covenant everyone prayed together at once. They prayed their own prayers and God sorted it all out. Of course, there is nothing wrong with that communal way of all praying together, but there is no relatedness to one another. They were saved as we are under the New Covenant, redeemed by the blood of the Lamb and looking forward to the cross, as we look back. They were, however, individuals although bound together. The distinguishing mark of the New Covenant is that God has put His Spirit within us and we are no longer merely individuals; we are members of a body. It was this which had in the early days of the Church such a colossal impact on the Jewish people. What was it with these people? They moved together as if some invisible conductor was there. It was not just a congregation of units; it was a body in the Messiah, joined to the Head, under the direction and government of the Holy Spirit.

LEARNING TO PRAY IN AN ORDERED MANNER

If a corporate prayer time is merely many individual units praying without too much regard for one another, praying their own prayers as if no one else was there, then we might as well suggest matters for prayer and send everyone home to spend a half hour on their knees in the quiet of their own homes. This would cut the wastage of time, and be as valuable.

The right kind of prayer time has an order and a design which stems from the Lord Jesus in our midst. In that meeting, the will and the mind of the Head results in a togetherness and harmony, even when some of us make mistakes. We will never be perfect, and the best of us will get it wrong at times, but we are all learners. It is amazing how patient the Lord is, and especially with those who have just begun to pray and put their foot in it. We only learn when we make mistakes and allow the Lord to correct us. The great problem is when there are those who are many years old in the Lord, and have never learned.

RECOGNITION OF THE ANOINTING AND SECONDING PRAYER

The key to corporate prayer is mutuality or togetherness, and the seconding of one another's prayers is of the most vital importance. In fact it is strategically vital. One does not have to be a great saint or to have lived many years in the service of God to discern an anointing on someone in prayer. As one listens one knows that the anointing is there, for we hear a clarity and an authority in that praying. It is at this point that we can make a real mistake with sad consequence. Often we think, "That is enough. It was so authoritative, so clear, we do not need to pray further on that matter." However, it is of paramount importance that the anointed prayer be seconded because it is the outworking of the phrase—*If two of you shall agree....*

By seconding such a prayer we are in effect saying "Amen." The word *Amen* is interesting because it comes from the Hebrew root *aman*, which means "to believe," "to have faith." The Hebrew *ma'amin* means simply "I believe." When we say "Amen," we are expressing our faith that the matter will come to pass. In other words, we are saying: "I believe; I have faith for that subject, Lord." Think about that the next time someone is praying about a subject and the Lord puts into your heart a witness confirming it, then say, "Amen. I have faith for that; I am with that; I am right behind that."

PRAYER—A MILITARY OPERATION

A corporate time of prayer has to be conducted like a military operation. So often, the idea seems to be prevalent among believers that as long as one has a gun and enough ammunition, one just fires it; that is all that matters! Getting your **enemy** in focus and firing accurately is a very secondary matter. The idea is that the Devil is so dim-witted that all we have to do is make a hullabaloo, shoot off a few Scriptures in different directions, make a huge noise, have lots of people saying prayers in the Name of Jesus, and the Devil will just run away.

The fact of the matter is that we are in a warfare, and the weapons of our warfare are not of the flesh but mighty through God to the pulling down of satanic strongholds. For our part we have to train our weapons or our guns on the target. We have to learn how to use the Word of God, which the Holy Spirit supplies as our weapon, and be focused on the target.

29

3
BAD HABITS
WHICH DESTROY CORPORATE PRAYER

In this chapter we will consider some of the bad habits which destroy corporate prayer. Those bad habits are to be avoided like the plague.

HORIZONTAL PRAYER

All genuine prayer is vertical. Horizontal prayer, on the other hand, is the giving of information through prayer and is for human consumption and not Divine attention. It would be far better to break into the prayer time and say simply, "I ought to mention this. Mrs. Smith lives just round the corner on Brewery Street, number twelve, on the third floor, in the back room. Her husband fell down the other day and broke his leg, her child is in the hospital with diphtheria, her son is becoming a gangster, and she is in dreadful need. Could we pray for her?" However, what normally happens is more like this: "Oh Lord, we pray for Mrs. Smith who lives in Brewery Street, number twelve, third floor up in the back room. Her husband has broken his leg, her child is in the hospital with diphtheria, her son is becoming a gangster, and she is in dreadful need." The Lord could say, "My dear child, I know all of this. Are you trying to identify Mrs. Smith for Me, lest I bless the wrong one? You really do not need to tell Me! Why are you giving Me all this information?" This is not praying to the Lord; it is giving information to other people, and the prayer time is being destroyed. The more quickly one learns that such prayer is a façade and valueless in the sight of Heaven, the better. The Lord knows all there is to know about Mrs. Smith and her problem. It can be, of course, a real help for others to hear about her condition and need, but to dress it up in prayer is wrong. When we fall into this error we are not praying.

We have to learn hard lessons. What point is it when you get to Heaven and say: "I did pray;" and the Lord says: "You did not! You spent most of your time giving information in the guise of prayer to others and with a lot of hot air; and as far as I am concerned, you were a dreadful bore." Do you think that our Lord is going to acclaim someone who has destroyed prayer meetings? Never! Our Lord is not a diplomat or a politician. He is not going to say, "You did very well," when in fact you did the opposite. He is going to say, "You were the destroyer of those prayer meetings. Why didn't you learn? Why didn't you allow Me to do something with you?"

Horizontal prayer is a plague. Ask God to keep you away from it. All prayer should be directed to God. Be aware that there is nothing that God does not know. It might be of help to share some information with others but not in the guise of prayer. Remember what the Preacher said: *Do not be hasty in word or impulsive in thought to bring up a matter in the presence of God. For God is in heaven and you are on the earth; therefore let your words be few* (Ecclesiastes 5:2 NASB). He did not mean for us not to pray much but to remember: God is in Heaven and you are on earth. He knows it all—and far more than you could ever understand. Therefore you can come to the point, be direct, and not use many words.

What did our Lord mean when He said: *For your Father knoweth what things ye have need of, before ye ask him* (Matthew

6:8)? This does not mean that we are not to ask, for He taught us to pray: *Give us this day our daily bread* (Matthew 6:11). But what He meant was: Do not go all around the bush. Your heavenly Father knows it anyway; He knows your need and your condition. It is the same with much greater needs, whether local, national, or international. There is nothing He does not know about those situations; therefore learn to be direct.

LONG PRAYER

There is nothing that can destroy corporate prayer more powerfully than the endlessly long prayers of some saints. I always remember the words of Golda Meir, who was at that time Prime Minister of Israel, and she said: "We do not need enemies when we have friends like these." She was speaking of some so called friends of Israel in positions of great authority in other nations who made much trouble for Israel. Sometimes, one wonders whether the Lord feels the same way. He does not have to blame Satan because left to some saints the prayer meeting and the work of the Lord will be destroyed anyway. In teaching us the pattern prayer the Lord Jesus said: *In praying use not **vain repetitions**, as the Gentiles do: for they think that they shall be heard **for their much speaking*** (Matthew 6:7 author's emphasis).

It is an interesting fact that it has been stated that not a single prayer recorded in the Bible, from Genesis to Revelation, lasts more than a few minutes! In this connection it is worth noting that the pattern prayer which the Lord gave us lasts no more than two minutes. Nevertheless many Christians pray unbelievably long prayers. Unwittingly, they become agents for the destruction of corporate prayer. By prayer they destroy prayer! In private prayer, of course, in the quietness of one's own home, one can pray for an hour or more. There is no problem. However, to hold forth in corporate prayer for such a length of time would kill any

33

prayer meeting! This has been a centuries' old problem. It reminds me of a story that is told of D. L. Moody, the great preacher, who had such a person in the Church prayer meeting. On one occasion Moody became so distressed over the length of the brother's prayer that he rose to his feet and said: "Let us all rise to our feet and sing hymn number so and so whilst our brother finishes his prayer."

SERMONETTES

Then there are the little sermons and Bible outlines which are another great destroyer of corporate prayer. Our beloved Lord is more preached at than any other person in the whole universe. If the unsaved were preached at as much as our Lord, no one could ever go to a lost eternity with the excuse that they never heard the Gospel! Sometimes, one wonders why people do not give the Lord a chance to come forward and answer the appeal.

With such believers there is nothing in the Word that is not rehashed. It would not be as serious or as destructive if it had something to do with the matter in hand. Rarely does it have any relationship to those matters! Marvellous thoughts are expounded from the Bible; from the Law, from the Psalms, from the Prophets, from the Gospels, or from the Letters. The trouble is that the corporate prayer meeting is often the venue for frustrated preachers. There is no other outlet for them; therefore, the prayer meeting becomes their platform. We have Biblical outlines and points one, two, and three—all the points beginning with the same letter. May the Lord preserve us from such sermonettes.

In corporate prayer there is a vast difference in rehearsing the promises, the declarations and the statements of the Word of God in prayer when they are in relation to His purpose and to the matters at hand—and preaching those truths back to God. In fact it is essential and necessary that we stand on the promises and the declarations of God which have much to do with the effectiveness of corporate prayer. However, to preach sermons or give Bible outlines is to preach at God, and that is appalling. It reveals an unawareness of the Presence of the Lord.

"Shopping List" Prayer

Then there is what we call the "shopping list" prayer or the "world tour" prayer. It is every matter that has been suggested for prayer, and a few more items added. Such believers probably had a great battle in opening their mouths, but when they finally have them open, they take the plunge and go through the whole list of matters that have been suggested. It is like having a shopping list that you tick off as you buy the items. The "world tour" prayers are much the same. You begin where you are and go from continent to continent till you arrive back from where you began; it is a kind of round the world trip!

Let me give an example. A person prays firstly for a Billy Graham campaign in Los Angeles; then he prays for a family in great need in Cape Town, in South Africa. After that he is off to Melbourne in Australia where there is a brother who has gone away from the Lord. Then he returns to London and prays for a group of believers there; and finally he prays for his grandmother's gangrenous toe. That is his prayer.

The next person comes in and he prays for the person in Melbourne who has gone away from the Lord, and then he comes back to the Billy Graham campaign in Los Angeles. Then he goes to London and prays fervently for the British people. Someone else prays for the grandmother's gangrenous toe and includes five other sick people, all with very different conditions. Then another one prays for Billy Graham's campaign in Los Angeles, goes to Melbourne; and then prays for all the believers behind the bamboo curtain and ends in the Czech Republic. Someone else prays for all those suffering everywhere, especially in Islamic countries and then prays for Russia.

What is happening in this prayer meeting? First we are here, and then we are there. We go backwards and forwards, and backwards and forwards. If you prayed like this at home the Lord would say that you needed some healing of the mind because you are in a confusion and all over the place.

In fact, when a believer prays in his or her home, he or she would kneel and pray for one thing after another, as one is prompted by the Spirit of God. You do not dodge backwards and forwards between different matters. The corporate prayer time should be the same. We proceed from one topic to the next, only together, and so on to the next topic. Thus we proceed under the guidance of the Holy Spirit. In such a time we may have seven saints praying on one topic, and five on the next, one on the next, and then twenty on the final topic.

When you have prayer that is all over the place, nobody knows where we are going. One would not dream of doing that privately or personally. In the corporate time, however, that is exactly what we do; we go all over the place and go through a whole number of items with each person trying to cover the whole list. In that kind of prayer time a heaviness and a lifelessness comes down upon it.

The "My," "Me," and "I" Syndrome

When we consistently use the personal pronouns in corporate prayer, it becomes a denial of the functioning of the body of Christ. It is obvious that we should use "we,' "our," and 'us," when we are praying together. If the Holy Spirit is leading us to pray in such a time we become, as it were, the mouthpiece of the rest. The other believers will either agree with the prayer and say, "Amen" or they will not and remain silent. Our Lord never taught us to pray corporately like this. In the pattern prayer which He gave us, He taught us to pray: ***Our*** *Father who art in heaven, Hallowed be thy name. Thy kingdom come. Thy will be done, as in heaven, so on earth. Give **us** this day **our** daily bread. And forgive **us our** debts, as **we** also have forgiven **our** debtors. And bring **us** not into temptation, but deliver **us** from the evil one* (Matthew 6:9-13). We need to note that it was to all the disciples and not to one disciple that He gave this pattern prayer. In other words, when they prayed together, they were to use the plural pronouns: "Our," "Us," "We." It is a sad evidence of the prayer time being a gathering of individuals praying individual and personal prayers when we use "I," "My," and "Me" rather than the Church at prayer. Furthermore, when those personal pronouns are used, one feels that one is shut out of that person's prayer. That child of God is praying as if there is only that one believer and the Lord in the room.

There, is, however, a place when personal pronouns should be used, even in a time of corporate prayer. For example, we often hear this kind of prayer when someone prays: "We all feel depressed!" It would be better if that believer said, "I am depressed; touch me, Lord, and revive me." There are other occasions when the personal pronouns are rightly used. It is normal however in corporate prayer to use, "our," "us," and "we."

When we begin to use the plural pronouns it is a sign or evidence that we are beginning to sense that we belong to the body of the Lord Jesus. The Holy Spirit is beginning to give us an understanding of what the Church is.

ARTIFICIALITY

Another very bad habit is the idea that we have to put on an artificial voice. W.P. Nicholson once said: "Why do people have to use strange voices when they speak to God?" It is obvious that we should be reverent in speaking to the Lord, but why can we not use our normal voice? We have, of course, to speak up so that others can hear our prayer and say, "Amen." The idea that we should use a kind of theatrical voice in speaking to the Lord is ridiculous. One pities the Lord having to hear all these strange voices which bear no resemblance to the normal voice of the person who is praying! As long as we speak up and our diction is clear, we need to be ourselves and speak to the Lord as we speak to one another—only reverently.

This habit is so prevalent that in united prayer times you can almost tell which denomination a believer is coming from. Anglicans and Episcopalians speak about the passion of our Lord and the agony of the cross and other tremendous truths as if they are talking over the fence to a neighbour about the tomatoes and other vegetables in their garden. It always has a level tone without any passion or emotion. Baptists tend to be very matter of fact and loud. Pentecostals are very much like the old-fashioned plane that revved up its engines before it finally took off. It then rises higher and higher until it loses power suddenly and descends. Presbyterians speak to God with great oratory and aplomb. The greatest need is not to take on some manner or voice which is not ourselves. We should be able to pray as ourselves, from our hearts, to the Lord, without artifice and pretence.

MECHANICAL NOISE

Another very bad habit is a kind of mechanical reaction that has nothing to do with the Holy Spirit. In a time of corporate prayer it destroys the anointing and power of the Holy Spirit, because it is not the Spirit of God but a totally human reflex. However, it can be uplifting when a believer exclaims, "Hallelujah" because that one has seen something by the Spirit; or someone says, "Amen" or another says, "Yes, Lord" out loud, or when a great chorus of "Amens" rises from all of us, because in the Spirit we are all witnessing to some matter.

I remember in a national conference of intercessors, after I had spoken, a lady approached me and thanked me for the message I had given. She then said that she had been greatly blessed by going to a Prayer Clinic.

I was immediately interested because I had led quite a number of Schools of Prayer in different places. I said to her, "But I have never heard of a Prayer Clinic!"

"Oh," she replied, "it has been very helpful to me in the different courses I have taken there. They have been very helpful to me; however I would like to ask you about the course I am taking at present because it troubles me."

"What is the present course you are taking, and why does it trouble you?" I said.

"Oh," she said "it is groaning in the Spirit."

I then said to her, "Well, I have never heard of such a course. How do they teach this? Does the teacher ask you to groan, and then says that is not good enough, and groans himself, and then says that is how it should be."

"Yes," she said, "that is how it happened, and I am not very happy about it."

So I told her that I thought she was quite right not to be happy about it, especially as the Scripture says these are groans which cannot be uttered, but are trapped within our spirit. Then suddenly the light dawned and I said, "Are you paying for these courses?"

"Yes" she said, "fifty dollars a course."

To teach people to mechanically groan is not a ministry of the Holy Spirit, and to make a charge for it is to add insult to injury.

On another occasion I was in a prayer meeting in one of the Southern states of the United States. I could not concentrate at all due to a fearful racket in the back of the meeting hall. In the end the pastor leaned over and said to me, "Is that noise disturbing you?"

And I said, "Yes, but what is it?"

"Oh," he said, "it is our brother who has a ministry of groaning."

At the end of the meeting the pastor said, "Would you like to meet our brother who has this ministry of groaning?"

And I said, "Yes, I would, since I have always understood that these groanings cannot be uttered." In my estimation it was not a genuine ministry, but mechanical hubbub.

Finally, to illustrate further this matter; I was preaching at a meeting in Southern Sweden and a man in the congregation loudly exclaimed every few minutes: "Takk og lov," which means "thanks and praise." I was preaching an evangelistic message and when I said, "There are many here who do not yet know the Lord," he said, "Takk og lov!" I even said, "Some, if they do not find the Lord Jesus, will end up in Hell," and he said, "Takk og lov." This kind of mechanical exclamation has nothing to do with the Lord. It is a mechanical reflex; like a sausage machine turning out sausages! This kind of mechanical noise needs to be avoided like the plague.

Making Sure that You are Heard when You Pray

It is obvious that when one leads in prayer one needs to be heard; otherwise there is no point in having a corporate time of prayer. If a number of believers who are praying are inaudible, it will destroy the whole time, since a large number present will not be able to hear them. What are the reasons for not being audible?

The first reason is the softness of some people's voices. If you have such a soft voice, it will always help if you stand up to pray. You do not have to use an artificial voice, but you do need to speak up and speak clearly. I have been amazed over the years to discover that powerfully built men often pray with incredibly soft voices. Normally, they speak like a fog horn, loudly and clearly, but when it comes to a prayer meeting you can hardly hear them. I have wondered to myself whether they want to appear before the Lord as humble and modest. Who are they kidding however? Not the Lord! Use a normal voice but obviously a voice that can be heard by all. If you have an inherently soft voice and cannot do anything about it, do not let that stop you from praying, but remember to speak out and keep it brief and to the point.

The second reason is that some people put their hands over their mouth or if they are kneeling, they pray into the seat of the chair. There is no way people can hear you like this. If you want to

41

kneel, and it is a good position to take, straighten up when you pray and pray out clearly.

INSENSITIVITY

Insensitivity to the leading of the Spirit of God or the anointing, can be a very great problem. Sometimes insensitivity can take the form of slavishly following through the whole list of prayer requests to the end. Why should we have to pray for every item that is suggested? Maybe the Lord does not want every one of those matters to be taken up in prayer. Some of those items which have been mentioned can be taken home and prayed through in our personal and family prayers.

Another evidence of insensitivity is the fear of a silence or quietness. As soon as a moment of silence comes we are on to the next point, because we are not being led by the anointing. There are times when a good Quaker silence can be greatly used of the Lord to speak to us. It is much easier for us to have a methodology. We have this list of matters and we feel that we have to cover every one of them. As we have said, however, some of those matters can be taken home and prayed through.

We need always to be sensitive to the Spirit of God and His leading. Sometimes, with some of us who suffer from deafness, there is a tendency to wait for someone who speaks powerfully or clearly and then jump in, but that may not be the Spirit of God. We have to learn even in that condition to be led by the Holy Spirit, and He will lead us in simple and clear ways.

LACK OF AWARENESS OF GOD

We cannot call this a bad habit, but it is the greatest problem in corporate prayer. If we were more aware of the Presence of the Lord, half of the bad habits we have in prayer ministry would be banished, and they would disappear. In a living awareness of the Lord's Presence amongst us, we would be delivered from the bad habits we have defined. Elijah used a phrase about himself a number of times: *The Lord before whom I stand* (see I Kings 17:1 cp. 18:10, 15). No one could see him standing before the Lord. In fact he may have been standing before King Ahab and Queen Jezebel, or someone else, but he had a consciousness or awareness of God. We need that same kind of consciousness or awareness of the Lord, even though we cannot see Him with our physical eyes. The Lord Jesus is in the midst of two or three or more believers. It is recorded in Hebrews 11:27b that Moses: ... *endured, as seeing Him who is invisible.* He also had the same experience as Elijah. It was his awareness and consciousness of the Lord that enabled him to endure and overcome.

By the Spirit of God we are in touch with the throne of God. If we were really aware of that, it would revolutionise our prayer, and we would be more direct. We would not feel that we have to beat about the bush or go all around a matter, but we will go straight to the heart of it. If we were aware that when the Church is at prayer we are actually in the throne room of God, in the Presence of Supreme Sovereign Authority and Power, such awareness would change our whole attitude to the events and problems we are facing. An awareness of the Lord's Presence would cause our prayer times to be powerfully effective and deliver us from the bad habits which destroy them.

A word in the ear of the King of kings and Lord of lords, the Ruler of the kings of the earth, is far more powerful than a word in the ear of the President of the United States or the Prime Minister of Great Britain, or the President of France, or anyone else. The Lord said: *And there I will meet with thee, and I will commune with thee from above the mercy seat, from between the two cherubim which are upon the ark of the testimony* (Exodus 25:22). This was a picture of the throne room of the Almighty; it was the Holy of Holies. There He said, "I will meet with you." As the redeemed of the Lord, could we have any greater privilege than this? This awareness of the Presence of God, of being in touch with His throne, would surely revolutionise our corporate prayer times and the way we pray together.

4
THE LEADING OF THE SPIRIT

Ephesians 6:17-18—And take the helmet of salvation, and the sword of the Spirit, which is the word of God: with all prayer and supplication praying at all seasons in the Spirit, and watching thereunto in all perseverance and supplication for all the saints.

Jude 20-21—But ye [in the plural], beloved, building up yourselves on your most holy faith, praying in the Holy Spirit, keep yourselves in the love of God, looking for the mercy of our Lord Jesus Christ unto eternal life.

Romans 8:26-27—And in like manner the Spirit also helpeth our infirmity: for we know not how to pray as we ought; but the Spirit himself maketh intercession for us with groanings which cannot be uttered; and he that searcheth the hearts knoweth what is the mind of the Spirit, because he maketh intercession for the saints according to the will of God.

Psalm 133—Behold, how good and how pleasant it is for brethren to dwell together in unity! It is like the precious oil upon the head, that ran down upon the beard, even Aaron's beard; that came down upon the skirt [or hem] of his garments; like the dew of Hermon, that cometh down upon the mountains of Zion: for there the Lord commanded the blessing, even life for evermore.

Without the Holy Spirit there can be no genuine corporate prayer. A prayer meeting without His known and practical

Presence is simply a number of human beings giving voice to many petitions. Real and effective prayer is when the Holy Spirit initiates, leads, directs, and empowers. He alone can bring us to the place where we can execute the will of God on earth; His leadership is vital and essential. Without Him, there can be no anointing, no togetherness, no harmony, and no ability to discover the weapons with which the battle will be won. We are then merely a gathering of saved individuals.

It is not that the anointing of the Lord is unavailable to us, but it has not been recognised and obeyed. If the Holy Spirit is not present, it is impossible to use the *sword of the Spirit, which is the word of God*. The weapons of our warfare are not of the flesh and only operate in and through the Presence of God (see II Corinthians 10:4). Those weapons do not belong to the realm of human genius, resource, or energy. If He is not present as conductor, leader, and director of the whole time of prayer, then however much we seek to stay focused on certain prayer matters, we will never reach the point where action can be taken by the Lord. There may be much prayer but nothing ever comes to a conclusion because it is trapped within the realm of human endeavour.

Who else but the Holy Spirit can make known to the members of the body of Christ the will, the mind, and the burden of the Head? It is only through the Spirit that Christ can make known to us His will. How does the risen and glorified Messiah bring about that harmonisation—that inner agreement, that functioning, spontaneous, organic oneness of the members of His body which is so vital to corporate prayer? Only the Spirit of God can do this; there is no other way!

THE ABSOLUTE SOVEREIGNTY OF THE HOLY SPIRIT IN CORPORATE PRAYER

We are told in Ephesians 6:18 that we are to pray: *With all prayer and supplication praying at all seasons in the Spirit.* Note very carefully the words: *Praying in the Spirit.* Jude also uses the same words: *Praying in the Holy Spirit* (Jude 20). There is a common idea nowadays that to pray in the Spirit is to pray only in a tongue. There is no question that praying in the Spirit includes praying in a tongue. The gift of tongues, when used in devotion and intercession, is a manifestation of the Spirit and is obviously part of praying in the Spirit. However, to equate praying in the Spirit with praying only in a tongue is quite wrong and devalues its meaning. Praying in the Spirit is a far greater matter. All genuine prayer is *in the Spirit*. It is under the leadership of the Spirit, under His direction and by His empowering. If we can get clear on this matter, it will help us very much. The source and power of all true corporate prayer is to pray in the Spirit. When we understand this, we recognise that corporate prayer is not merely a "get together" of saved human beings, giving voice to their own burdens, petitions, and feelings. It is in another dimension and is under the sovereign leadership of the Spirit of God. That is praying *in the Spirit*.

Unless His sovereignty is recognised by everyone at the very commencement of a time of prayer, there will be a blockage from its start, and a shadow will come over the whole time. It is not only that any Tom, Dick, or Harry can quench the Holy Spirit; sometimes prayer leaders do so. A prayer time is not just a cosy free-for-all. It is not for some sort of spiritual self-expression, where you say your little piece and I say mine, and it helps us all. If we view a prayer time like that, there can be no question of seeing anything completed, of touching matters in the heavenlies,

47

or of overcoming principalities or powers and breaking their influence. The prayer time is not even just a time for the expression of petitions as *we* see the need. Just because a believer sees a need or feels a need, it does not necessarily mean that the Lord Himself wants that particular need brought into that time of prayer.

CHRIST AS HEAD OF THE BODY

The apostle Paul wrote: *Not holding fast to the head, from whom the entire body, being supplied and held together by the joints and ligaments, grows with a growth which is from God* (Colossians 2:19 NASB). In these words we discover the essential meaning of the Church.

Christ is the Head of the body which is the Church (see Colossians 1:18 and Ephesians 1:22-23). This is repeatedly emphasised in the New Testament. The phrase *the head of the body* does not occur in the Old Testament. It is introduced by the Spirit of God in the New Testament with enormous significance and meaning; it has very much to do with God's new Man.

When every member holds fast the Head, we discover the body. One never discovers the body of Christ by trying to hold fast the body. When we are Church-centred and not Christ-centred, we lose the real Church and are left with only the format. It is the system, the pattern, and the methodology with which we are left. We know little and experience less of the heart and meaning of the Church which is Christ! When we hold fast the Head, we experience the body in life and function. It is obvious that without a head, the body cannot function. It is lifeless! When the Church does not hold fast the Head, it has to resort to its own natural energy and natural schemes. It produces a system and an organisation which is able to continue whether the Lord is there or not.

What does this vital truth mean if the "Head" does not represent the mind and will of the Lord Jesus? A head is not meant to be empty! A person's intelligence is centred in their head. It is there that he or she thinks, and from the head he or she wills and purposes. This unique statement, that the Lord Jesus is the Head of the body, means that from Him comes all our spiritual intelligence and understanding. It is the Holy Spirit who makes the Headship of Christ a living reality to the members of the body. We cannot know the mind or the will of our Head except through the Holy Spirit. It is His work to reveal and illuminate the Lord's mind and will to us, and then to enable us to execute it on the earth.

Many believers think of the Headship of Christ in the manner in which we think of a President or a Prime Minister or a Principal of a hospital or a Chancellor of a university. He is the Head, we are the staff. That is not how it is expressed in the New Testament. One has never seen a *living* headless body or a *living* bodiless head; they are one organic whole! They cannot exist without each other. The Holy Spirit alone oversees the vital and strategic communication of the Head with the body.

Therefore, it is extremely important that we recognise, obey, and begin to experience the Headship of Christ by the Spirit. Then the youngest believer will learn lessons that will stand him or her in good stead for the whole of his or her life on this fallen earth and for eternal service. In corporate prayer we will all learn to distinguish between soul and Spirit, to discern and understand the government of God, and to discern His leading. These are all foundational and practical lessons to learn.

Corporate prayer illustrates this vital and essential principle more than any other aspect of the life of God's people. In a prayer time one can tell the state of health of a Church. In other words, it becomes clear through a time of corporate prayer whether the Head and the body are functioning as they should—or not. When there is the direction and anointing of the Spirit of God, when there is harmony and cohesion, there is fulfilment. The body of Christ grows with a growth which is from God. If we hold fast the Head there is a supply of His life and power; there is spiritual equipment; there is the manifestation of the Spirit for the good of the whole body and for its increase. The Head, by the Holy Spirit, is able to execute and perform His will through His body in corporate prayer. Such a prayer time then becomes a thrilling experience.

In a corporate time of prayer the Spirit of God is like the conductor of an orchestra. And all the members of the orchestra must keep their eyes on the conductor. It is no good just having your instrument in hand and the music in front of you; you must keep your eye on Him as well. If you do not keep your eye on the conductor and his baton, the whole symphony or concerto will become a disharmony. The Holy Spirit is symphonising us; He is blending us together. If we will only keep our eyes on Him, then every one of us has a part to play in the prayer time. If we are wholly with Him, we shall give what He gives us as He directs.

Even when we do not actually contribute in the prayer time, we can be a living part of it. Some people will hide behind that statement saying: "Well, I am so glad he wrote that because I never take part, or very rarely. I do not think the conductor would ever point his baton in my direction." Needless to say, the Lord is a perfect gentleman, and if you say, "I do not want to take part in this session, Lord," He will ignore you. He will never draw you in unless you are willing. We need to learn to overcome our reluctance and contribute what we have of the Lord under the direction of the Spirit of God. Sometimes we will make mistakes and learn from those mistakes. Otherwise, we shall not be truly qualified for the eternal service for which God is seeking to train us. Everyone has something to give and, until we give what we have, we will not learn. When we all obey the Holy Spirit in a time of corporate prayer, there will be design, harmony, and cohesion. This is what it means to pray in the Spirit—we are under His direction. If we are under His direction and leadership, and we are contributing by His prompting and enabling power, there will be harmony, cohesion, and fulfilment in that time.

THE PURPOSE OF THE PRAYER TIME

The Lord Jesus taught the disciples to pray: *Thy kingdom come. Thy will be done, as in heaven, so on earth* (Matthew 6:10). As the body of our Lord Jesus, the aim and purpose of corporate prayer is to see that the will of God is done as it is in Heaven so on the earth. As the body of the Messiah, in union with the Head by the Holy Spirit, we are to bring the throne of God or the government of God to bear on situations in this fallen world.

It is therefore obvious that we have first to discern what the will of God is in any given situation or circumstance—whether family, local, national, or international. Until we come to a conclusion together as to what the will of the Father is, we cannot take action. In other words, the keys of the Kingdom of heaven cannot be used. Those keys should always be used corporately and in fellowship with others. It is folly when one hears believers personally trying to use the keys of the Kingdom without any knowledge as to what the will of God is or without regard to the other members of Christ.

51

Supposing we are involved in evangelism, and suddenly we are spiritually besieged by the powers of darkness; what are we to do? We may preach more fervently and loudly, thinking that might be the answer; or we may decide to change the whole format of the time. Whatever we do we discover that the spiritual blockade is still in place. The real solution is that the workers need to go behind the scenes and bring the throne of God or the Kingdom of God to bear on that situation.

Is it possible that Satan and his host could ultimately blockade the work of Christ? Can the gates of hell prevail against the building work of the Lord Jesus, in flat contradiction to His words: *"Upon this rock I will build my church; and the gates of Hell shall not prevail against it"* (Matthew 16:18). Many times one has seen that blockade building up, and the people of God have found it increasingly hard to break through. A mere appeal to the Lord does not bring an end to such an onslaught. The moment, however, we declare that Jesus is Lord and assert that the throne of God has the final say in the situation, we see the grip of Satan losing its power, and the blockade is broken.

There can be all kinds of complex situations and problems that we face—in our families, in our business and workaday life. It may be locally in our life together as the people of God, or as workers in the work of God that we face mountainous obstacles. In another dimension of corporate prayer there are national and international situations. In the pattern prayer that our Lord Jesus gave us, we are taught to pray: *Thy kingdom come. Thy will be done, as in heaven, so on earth.* Of course, the final and glorious manifestation of the Kingdom of God is yet to come, and we await it with joy. However, our work in corporate prayer is to bring His Kingdom authority to bear on our problems, situations, and circumstances—situations often inspired and manipulated by the powers of darkness. It is as we assert the will of God over the problems and situations we face, that the power of the enemy is broken, and the will of God is realised.

At the heart of the Kingdom of God is the throne of God. It is: *The kingdom of our Lord, and of His Messiah* (Revelation 11:15). The Father has said to the Son: *Sit thou at my right hand, until I make thine enemies thy footstool. The Lord will send forth the rod of thy strength out of Zion: Rule thou in the midst of thine enemies* (see Psalm 110:1-2). There is no question about the enthronement of our Lord Jesus at the right hand of the Father or of His total victory. There is nothing Satan or the Powers of darkness can do about it. They can only attack *us*. We need to declare and proclaim the Kingship of Jesus, and that in His hands all authority and power in Heaven and on this earth reside. He has won and: *He must reign, till He hath put all His enemies under His feet* (I Corinthians 15:25). It is this glorious victory of our Lord Jesus that we must learn to declare and proclaim.

THE ANOINTING OF THE PRAYER TIME

People travel many miles to hear someone who is anointed, for every believer is clear on the need for anointed preachers, leaders, or Christian workers. However, very few people ever see the need for an anointing on a meeting. It is noteworthy that under the Old Covenant we find everyone and everything that God used had to be set apart and anointed—the King, the Priest, the Prophet and the Levite all had to be anointed. Believers are often unaware that all the furniture in the Tabernacle and the Temple had to be anointed in the same way that the King, the Prophet, and the Priest were anointed (see Exodus 30:26). Even the Tent of Meeting where God met with His people had to be anointed. From this we learn that there is an anointing for our meetings with God and God's meeting with us!

Under the Old Covenant, anointing was the Divine sign that someone or something was set aside for His use. There was to be no flesh involved. That is why it is stated concerning the anointing oil in Exodus 30:32: *Upon the flesh of man shall it not be poured, neither shall ye make any like it, according to the composition thereof: It is holy, and it shall be holy unto you.* The apostle Paul also writes concerning spiritual warfare in corporate prayer: *We do not war according to the flesh ...* (II Corinthians 10:3). There is an anointing for the meetings of God's people, and in particular as we are considering the prayer meeting. The flesh ought not to come into that time. It is not the place for man's ingenuity or creativity or for his ideas or opinions—not even man's ability or resources. The whole time should be set aside for the Lord. Even if we meet for corporate prayer in a secular setting we should sanctify and cleanse such a meeting place in the name of the Lord before we use it for such prayer.

Psalm 133 has much to teach us about this anointing: *Behold how good and how pleasant it is for brethren to dwell together in unity!* This is not a fleeting experience of unity for a limited time. This blessing, and the grace and the power which comes with it is for those who *dwell in unity.* This living in unity is *like the precious oil upon the head, that ran down upon the beard, even Aaron's beard; that came down upon the hem of his garment.* I remember the first time I ever read this Psalm. I thought what an odd Psalm it was—heads and beards and hems of the garment and oil being poured on the whole. Then it talks about the dew of Hermon coming down upon the mountains of Zion. This Psalm in fact goes right to the heart of the matter. Aaron, as the High Priest, is a perfect picture of the Messiah Jesus as our High Priest. The oil is a symbol of the Holy Spirit being poured out on his head, never touching his flesh, trickling down his beard, onto his High Priestly garments and reaching to the very hem. Our dwelling in unity can only endure and function in practical ways under the anointing by the Spirit of God. Every single member of Aaron's body was included in this anointing. It was from the head to the hem of his garment. That alone is sufficient for us to believe that there is an experience of the Holy Spirit into which every believer must enter. We all need to experience the anointing.

One of the titles of our Lord Jesus is Christ, which is the anglicised Greek *Christos*. The anglicised Hebrew, *Maschiach*, is Messiah. Both the Greek and the Hebrew mean the "Anointed One." What does it mean to be *in Christ*? It means that we are in the Anointed One. There is an anointing for you in Christ. This is the meaning of Pentecost. When the Lord Jesus ascended, He sat down at the right hand of the Father and received the Father's promise of the Spirit, and poured out the Spirit on His body. The anointing oil came down from the Head, the Lord Jesus, onto one hundred and twenty members of His body, and every one of them was saved and entered into a union with Him and into the anointing that was theirs. So powerful was this anointing that within hours three thousand people were saved! What would have normally taken weeks or months or years in evangelism, with the anointing it took an hour or two. This is a reflection on much Christian work and testimony. Without the anointing it is hard labour and little result. With the anointing the will and purpose of God is accomplished.

This has much to say about our prayer times. Nothing suffers more from our opinions or sentiments than those prayer times. Yet the Word of God stands: *Upon the flesh of man it shall not be poured.* We have to recognise that the time of corporate prayer is set aside for the sole purpose of God. There is an anointing for every single time of prayer. If we were to meet seven times a week, there would be a fresh anointing for every one of those times. The whole value of that time will depend on whether all the leaders and people alike stand into that anointing, from the beginning of the time and right through to the end of it.

Psalm 133 proclaims: *For there the Lord commanded the blessing, even life forevermore.* When there is a time of prayer that is under the anointing, there is life, and it floods through the whole time. It is just like the dew coming down from Hermon. The cold air of the North and the warm air of the South meet over the mountains of Zion, and it comes down as dew. Jerusalem does not normally have rain for seven months of the year, and therefore relies in the summer months on this heavy dew. In a time of corporate prayer, when we all stand into the anointing and follow the leading of the Spirit, there is a reviving and renewing dew of the Spirit. We may come into the meeting worn out but we go out revived and renewed. The prayer time can be a battle, but we will go out with a spring in our step. Many times in un-anointed prayer meetings we come in worn out and go out nearly dead! Senility overtakes us during the time. The reason for this is that the anointing has not been recognised or obeyed by us, and therefore there is no dew and no life everlasting. Few believers are able to recognise when that blessing of eternal life has been smothered. We just go on with a routine of prayer.

It is part of our spiritual education to learn to discern and to abide under the anointing. If the burden of Christ for a particular prayer time is centred on Nepal, it is no good praying for Laos. Someone may have had a letter hot from Laos with urgent needs and strongly feels we should pray for that country. But if the burden of the Lord for that time is for Nepal, we discover that when we obey the leading of the Spirit, the problems and needs in Laos are also answered by the Lord.

AN EXAMPLE OF UN-ANOINTED PRAYER

A number of years ago I led a School of Prayer in the United States. In one of the practical sessions of prayer we were praying about a certain backslider. It was amazing to me that although I had said nothing about him and the people praying did not know him or his situation, it was like peeling an onion; little by little they came to the heart of the matter. It was through the leading of the Spirit; it was the anointing at work!

Earlier, however, someone had brought up the name of a dear sister who was extremely ill. We talked about her for some ten minutes or so at the beginning of the prayer time. When the session began, we prayed for this backslider with great power. Then suddenly an old missionary prayed and said, "How can we pray about other matters when our dear sister is so ill." From that point it became one of the worst times of prayer I have ever been in. The former sessions of this School of Prayer had been marvellous times of genuine prayer and practical instruction. Now in this session it took a nose dive, and all of us were fumbling around. The dear lady's name would go back and forth across the meeting, over here and back again. The gist of it was a fight between those who believed that she should be instantaneously healed, and others who felt that she should be healed only if it was the will of God. It was theological warfare! Instead of having their guns trained on the enemy, they had their guns trained on one another. Finally, one brother, speaking to the Lord, said: "You are a liar if you do not heal her." That was enough for the other side! An outraged sister said: "How dare we tell the Lord that He is a liar!" We rumbled around in a mess and confusion that was very hard to bear. At the end of it one brother said: "Oh, Lord, we have fallen flat on our faces; help us." I concluded the session with a prayer: "If it is possible, Lord, bless this mess." Then we went to lunch. In fact, this session of prayer in the end became one of the most marvellous times of instruction for everybody there. When we got back on track, it was tremendous.

Whilst having lunch we received a phone call. Our dear sister had passed away to be with the Lord that morning at 8 AM long before the prayer session had even begun. We had obviously not been led by the Spirit for she was already with the Lord. I could not wait for the next session to begin. I said: "It is clear to me that many of you dear brothers and sisters must be Catholics, because we spent much of the time in the last session praying for the dead. Our sister was already in the presence of the Lord at 8 AM!" This is an illustration of how sentiment and emotion can replace the anointing of the Holy Spirit. It was flesh that operated in that previous session.

The whole matter of the anointing or the leading of the Holy Spirit in corporate prayer is not only a matter of Divine government; it is a matter of Divine discipline. We have to be disciplined practically by the Spirit of God, and very often by one another. We only learn if we are prepared to make mistakes. Sometimes we learn more from making a mistake than by any other means. As long as we learn from the mistakes we make all is well. It is when we make the same mistake time and again that there is something radically wrong.

PRACTICAL POINTS

"Firstly: We must not only look to the Holy Spirit to lead us at the beginning of the prayer time, but right through the whole time.

Secondly: Brothers with responsibility for leadership over the prayer time should always assert the Headship of Christ over it before it begins. Never go into a time of prayer without two or three brothers coming before the Lord and declaring that Jesus Christ is Lord of that time and has been made Head over all things to us.

Thirdly: We must learn to know when to pray and when to stop praying. That may not always be easy when, finally, after a great battle one has opened one's mouth in prayer and is in full swing. It is sad when people cannot stop and are unable to distinguish that the anointing has gone from them. We must learn when to pray and when to stop praying.

Fourthly: We must learn to assess when a topic is settled, and when the anointing is moving on from it. Do not get the idea that every single matter raised in a prayer time has got to be settled in that time. That can be a legalistic idea. It is much easier to go by regulations or by methodology than to be led by the Spirit. There are times when the Lord brings up a matter and many people may pray for it from different angles. The Lord may then say, "Drop it; that is enough for this evening; we shall take this matter up again at a later date."

There are some people whose idea is to walk around Jericho until the walls drop. However, it will not be the walls that drop, but you will wear yourself out in that matter of prayer because you are not under Divine direction. Listen carefully to what the Lord said to Joshua and the people of Israel. They were to compass the walls of Jericho once a day for six days, and on the seventh day they were to compass it seven times. It would have done them no good on the first day to have compassed the walls many times because the Lord had not so directed. They would have had many blisters and terrible foot sores and still the walls would not have come down.

It is true that when the children of Israel came to the River Jordan, the priests who were carrying the Ark, put their feet down into the water onto the riverbed. It instantaneously dried up, and they went over. It was exactly as the Lord had directed them to do, for He had said: *Every place whereon the sole of your foot shall tread shall be yours* (Deuteronomy 11:24). They had precisely obeyed the Lord in obedience and living faith and the Divine promise was fulfilled. When it came to taking Jericho, the people could have said to one another: "Why do we have to walk around the walls of Jericho once a day for six days and seven times on the seventh? Why does Joshua lack faith? All we have to do is to obey the Lord's word!" The truth is that the Lord has to direct us. At the River Jordan it was immediate, but with Jericho it was seven days. The point that we ought to underline is the leading of the Spirit of God. It is essential to follow His leading. By faith and patience we inherit the promises.

Fifthly: Learn to assess when a matter is settled and be ready to introduce a new matter under the government of the Spirit. Be careful of slavishly and mechanically following through all the items for prayer. Be alive and sensitive to the Spirit of God.

Sixthly: We must learn how to respond when some matter not under the anointing is introduced. When someone begins praying and we do not have a witness in our spirit that it is right, we need to look to the Lord to bring us back to the anointing. It may be a sermonette, or a horizontal prayer, or just a long lifeless un-anointed prayer. Do not be tempted to think that is the end and give up. Maybe the Lord will teach you through such mistakes. Sometimes our prayer times go in and out; one moment we are on track, the next moment we go astray. The Lord, however, may judge that it was a good time of prayer, because basically we kept on track, and at the end of it we went out under the anointing.

Seventhly: Be careful not to allow sentiment to govern your sense of priorities. Apparent emergencies may arise that seem to require immediate attention. If the Lord directs that we should take them up, then we should do so. There are also times when the Lord does not direct us to do so and we should listen to Him at all times.

Eighthly: We should always listen carefully to the suggested matters for prayer. Remember that they are only *suggested* matters. It is our responsibility to look to the Lord as to what He wants us to concentrate on, or even to be alive to the possibility that He would introduce a matter that was not suggested.

Ninthly: On occasion those with responsibility for leadership should be alive to the need to encourage and if necessary to correct. When there are people who are failing again and again, then there is a need for a word of correction. Alternatively, when someone is really a means of bringing life into a time of prayer, that person should be encouraged. So often the person who is alive and under the anointing is discouraged and the person who is making mistakes proceeds like a tank.

Lastly: Remember that *all* of us are disciples. We are *all* learning in the School of Prayer.

5
WATCHING AND PRAYING

Matthew 26:41—Watch and pray, that ye enter not into temptation: the spirit indeed is willing, but the flesh is weak.

Mark 13:33-37—Take ye heed, watch and pray: for ye know not when the time is. It is as when a man, sojourning in an-other country, having left his house, and given authority to his servants, to each one his work, commanded also the porter to watch. Watch therefore: for ye know not when the lord of the house cometh, whether at even, or at midnight, or at cockcrowing, or in the morning; lest coming suddenly he find you sleeping. And what I say unto you I say unto all, Watch.

Luke 21:34-36—But take heed to yourselves, lest haply your hearts be overcharged with surfeiting, and drunkenness, and cares of this life, and that day come on you suddenly as a snare: for so shall it come upon all them that dwell on the face of all the earth. But watch ye at every season, making supplication, that ye may prevail to escape all these things that shall come to pass, and to stand before the Son of man.

Ephesians 6:18—With all prayer and supplication praying at all seasons in the Spirit, and watching thereunto in all perseverance and supplication for all the saints.

Many people learn to pray but few learn to watch. Our Lord Jesus said: *Take ye heed, **watch** and pray ... **Watch** therefore ... And* *what I say unto you I say unto all,* **Watch** (Mark 13:33, 35, 37). And again: *But* **watch** *ye at every season making supplication, that ye may prevail to escape all these things that shall come to pass, and to stand before the Son of man* (Luke 21:36). The apostle Paul also encouraged us to watch: ... *at all seasons in the Spirit, and* **watching** *thereunto in all perseverance and supplication for all the saints* (Ephesians 6:18 author's emphasis). The fact that the Lord Jesus warned us to *take heed, watch and pray* should be enough to make us seriously consider this matter. As also the words which Luke records: Watch ye at every season making supplication ... Paul adds to the significance of this with his words: Praying at all seasons in the Spirit and watching thereunto ... These are just a few examples in which we are commanded not only to pray but to watch. We should carefully note this emphasis. In fact there are at least twenty references to *watching* in the New Testament; not all of them, of course, are connected with prayer.

THE LORD TEACHES US TO WATCH AND PRAY

The Lord told His disciples to watch and pray that they might not enter into a time of severe testing, and then added: *The spirit is willing but the flesh is weak.* One wonders what would have happened if those disciples had not merely heard the words but understood His meaning behind them, and in obedience had taken positive action. The moment of their test—the temptation to compromise and even to deny Him—was about to come on them. The Lord Jesus had taught the disciples in the pattern prayer to pray: *Lead us not into temptation, but deliver us from the Evil One.* This Greek word, translated so often by the English word *temptation*, is better understood as "testing." The most severe test of their lives was just at hand, and they were unaware of it. Every one of them failed that test, including John.

64

In His incredible understanding of them the Lord Jesus had sought to warn them. He understood their frame and remembered that they were dust. He knew that their spirit was willing but their flesh was weak. He understood everything about them; their lives and personalities were an open book to Him. If they had truly listened they would have understood the meaning behind His words. In Gethsemane the Lord Jesus was also about to face the most severe test of His earthly life, and in His humanity, when He most needed their support, their fellowship, and their comfort, they all fell asleep. They could not even watch for one hour.

How much this has to speak to us! None of us would know times of defeat and failure if we had learned to *watch* and pray. Instead, so often we find ourselves in the midst of a deep crisis and conflict before we are even aware of it; and at that moment we panic, as did those disciples. It was in that crisis that they were tempted to compromise, to lose heart and faith, and even to deny Him. The apostle Paul describes such a time as *an evil day*. In such a day it seems that Satan is in charge; all is dark and devilish, and the Lord is seemingly nowhere to be found. It is as when the disciples were in the boat, and Jesus, on that occasion, had refused to enter it with them. A great storm arose, and they feared for their lives, but Jesus seemed nowhere! When He did appear it was in the midst of the stormy billows, walking on the water. To the disciples He appeared to be a ghost or a phantom and not the Lord! Such is the power of darkness in an "evil day"—that Jesus appears to be a phantom, an apparition and not reality! The fact is the Lord Jesus wanted to teach them how to walk on a stormy sea—to learn to walk through the storms of life with Him.

What is Watching?

If this subject of watching is so strategically important in prayer, we must ask the question: What is *watching*? The Greek word translated by the English word watching simply means to "keep awake and alert." We might better comprehend the meaning of this word if we understood the opposite to it—to be spiritually careless, drowsy, or laid back and half asleep. The Hebrew word *shomer* also means "to watch over, to keep, to guard," and gives an added understanding to the word *watching*.

The Watchmen He Seeks

This association of the word *watching* with prayer therefore gives us the idea of safety and security. In our prayer ministry we are to watch over the interests of the Lord and to guard His rights. In this part of the world watchmen are often old and decrepit. Their presence on a property is supposed to be a deterrent. But in fact, they may be half blind and deaf with not much muscle left. So when we hear of the Lord setting *watchmen on the walls of Jerusalem*, we might think that they have to be very old retired people; only such could be candidates for watchmen! Our whole understanding of this matter of watching will be transformed by seeing watchmen as "security guards." A security guard must be healthy with plenty of strength and muscle and with good sight and hearing. The candidates for which the Lord is seeking are not found in an old age retirement home, as if watching and praying are only for the aged and white haired when they can do nothing else! The Lord's candidates are to be spiritually healthy and strong believers of whatever age—old or young; even very old and white haired! They must have good spiritual sight and hearing and be able to watch over the fulfilment of the will of God in any situation. Remember the words of the apostle Paul: *Be on the alert, stand firm in the faith, act like men, be strong* (I Corinthians 16:13 NASB).

GUARDING AGAINST SATANIC AGENTS

It is very interesting to note that in the New Testament watching is often related to guarding against thieves or robbers or spoilers. These all symbolise spiritual forces or satanic agents who are out to spoil and destroy the life of the believer, the testimony in believing households, the building up of the true Church of God, and the health of the work of God. They are the spiritual beings whom the apostle Paul defines as principalities, powers, world rulers of darkness, hosts of wicked spirits in the heavenlies.

Luke recorded the words of our Lord Jesus: *Blessed are those servants whom the lord when he cometh shall find **watching**: ... But know this, that if the master of the house had known in what hour the thief was coming, he would have **watched**, and not have left his house to be broken through. Be ye also ready: for in an hour that ye think not the Son of man cometh* (Luke 12:37, 39-40 author's emphasis).

The apostle Paul also writes in the same vein: *For yourselves know perfectly that the day of the Lord so cometh as a thief in the night. When they are saying, Peace and safety, then sudden destruction cometh upon them, as travail upon a woman with child; and they shall in no wise escape. But ye, brethren, are not in darkness, that that day should overtake you as a thief: for ye are all sons of light, and sons of the day: we are not of the night, nor of darkness; so then let us not sleep, as do the rest, but let us **watch** and be sober* (I Thessalonians 5:2-4 author's emphasis). It is interesting to note that a number of Scriptures, on the one hand, refer to **Satan and his hosts** as coming like thieves, spoilers and destroyers; and other Scriptures, on the other hand, refer **to the coming of the Lord** as being like a thief in the night, as do these two previous Scriptures we have mentioned. The key matter is to be ready for the Lord and also to guard against satanic agents and devices. The apostle Peter adds his voice to this when he wrote: *Be sober, be watchful; your adversary the Devil, as a roaring lion, walketh about, seeking whom he may devour* (I Peter 5:8).

AN EXAMPLE OF BEING AWAKE AND ALERT

At one time there was a German organization which planned to open up a chain of sex shops in Britain, and they planned for the first one to be in Richmond. As a fellowship of believers we were aware that such shops were becoming a problem all over the country, and we were keeping awake and alert to the whole situation. We were praying against the possibility and watching for the first sign of its appearance. There was no doubt in our mind that the powers of darkness used this kind of outlet to corrupt, to spoil, and to mess up human beings. We had seen the effect and damage it had done on a number of the fellows who had been saved amongst us that "had been delinquents."

One day, a brother in the fellowship came to Halford House and told us that the shop had actually opened opposite the Richmond Railway Station. We decided as a fellowship that we would spend some days in prayer. Those were marvellous times of corporate prayer, and in them the Holy Spirit gave us various promises in the Word of God. On the basis of those promises we stood in the Name of the Lord for the destruction of the sex shop.

On the last evening of prayer we all felt that the Lord had heard our prayer and we began to praise Him. I was quite carried away by the excitement of it all and summed up all our prayer by saying: "Oh, Lord, we put a bomb under this sex shop and blow it up!"

The next morning, Margaret Trickey, who looked after Halford House, came in giggling so much that for a long time she could not tell us what was so funny. Finally, leaning on the doorframe she managed to say, "The sex shop, the sex shop." I said "Margaret, surely you have not been in the sex shop, have you?" She said "No," and at last managed to say, "The porn shop! It is blown up!"

Then it was my turn to have kittens because I thought the police would be around shortly to see us. I imagined them confronting me: "Mr. Lambert, do you have any reason to suspect that a member of your congregation would possibly put a bomb under this shop?" I would say, "Of course not, we would not dream of doing such an unlawful thing!" However, I thought to myself that in our fellowship we have a number of boys who have a police record and had been saved. If the police were to ask one of them he might say, "No, I do not know anyone in the fellowship who would put a bomb under the sex shop, but when our leader prayed, he said, 'Lord, we put a bomb under this sex shop and blow it up.'" I had visions of trying to explain to some magistrate or judge what I had meant.

The truth was different. Margaret had gone into the shop next door and found that they were very annoyed about what had happened. They said the sex shop's gas heating had blown up and had destroyed the building. That was the end of that sex shop! We had been watchful on this issue and sought to deal with it in prayer, and the Lord had acted on our behalf.

WATCHMEN WHO ARE READY, SPIRITUALLY ALERT, AND ALIVE

The need to watch and not only to pray has very much to do with being aware of the events that will usher in the coming of the Lord. Again and again the Lord Himself warns us that we could be caught out by His coming. For those who do not watch, He will come like a thief in the night, suddenly and unexpectedly. The Lord Jesus declared, as recorded by John, in Revelation 16:15: *"Behold, I come as a thief. Blessed is he that watcheth, and keepeth his garments, lest he walk naked, and they see his shame."* Thieves are not in the habit of phoning their victims about their visit. They do not send in a business card with the date and hour of their visiting; they come stealthily, and unexpectedly.

Many years ago my mother was away for a few days, as was also my stepfather, and an aunt came to look after my sister and I. At about two in the morning, my aunt burst into my bedroom and said: "Lance, get up quickly; the whole avenue is filled with police and police dogs and black police vans. They are going in and out of the gardens of different houses. Teresa and I are wondering which neighbour has been burgled."

I quickly got up and rushed into the main bedroom. There my sister and aunt were hanging out of the window, watching with avid interest all that was happening. My aunt thought that a certain neighbour was the one that had been burgled; but my sister said, "That neighbour owns a huge Alsatian dog, which is quite ferocious." Suddenly, my aunt said: "Oh, I feel thirsty; I think I will go downstairs and make myself a cup of coffee." And with that she disappeared downstairs. A moment later there was a blood curdling scream that could have caused the dead to rise from the Parish cemetery a mile across the river. Less than a minute later, like a rocket fired from Cape Canaveral, she was up the stairs and on the top landing, white-faced and shaking. "The thief, the thief," she spluttered; "he is in our kitchen."

My sister said: "Did he say anything?"
"Yes." He said, "Good evening, madam."
"Well, what was he doing?" I said.
"He was eating one of our blancmanges," said my aunt.

It turned out that he was a famous cat burglar. He had burgled thirteen houses that night, and still the police had not been able to catch him. It was a year later when they caught him. He went out of our kitchen in the same way he came in, through a small window in the larder. We had all been discussing who the burglar was visiting—and he was actually in our own house! This illustrates how it is possible to believe that others will be caught out by the coming of the Lord as a thief when it could be us!

Indeed, we will have no excuse if we are caught out by the Lord's coming. We have such a proportion of the Word of God, which accurately and precisely describes the conditions and the events that will lead up to His coming. If we believe in a rapture of those who are ready, as I do, then we need not only to pray but to watch. If we watch what is happening in our nations, or in the world at large, the Spirit of God will alert and prepare us to be ready. The Lord Jesus warns us in the words: *But watch ye at every season, making supplication, that ye may prevail to escape all these things that shall come to pass, and to stand before the Son of man* (Luke 21:36). We are to watch at every season, making earnest enquiry and beseeching appeal that the Lord will keep us awake and alert. To those who watch and are spiritually alive and alert the Holy Spirit will give an "understanding of the times."

He said also: *And there shall be signs in sun and moon and stars; and upon the earth distress of nations, in perplexity for the roaring of the sea and the billows; men fainting for fear, and for expectation of the things which are coming on the world: for the powers of the heavens shall be shaken. And then shall they see the Son of man coming in a cloud with power and great glory. But when these things begin to come to pass, look up, and lift up your heads; because your redemption draweth nigh* (Luke 21:25-28). It seems to me that these words of our Lord are very important and timely. Are we at the beginning of the fulfilment of them? If so, we not only need to pray but to watch and be ready!

WATCHMEN OF SOBER AND BALANCED MINDS

It is not only that we need to watch world events which herald His return, but whilst we have time, we need to grow in the grace and the knowledge of our Lord Jesus Christ, and by that grace be overcomers. It is noteworthy that we are told to be sober and watch: *Wherefore girding up the loins of your mind, be sober and set your hope perfectly on the grace that is to be brought unto you at the revelation of Jesus Christ* (I Peter 1:13). And again: *Be sober, be watchful: ...* (I Peter 5:8a). Furthermore, the apostle Paul writes: *So then let us not sleep, as do the rest, but let us watch and be sober...But let us, since we are of the day, be sober* (I Thessalonians 5:6, 8).

Some believers, who watch these events beginning to take place, go overboard and are anything but sober! In watching, we need to be of a balanced and sound mind. Some of us become prophetic cranks who bring God's prophetic Word into disrepute by our babblings. Some years ago a brother wrote a book entitled: "88 Reasons Why The Lord Is Coming Back On The Festival Of Trumpets (Rosh Hashanah, the Jewish New Year) in September 1988." Everywhere I went Christians asked me about this booklet, and I told them to get in touch with me in October 1988. I was greatly surprised by some of those who questioned me because they were believers who really knew their Bibles. Then in the last months of 1988 it transpired that the brother felt that he had been wrong in his prediction due to a miscalculation he had made. He then proceeded to write another booklet entitled: "89 Reasons Why The Lord Is Coming Back On The Feast of Trumpets, September 1989." Since then we have not heard anymore. The truth is simple and should keep us from making this kind of mistake. The Lord Himself has told us clearly that we would not know the day or the hour of His return: *But of that day or that hour knoweth no one, not even the angels in heaven, neither the Son, but the Father* (Mark 13:32). Hence, the vital need to be ready!

We need to be of a sober and sound mind as we watch these events taking place—earthquakes, tsunamis, volcanic eruptions, huge floods, great fires, and climate change, with the possibility of coming serious famines. To this we must add economic distress, financial instability, and the growing unrest in many nations. All these events have the effect of exciting and unhinging some believers, so much so that their minds become unbalanced. We need, as we watch, to be of a sober and sound mind, being able to view these matters with a cool mind. Indeed we are told to straighten up and lift up our heads, and the Messiah was referring to the Jewish way of worshipping and praying. With living faith we are to worship and to pray because our redemption draws near.

WATCHING AND PRAYING FOR THE HEALTH AND BUILDING UP OF THE CHURCH

The Lord Jesus clearly and dogmatically declared: *Upon this rock I will build my church; and the gates of hell shall not prevail against it* (Matthew 16:18 AV). The history of the Church which the Messiah has been building is an extraordinary one. Again and again, when the gates of hell have seemingly prevailed against His building of the Church, He has launched a new initiative by the Holy Spirit. It is the story of the true and pilgrim Church. The fact that He spoke of the keys of the Kingdom has great significance. Keys represent authority. With keys you lock and unlock. The Lord Jesus had prefaced this statement with the words: *Thou art* **Peter**, which in Greek is *Petros*, "a small stone or pebble." *But upon this* **rock**—*Petra*—"the massif of the rock or the bedrock" *I will build my church.* Peter was always a man of action. He wanted to accomplish matters; unfortunately, it was his flesh which powerfully operated. He was always opening his mouth and putting his foot in it! We have many examples of this in the Gospels. It is amazing that upon the Rock which is the Messiah Jesus, He builds His Church and takes "Peters" and makes them living stones in the House of God!

However, the grace of God goes much further than that. The Lord Jesus says: *I will give unto thee the keys of the kingdom of heaven: and whatsoever thou shalt bind on earth shall be bound in heaven; and whatsoever thou shalt loose on earth shall be loosed in heaven* (Matthew 16:19). As the chief apostle, Peter represents the members of the body of Christ. How amazing that God could take a man, an enormously active man, but a man of the flesh, and make him not only part of His building but give to him the keys of the Kingdom of Heaven. We should note that it is not people who are being bound or loosed. The word "**what**soever" is neuter and is therefore not "**who**soever." It is circumstances that are being locked up or unlocked—not people! These two verbs translated into English as "to bind" or "to loose" are both perfect passive participles. It will help us to understand what the Lord was saying if we translated His declaration as: "Whatever you bind on earth, shall have been bound in heaven, and whatever you loose on earth, shall have been loosed in heaven." As born again believers we are called not only to pray for the will of God to be done but to watch over the performance of it.

In other words, the Church cannot bind that which the throne of God has not bound or loose that which it has not loosed. Nevertheless, the Church has a Divine responsibility, an authority delegated by God the Father to watch and pray, and not only to watch but at times to take action in the Name of the Lord. Maybe the history of the Church would have been very different if we believers had understood that. If only, when matters had begun to deteriorate and backslide in the Church, there had been those who in corporate prayer had used the keys of the Kingdom of Heaven to unlock resurrection life and power and lock up the powers of darkness. Then the history of the Church could have been different and certainly more glorious.

The apostle Paul was a vivid illustration of this when he gave his farewell address to the Church in Ephesus. He said: *Take heed unto yourselves, and to all the flock, in which the Holy Spirit hath made you overseers, to feed the church of the Lord which he purchased with his own blood. I know that after my departing grievous wolves shall enter in among you, not sparing the flock; and from among your own selves shall men arise, speaking perverse things, to draw away the disciples after them. Wherefore watch ye, remembering that by the space of three years I ceased not to admonish every one night and day with tears* (Acts 20:28-31 mg and author's emphasis).

Why do we need to watch in praying for the building, the progress, and the health of the Church? For the very simple reason that the gates of Hell never cease in their attempts to destroy the building work of the Lord Jesus. From the beginning, when the Holy Spirit birthed the Church, Satan has sought to

75

destroy every new initiative that the Lord Jesus has taken. Within a few generations of every such move of the Holy Spirit, it has started to deteriorate, to stagnate, to crystallise, and to become a human system. What happened in the Church in Ephesus is a cameo of what has happened again and again throughout the history of the Church. The good and healthy spiritual food the Church had in the beginning of each great move of the Spirit of God gradually became a watery and milky substance with little real value (see Hebrews 5:12-14). Thus the Church became spiritually anaemic and unhealthy. Within generations it had almost completely moved from its original foundation and course. As in the Church in Ephesus, *savage wolves* from without came in and destroyed the progress and upbuilding of the Church, and men arose from within it speaking perverse things which produced confusion, division and paralysis.

All of this brings home to us the great need, not only to pray but to watch. If those members of the body of Christ in Ephesus had only watched they would have spotted that it was not any more the whole counsel of God that was being given, but rather a watered down Gospel. They would have recognised the savage wolves in sheep's clothing that came in with the world's philosophy, wisdom and methodology; and they would have been alive to those men teaching "perverse things" and bringing confusion and heresy.

WATCHING AND THE WORK OF THE LORD

The work of the Gospel is a vastly important work of God. We have no right to contradict or water down the command of the Lord to go and preach the Gospel to the whole creation, whether that means staying at home and evangelizing in our local setting or going to the ends of the earth. The Lord Jesus prefaced the Great Commission with this declaration: *All authority hath been given unto me in heaven and on the earth*. It is a tremendous statement. He has been given by the Father all authority in Heaven and on this fallen, demonised earth. He then went on to say: *Go ye therefore, and make disciples of all the nations, baptizing them into the name of the Father and of the Son and of the Holy Spirit: teaching them to observe all things whatsoever I commanded you: and lo, I am with you always, even unto the end of the world* (Matthew 28:18-20). We should note the word therefore. It is because all authority in Heaven and on this fallen earth is given into His hands that He commands us to *go* and make disciples of all the nations. This commission comes to us because He is all powerful. The command to go is reinforced by the words with which He concludes the commission: *And lo, I am with you always, even unto the end of the world.* In other words, He is not throwing us out into a world of darkness and evil in which the Devil seems to have the upper hand, and there to make do as best we can out of our own resources and ingenuity. On the contrary, it is because Jesus has all authority and power in His hands that He sends us with all the resources of the throne of God. It is no small thing to have behind us all His resources, His authority and power. The promise is simple and clear: if we obey His command, He will always be with us to the end of the age.

DENNIS CLARK AND THE BIENNIAL INTERCESSOR LEADERS' CONFERENCE

Dennis Clark, of blessed memory, used to lead a time of prayer for intercessor leaders every two years somewhere in the world. There were over forty-two national prayer movements spread across the whole globe. When those intercessor leaders came together, the times we had were powerful. They were times, not only of close fellowship, but of intercession for international matters and for particular nations. During the times of intercession, the Lord very often illuminated our minds concerning international matters and the problems certain nations were facing.

For myself, I discovered that those biennial get-togethers were times when the Lord Himself gave intelligence from His throne. Listening to the prayer of my fellow intercessors, I learnt more about the spiritual condition of whole areas of the world as well as of particular nations. For me it was not only prayer but watching that was so helpful.

WORKERS IN THE WORK OF THE LORD

We have here two vitally important facets to this matter. One is the work of the Lord, which not only includes the work of the Gospel, but also the planting and building up of the Church. The other is to do with the workers, the servants of the Lord who are called into His work. It is obvious that if the workers have little spiritual character and shallow experience of the Lord, the work itself will suffer and even die. The apostle Paul writes: "Building on the foundation which has already been laid, which is the Messiah, the Lord Jesus." He then writes of building on that foundation: *Gold, silver, costly stones, wood, hay, stubble* (see I Corinthians 3:10-15). There is a huge difference between the gold, silver, and costly stones of the life of the Lord Jesus, and the wood, hay, and stubble of our self-life. He prefaces what he has to say here with the words: *We are God's **fellow**-workers* (I Corinthians 3:9). We have here two kinds of work—the work **of** the Lord and work **for** the Lord. The work of the Lord is that which He calls us into, and it is under His government and direction. He promises to be everything in it that the worker needs. The second is work for the Lord, which is our work for the Lord, and it is performed out of our own energy, wisdom, knowledge, and strength. We then need the Lord to get behind us and support and bless us. The first is a matter of gold, silver and costly stones—the treasures of Christ's nature and life. The second is wood, hay and stubble, which can look very beautiful, impressive, and even magnificent, but is in a totally different dimension.

THE V.I.P. GUESTHOUSE IN MANILA

Many years ago in Manila, the capital of the Philippines, I was taken by dear believing friends to see the V.I.P guest house of the previous President of the Philippines which was built by his wife. It was a beautiful and impressive place. Everything within its walls was built out of the palm tree. I could not believe that so much could be created out of the palm tree! It was, however, all wood, hay and stubble, even if it was beautiful and tasteful! Many Christian works are much like the V.I.P guesthouse which Imelda Marcos had built. Outwardly, it looks fine, but it is all the work of human ingenuity and energy.

MAKING DISCIPLES OF ALL THE NATIONS

The commission is not merely to preach the Gospel, vital and important as that is, but it is to make disciples of all the nations. Making a disciple of Jesus out of a saved sinner is the work of the Holy Spirit. We who obey His command "to go" are to be the bondslaves of the Lord. We are called to be the means and the instrument by which the Holy Spirit makes such disciples. If the Spirit of God has been unable to produce spiritual character in us, it will be impossible for Him to use us to make disciples.

SPIRITUAL CHARACTER IS ESSENTIAL IN THE WORKERS

We need to pray for the workers in God's work, that He will produce spiritual character in them, causing them to grow in such a way that they become examples to those whom they lead to the Lord. In watching we need to pray that those workers will have deep and living experience of the Lord. It is interesting to note that when the Lord speaks to the Church in Laodicea, He says: *I counsel thee to buy of me gold refined by fire, that thou mayest become rich ...* (Revelation 3:18). If there is no gold in our spiritual character, how can we use it in God's building work? If our understanding of the Lord falls far below "the whole counsel of God," how can we teach others to observe *all* things that He has commanded? We need the gold, silver, and precious stones of His life and nature in us if our preaching and teaching is going to produce discipleship. The history of the Church teaches us that if our leadership, preaching and teaching ministry of the Word do not come out of deep and costly experience of the Lord, it is wood, hay, and stubble. The Lord Jesus told us to **buy** of Him gold. Since this gold is given to us by the grace of God, what is the price? It is deep and costly experience of Him. We who are workers in the work of God need to watch and pray. We need to be aware that our Lord is not interested in a mere façade. If we are in the work of God, rather than work for the Lord, the Lord Himself will see to it that we come into crises and experiences in which His character is formed in us.

IMPOSSIBLE SITUATIONS AND DIFFICULTIES WHICH FACE THE WORK OF THE LORD

Finally, in this matter of the work of the Lord we need to watch and pray over it. There are situations in nations which, humanly speaking, make the progress and advance of His work impossible! There are not only national situations which create massive problems but local situations. We are called as workers in His work to recognise that whilst these situations may be humanly impossible, with Him there is nothing which He cannot overcome and achieve. With God nothing is impossible! These situations—international, national or local—can range from very large problems to very small ones. The aim of the powers of darkness, however, is always the same. It is to frustrate, paralyse, and destroy the advance of the work of the Lord. We need to learn, not only to pray but to watch and to become aware by the Spirit of God where the problem lies, and how to deal with it.

When at last the whole story is rehearsed, it seems to me that we shall discover that every genuine advance of the Gospel throughout the history of the last two thousand years has involved those who have watched and prayed. Likewise in the great moves of the Spirit of God in the history of the Church, there have been those who have watched and prayed. In those times of renewal by the Spirit, there have been great advances and building up of the Church.

The Lord Opening Closed Nations to the Gospel

Nepal

Years ago it seemed that to preach the Gospel in Nepal was impossible. It was totally closed to any Christian work. The Lord, however, had called two sisters to preach the Gospel in Nepal, Dr. O'Hanlon and Lucy Steele. Since there was no human possibility of entry they lived for quite a time on the slopes of the Himalayan foothills near the border with Nepal. They were quite clear that it was the Lord who had called them. I can remember when the cable came to the little group praying for Nepal, of which I was part, that a miracle had taken place, and they had permission to enter Nepal the following day. Out of that and many more miracles, came the work of the Lord in Nepal. That little prayer group, in my estimation as a teenager, were all very old—gray haired or white haired. I went to the prayer time weekly, but the other young people thought I was mad and wasting my time. "Why do you want to go and spend a whole evening with those old fogies?" they said. I replied to them that we were praying for the Kingdom of Nepal to open to the Gospel. "It will never happen," they said, "not in a thousand years." However, it did happen and I was so excited that I had been part of that prayer meeting. Of course, there must have been many other groups praying for Nepal, but I felt that I had been part of the opening of a closed nation. This is an example of watching and praying.

Afghanistan

Another vivid story that I well remember is the story of Ellen Rasmussen. I met her in Denmark when she was in her late eighties. She recounted to me how when she was a girl of eighteen, the Lord had told her to go to Afghanistan. However, the problem was that Afghanistan was completely closed to any Christian work. She was faced with impossibility. She felt that the Lord would have her go to the Northwest of India, and to an area near the border of Afghanistan which is now Pakistan. For all those years she served the Lord in that area, still believing that the Lord would keep His word to her. The mission in which she served the Lord had a strong stipulation that when their workers reached their mid-sixties, they had to retire. Ellen Rasmussen felt that she could not return to Denmark with the commission which the Lord had given her unfulfilled. So she rented quarters in that area and went on with her work of watching and prayer, continuing to intercede for Afghanistan. When she reached her eightieth year, on one particular day, a man knocked on her front door. When she went to open it, she found a man dressed in the Afghan way and quite obviously from the ruling class. He said,

"Are you Ellen Rasmussen?"

"Yes" she replied "I am."
"Are you a nurse specialised in eye trouble?"
"Yes I am."

Then he said, "I am come from the King of Afghanistan to ask whether you would come to Kabul to nurse the Crown Prince who has eye trouble."

Thus in her eightieth year Ellen Rasmussen saw the Lord fulfill her original calling. As a result of her going, she was able to speak to the king about the need to bring in a specialist eye doctor. The missionary doctor, who came with the king's protection, was able to preach the Gospel. The consequence was that a whole assembly of believers came into being in Afghanistan. It is interesting to note that Ellen had to endure patiently many years of service in North West India before her calling was fulfilled. With God nothing is impossible!

WATCHING AND THE SPIRITUAL GROWTH OF BELIEVERS

There is a further topic I feel I must raise before we conclude this chapter. There is a colossal need of intercession for believers that they would grow up in the Lord. He is not interested in millions of spiritual babies. There is nothing more beautiful than a baby when it is healthy and well formed, but when a baby does not grow, we know that something is wrong. The Kingdom of God into which we have been born by the work of the Spirit of God is sadly filled with spiritual babes who are ten, twenty, thirty or fifty years old in the Lord, but have remained immature and stunted in their growth. They should have long ago grown up and left behind the toys, the dummies and pacifiers of babyhood, or the self-centeredness of their teen years. They should have become good soldiers of the Lord Jesus.

The apostle Paul, writing to the Galatians, wrote: *My little children, of whom I am again in travail until Christ be formed in you* (Galatians 4:19). Conybeare and Howson translate this: *My beloved children, I am again bearing the pangs of travail for you, till Christ be fully formed within you.* The apostle uses a Greek word that speaks of the agony or labour of childbirth. It describes his spiritual experience when he prayed for them. It is not a description of a few easy words in prayer but a condition in which something is being born. It is through spiritual travail and pain. Note carefully that it is "little children" and he uses the word "again." In other words, at some point earlier he had travailed for their spiritual birth. Now he is praying that Christ be fully formed in them.

This kind of prayer ministry is rarely found in these days. It is not only for the spiritual birth of sinners, but it is for the formation of the fullness of Christ in the believer, their growing up into full stature. This is another dimension of watching and prayer. For the lack of it the Church is filled with spiritual babes. The self-centred type of Christianity to which we have now become accustomed is centred in our or my satisfaction, in our or my needs being met. It is what we can gain out of the Lord rather than what we can give Him in service. Who in their right mind, in this type of Christianity, would ever think of laying down their lives for Him, or going to the ends of the earth for Him, or even going into living conditions that would not be comfortable or pleasant in order to serve Him? That kind of Gospel is out of sorts with much modern Christianity.

Of course, I do not mean that our needs should not be met, or that we should not be spiritually satisfied. To stay at that point is not, however, the Gospel that our Lord Jesus preached. If we would know spiritual growth, a growth to full stature, if we would grow up to be soldiers of Christ, we will need to hear and obey the words that He gave: *If any man would come after me, let him deny himself* (give up all right to himself), *and take up his cross, and follow me. For whosoever would save his life shall lose it; and whosoever shall lose his life for my sake and the gospel's shall save it* (Mark 8:34-35 author's emphasis).

With this type of Christianity we will never find believers who, called of God, will give themselves to the Lord and know the Holy Spirit conceiving in them burdens for the full spiritual growth of other younger children of God. Those burdens will involve a kind of travail. How thankful many of us are for older believers who, when we were saved, without our having any knowledge of it travailed for us behind the scenes. They travailed that we would be kept from the powers of darkness, from the enticements of the world, and experience a spiritual growth to full stature.

It is not only travailing prayer which is needed, but a sensitive and loving watching. Spiritual babes do not need harsh and impersonal legalism, nor a critical attitude or spirit but loving care. There are not so many Christian workers who would open themselves up to the Holy Spirit for such burdens to be conceived within them. The Lord had this kind of loving and sensitive care for Peter. Apparently He had watched and had already interceded for him: *Simon, Simon, behold, Satan asked to have you, that he might sift you as wheat: but I made supplication for thee, that thy faith fail not; and do thou, when once thou hast turned again, establish thy brethren* (Luke 22:31-32). Due to the intercession of Jesus, the Lord received the wheat and Satan obtained the husks! This is the kind of intercession that comes through watching and praying.

For want of this type of intercession, we have so many babes in the Church of God. This ministry of travail will always be successful since it is conceived by the Holy Spirit. It came from the enthroned Lord Jesus, by the Holy Spirit, into willing and committed believers. It will end in the throne of God. *They that sow in tears shall reap in joy. He that goeth forth and weepeth, bearing seed for sowing, shall doubtless come again with joy, bringing his sheaves with him* (Psalm 126: 5-6).

COUNT ZINZENDORF AND THE MORAVIANS

When Nicholas, Count Zinzendorf was saved as a young man, one of the most brilliant chapters in the history of the Church and the work of God was written. He had been in a museum where he saw a painting of the crucified Christ. He was so captivated by this painting that he stood before it for more than an hour without moving. Underneath the painting were the words, "I have done all this for thee, what hast thou done for Me?" Those words were burnt into the heart of Zinzendorf by the Holy Spirit. At that point he committed his whole life and being to the Lord; he surrendered his will to God. The Lord produced in him the kind of spiritual character that was to influence all the leaders of the Moravian movement and many others. He used his castle and his estate as a sanctuary for persecuted believers in that area of Central Europe; they came to him for refuge from all the surrounding region.

When the Holy Spirit fell upon them in one particular meeting, that movement was to touch the whole world. The hundred year's long prayer meeting began, and workers were sent out to all the most difficult places on the face of the earth. The spiritual character which the Holy Spirit produced in Count Zinzendorf was to be reproduced in many others. In order to reach slaves, workers became slaves; in order to reach lepers, the workers contracted leprosy, not willingly but joyfully that they might reach lepers. The total commitment of the leadership and workers to the Lord Jesus in this move of the Spirit of God became proverbial. They went to all the places which were impossible and shunned by so many other Christian workers. No self-sacrifice was too great or too painful for them.

JOHN WESLEY

It was in a small meeting in Fetter Lane in the City of London that John Wesley, a failed missionary, came to the Lord. John Wesley had his first contact with the Moravians in the ship which took him to the colonies in America. He did not even know the Lord, but he was going to preach the Gospel to the Red Indians! In the midst of the Atlantic a huge storm hit the ship and it seemed that it would be shipwrecked. The sailors panicked and so did John Wesley. He was in the hold of the ship when he thought he heard singing and wondered whether he was already in Heaven. Moving towards where the singing was coming from, he slowly opened the door and saw to his amazement that the whole room was filled with Moravians. They had children sitting on their knees and babies being nursed in their arms, and all of them were in perfect peace. He marvelled at it and thought to himself: "I wish I had faith like these people." After having worn himself out in seeking to save Red Indians, he returned to Britain a failure. He wrote in his journal, "I came to save the Red Indians, but Oh, God, who can save me?"

At this small meeting in Fetter Lane a Moravian preacher was reading the preface to one of Martin Luther's books. As the Moravian preacher read it, John Wesley felt a strange warming in his heart: The Lord had saved him. It was the beginning of the Great Evangelical Awakening in the British Isles. The spiritual character of Count Zinzendorf and the Moravian believers infected John Wesley. From the moment he was saved, he committed himself totally to the Lord Jesus. The labours of John Wesley throughout the British Isles and the colonies of America are memorable. At ninety-four years of age he was still preaching some four times a day, travelling by horseback in all kinds of British weather. He was a living sacrifice. When Wesley went to be with the Lord, King George III who was not a believer decreed three days of mourning. John Wesley was buried by Royal decree in Westminster Abbey. No one has ever been able to compute the enormous influence of the Wesley brothers and of Count Zinzendorf on the building up of the Church and the advance of the work of God. We only know that untold thousands came to a saving experience of the Lord Jesus.

THE THREE MORAVIAN SISTERS SERVING THE LORD ON THE MOUNTAINS OF SAMARIA

Many years ago I was visiting the sisters who ran the Evangelical Girl's Home in Ramallah. Gladys Roberts, who had been with Rees Howells throughout the war years in the prayer meetings in Wales, told me of three remarkable Moravian sisters in the mountains of Samaria. They were living and serving in a small cluster of white buildings which you could easily pass by without noticing. They were all in their late seventies or eighties and had been cut off from all Moravian support and fellowship due to communism in Eastern Europe. They cared for a few lepers in advanced leprosy. They had to carry them to the bathroom, wash them, feed them, and care for them. Gladys asked me whether I would like to visit them. "It will mean much to them," she said. For me it was an incredibly moving experience to meet these frail old saints. No one knew about them, nothing was ever written about them, but they had unfailingly served the Lord in caring for those lepers. They served them as if they were serving the Lord Jesus. All these centuries later, they still had the same spiritual character as Count Zinzendorf. They were totally devoted and committed to the Lord Jesus. He was their life, and they were living sacrifices for Him.

There is a hymn composed by Charles Wesley which sums up the kind of spiritual character that lies behind true watching and prayer. If we are to serve the Lord, the growth of that character is an absolute necessity. This hymn certainly describes the secret that lies at the heart of the service of Count Zinzendorf and the early Moravians, John and Charles Wesley and the early Methodists. Indeed it lies at the heart of the service of all those who have followed the Lord wholeheartedly from the beginning until this day.

> Oh Thou who camest from above
> The pure celestial fire to impart,
> Kindle a sacred flame of love
> Upon the mean altar of my heart.
>
> There let it for Thy glory burn
> With inextinguishable blaze;
> And trembling to its source return,
> In humble prayer and fervent praise.
>
>
> Jesus, confirm my heart's desire
> To work, and speak, and think for Thee;
> Still let me guard the holy fire,
> And still stir up Thy gift in me.
>
> Ready for all Thy perfect will,
> My acts of faith and love repeat,

Till death Thine endless mercies seal,
And make the sacrifice complete.

CERTAIN PRIORITIES DEFINED

Firstly: There has to be a total and undivided commitment to the Lord Jesus. If we are not devoted to Him there is no possibility of the Spirit of God producing spiritual character in us. He has to be the beginning and the end of our life, and of our service. In the final analysis it is an ongoing, living, and fresh experience of Him which determines everything.

Secondly: The worker is far more important than the work he does. If the Lord cannot do a work in the worker, his work will be shallow and superficial. This is the reason why the question of spiritual character is so important. The difference is, on the one hand, the gold, silver and costly stones of what He works in us; or on the other hand, the wood, hay, and stubble of our self-life.

Thirdly: The major part of our problem is centred in our will. To surrender our will entirely to the Holy Spirit is no small or easy matter, but it is that surrender which opens the gate to a new dimension of spiritual life, power, and experience.

Fourthly: The aim of the Gospel is that we should present our bodies as a living sacrifice, which is our spiritually intelligent worship and service (see Romans 12:1). All true spiritual character and service flows from this.

Fifthly: Without these four qualities, it is impossible to be led of the Holy Spirit, consistently and continually. *For as many as are led by the Spirit of God, these are sons of God* (Romans 8:14). We should note that it is not "babes" that are led by the Spirit, but those in whom there is some spiritual growth and stature.

90

Lastly: The whole subject of watching and praying springs out of these qualities! Without total commitment and devotion to being conformed to the likeness of Christ, without a surrender of our will to the Spirit of God—which results in a readiness to be a living sacrifice—without a progressive experience of being led by Him, there can be no genuine watching and prayer.

6
THE MANIFESTATION OF THE SPIRIT

I Corinthians 12:4-11 NASB—Now there are varieties of gifts, but the same Spirit. And there are varieties of minis-tries, and the same Lord. And there are varieties of effects, but the same God who works all things in all persons. But to each one is given the manifestation of the Spirit for the common good. For to one is given the word of wisdom through the Spirit, and to another the word of knowledge according to the same Spirit; to another faith by the same Spirit, and to another gifts of healing by the one Spirit, and to another the effecting of miracles, and to another prophecy, and to an-other the distinguishing of spirits, to another various kinds of tongues, and to another the interpretation of tongues. But one and the same Spirit works all these things, distributing to each one individually just as He wills.

Romans 8:26-27— And in like manner the Spirit also helpeth our infirmity: for we know not how to pray as we ought; but the Spirit himself maketh intercession for us with groanings which cannot be uttered; and he that searcheth the hearts knoweth what is the mind of the Spirit, because He maketh intercession for the saints according to the will of God.

THE MANIFESTATION OF THE SPIRIT

All true and genuine corporate prayer is a manifestation of the Presence of the Holy Spirit. The Greek word translated by the English word *manifestation* literally means "to make visible, or observable; to make known, or to make clear." Essentially, it has the idea of uncovering, of laying bare, or of revealing a matter. When we understand this, we begin to comprehend the real meaning of the manifestation of the Spirit. The Holy Spirit is uncovering the mind and the will of the Head—revealing His burden and concern. The aim of the Spirit is to enable us, through the spiritual weapons which He supplies to us, to realise a successful outcome or to take executive action when necessary. Sometimes in prayer we only dimly understand what the mind of the Lord is on any given matter, because His mind is not clear to us. The manifestation of the Spirit however gives crystal clarity to our time of corporate prayer. Sometimes we only need to know what we are up against; we may feel all kinds of currents in the atmosphere. It may be a heaviness, or an onslaught of the powers of darkness, or it may be something else; but we are not aware as to what those currents might be. Other times we are not clear as to what the goal and aim of the Lord is in particular situations.

It is the grace of God when there is a manifestation of the Spirit through which we come to a revelation of the mind of the Lord. If the Lord Jesus has been made Head over all things to the Church, then it seems only spiritually logical to expect that He will make known practically how we are to pray and proceed. The uncovering and laying bare of the heart of God is the strategic significance of the manifestation of the Spirit.

We are told that this manifestation of the Spirit is for the *common good* (NASB), *to profit withal* (AV and ASV). The Spirit of God manifests Himself to the advantage of the whole body. It is interesting to note that *to each one is given the manifestation of the Spirit*. It is in fact the body of Christ in action or the members of His body functioning as they should. Furthermore, if there is to be an outcome to our prayer through the Holy Spirit, we need to be harmonised, to be together, or to be "agreed." Thus a time of corporate prayer becomes a thermometer of the health of a congregation or a fellowship. If we do not know how to move together, we are merely a collection of individuals saved by His grace but strangers to the functioning of His body.

We are urged by the apostle Paul: *With all prayer and supplication praying at all seasons in the Spirit.* As we have already explained in chapter four such "praying in the Spirit" can only be experienced when we are under the sovereign leading and enabling power of the Holy Spirit (see Ephesians 6:18). It is a spiritual dimension into which we enter; it is His burden that is conceived in us; He is the One who prompts us, leads us, and enables us to pray. That means we are under and in the anointing of the Spirit. He is also the One who harmonises us and empowers us not only to understand what the will of God is but to see His will fulfilled in practice on this fallen earth. Corporate prayer is thus in the realm and dimension of the Spirit of God. If that is true, then there must be times when the Holy Spirit manifests Himself in specific ways.

THE GIFTS OF THE SPIRIT

The gifts of the Spirit are the equipment, the tools, and the weapons with which we can accomplish the work. Whilst these gifts apply to much more than corporate prayer, they are strategic and vital to such prayer if the Lord is to direct us accurately and efficiently. No one would think of fixing a car engine with a paint brush or of trying to paint a house with a wrench. One needs the right tools! It would be a shock if one had to have an appendix operation, and the surgeon came with a tree saw and a mallet. If a patient were to ask him, "Why have you come with a tree saw and a mallet?" It would be no small shock to hear him say, "The mallet is to knock you out, and the tree saw is to cut you open!" One would feel that he was not in possession of the right equipment! When we have the right equipment, or the correct weapons for the time of prayer, the work that the Lord wants us to do can be done properly and efficiently.

The Holy Spirit manifests Himself in many ways. In corporate prayer He uses a number of the gifts which He manifests amongst us. By the Holy Spirit Paul, in fact, writes of nine gifts: The *word of wisdom*, the *word of knowledge, faith,* the *gifts of healing,* the *effecting of miracles, prophecy,* the *distinguishing of spirits, various kinds of tongues,* and the *interpretation of tongues* (see I Corinthians 12:8-10 NASB). All of these are to the advantage of the whole body—to its building up, its functioning, and its spiritual health. Some of those gifts are particularly useful in corporate prayer. Let us consider some of them.

The Word of Knowledge

For example, in corporate prayer a word of knowledge can be a key to unlocking so much. It is the explanation of the facts in any situation, problem, circumstance, or satanic onslaught. To know those facts is at least fifty percent of the way towards victory. Many times we are completely nonplussed by situations which confront a fellowship or an assembly, or which confront the work of the Lord, and we cannot make any headway at all. The reason is that we are ignorant of the facts. To know the facts in any given situation may immensely help us, but it is not the full answer.

The Word of Wisdom

A word of wisdom can change the whole atmosphere of a time of corporate prayer. The manifestation of the Spirit in a word of wisdom gives us the understanding of how to *handle* the facts. This means that we are seventy-five percent of the way towards victory. Simply because we have knowledge of the facts of any situation or problem does not mean that we know how to proceed in prayer. To know how to handle those facts means that we can proceed with great confidence in the Lord and witness the fulfilment of our prayer.

In the early part of the Yom Kippur War in Israel in 1973, a number of local believers had met together in Jerusalem for intercession. The war was in a "touch and go" state. The matter that was so much on the hearts of Israel's Defence Minister, Moshe Dayan, and the Chief of Staff, David Elazar, was the possibility that the Hashemite Kingdom of Jordan would join Syria and Egypt in attacking Israel. Of all our neighbours, Jordan has the longest border with Israel.

We were praying with great passion and purpose when suddenly Colonel Orde Dobbie broke in to our prayer with the words: "Would you all please judge this? Three times I have seen the same picture of large clouds coming down and blotting out the mountains of Moab. (The Mountains of Moab are in modern day Jordan.) I do not understand it, but I wonder does it have some meaning for our prayer time?" Orde Dobbie was not an emotional man and was from a military family, which for many generations had served in the British army. We all began to pray that the Lord would show us whether this was from the Lord and what it signified. Suddenly one of those present said, "Should we not pray that Jordan will be so confused by the Lord that they will not enter this war?" If Jordan had come into the war, in all likelihood, it would have tilted the war in favour of the Arabs. We all felt that we should pray in that manner, and we did with great fervour. The Hashemite Kingdom of Jordan, in fact, never came into the Yom Kippur War and was roundly criticized for not doing so by Syria, Egypt, and other Arab states.

At least a month later I was staying with my mother in the family home in Richmond, England, when I suddenly heard my mother calling my name and saying, "Lance, come down quickly. King Hussein is being interviewed on the television." I came down in time to hear the interviewer saying, "But, your majesty, you must know that all the Arab states around you are criticizing you for not coming into that war." King Hussein replied, "We had made the decision to enter the war, but suddenly, we became greatly confused by the fact that we did not have sufficient air cover, and thus we decided we could not enter it."

This is a good illustration of the Holy Spirit manifesting a word of knowledge and then a word of wisdom, and thus leading us all in prayer, with perfect result.

The Gift of Faith

When the Holy Spirit manifests Himself in a gift of faith, and it is expressed, it can make all the difference between defeat and failure or victory. Many times in corporate prayer the expression of God given faith spells a breakthrough, and the realisation of victory. There are many occasions when one has witnessed this. After much prayer, sometimes prolonged prayer, suddenly one child of God expresses with their lips their faith that the Lord has heard and answered. Almost immediately, there is a witness in others that it is true; and the prayer time changes from earnest appeal and petition, or spiritual warfare, to praise and worship.

In one prayer time in Jerusalem, when we were in prayer concerning a very prickly and complex situation, which seemed to be as unyielding as iron, someone expressed their faith that we had been heard and that the Lord would act. We then began to praise and thank the Lord. One of the brothers took down a large and ancient shofar which was hanging on the wall, and gave it to another brother who could blow it properly. When he blew the shofar, the sound resonated in the spirits of all who were present and lifted us onto another level. We saw in the weeks that followed the practical answer to that prayer; and we worshipped the Lord.

The Discernment of Spirits

In many situations which are being raised in corporate prayer, there are some problems that are very complex. On occasions when no solution can be found for a problem, and it is unusually complex, more often than not it is a sign that there is demonic influence involved. Sometimes it is more than an influence; it is a bondage which appears to be unbreakable; a blockage which is immovable. It is here that the manifestation of the Spirit in the gift of discerning or distinguishing spirits is vital. Once there is a demonic hold on the problem, it cannot be broken or moved until we recognise and know which kind of spirit is involved. The Word of God is absolutely clear on this: *That through death He might bring to nought him that hath the power of death, that is, the devil; and might deliver all them...*(Hebrews 2:14b-15a). The finished work of the Messiah spells total victory over all the works of the Devil involved in situations, problems, or in people. Once we know what we are facing in the problems, we can stand firmly on the finished work of the Messiah and see the demonic grip and hold on them broken.

Prophecy

Many times international, national, or even local situations appear dark and confusing, and we cannot make head or tail of them. When the Holy Spirit manifests Himself in prophetic utterance, it is like a light shining on them. Of course, we need to test every prophetic utterance by the Word of God, and the witness within our spirit. However, when it is truly of God, it can be like a beacon illuminating the way in which we ought to pray. The unfailing test of whether a prophecy is genuine or not is whether what is uttered is fulfilled.

DAVID WILKERSON'S PROPHECY

Years ago the Holy Spirit used David Wilkerson to warn the United States that serious trouble and judgment was coming on that nation. That prophetic utterance has not yet been completely fulfilled. The beginning of that fulfilment was 9/11, but there is much more to come. The prophetic utterance the Lord gave him should have been enough, however, to activate and energise prayer warriors in the United States to intercede on behalf of their nation. In a real sense David Wilkerson's prophecy is a light illuminating the way in which we ought to pray for the United States. Certainly it seems that America is on a downhill path, and much more serious judgment is coming. I have myself likened the States to the ship, Titanic, which was thought to be unsinkable but was, in fact, sailing into an iceberg with all lights blazing and the bands playing. It sank within a very short time.

In 1998 David Wilkerson published a book entitled, *God's Plan to Protect His People in the Coming Depression*. It was prophetic and began to be fulfilled in 2008. This kind of prophetic utterance or writing is a light on our path that we might understand how to pray and intercede.

THE PROPHETIC CONFERENCE IN CARMEL AND JERUSALEM, APRIL 1986

There was a conference of Christian leaders on prophecy in April 1986 that was held on Mount Carmel and concluded with a final meeting in Jerusalem. There was a prophetic utterance that the Lord would judge the Soviet Union and the Kremlin for all that it had done. I will only quote a part of it:

"It will not be long before there will come upon the world a time of unparalleled upheaval and turmoil. Do not fear; it is I the Lord who am shaking all things. I began this shaking with the First World War, and I greatly increased it through the Second World War. Since 1973 I have given it an even greater impetus. In the last stage, I plan to complete it with the shaking of the universe itself, with signs in sun and moon and stars. But before that point is reached, I will judge the nations and the time is near. It will not only be by war and civil war, by anarchy and terrorism, and by monetary collapses that I will judge the nations, but also by natural disasters—by earthquake, shortages and famines, and old and new plague diseases. I will also judge them by giving them over to their own ways, to lawlessness, to loveless selfishness, to delusion and to believing a lie, to false religion and an apostate Church, even to a Christianity without Me.

Do not fear when these things begin to happen, for I will disclose these things to you before they commence, in order that you might be prepared, and that in the day of trouble and of evil, you may stand firm and overcome. For I purpose that you may become the means of encouraging and strengthening many who love Me but are weak. I desire that through you many may become strong in Me, and that multitudes of others might find My salvation through you.

And hear this! Do not fear the power of the Kremlin nor the power of the Islamic Revolution, for I plan to break both of them through Israel. I will bring down their pride and their arrogance, and shatter them because they have blasphemed My Name. In that day I will avenge the blood of all the martyrs and of innocent ones whom they have slaughtered. I will surely do this thing, for they have thought that there was no one to judge them. But I have seen their ways, and I have heard the cries of the oppressed and the persecuted, and I will break their power and make an end of them. Be therefore prepared, for when all this comes to pass, to you will be given the last great opportunity to preach the gospel freely to all the nations."

This prophetic utterance gave us all much illumination as to the course that contemporary history was taking. It also gave us clear direction as to how to pray for the Soviet Union and its empire, and its many satellites. The Lord would break its enormous power and the grip it had on so many. We were also warned to take seriously the Islamic Revolution and Revival.

A few years before this prophetic utterance, the Soviet Empire was led by a highly influential KGB officer, Yuri Andropov. His influence permeated even the immediate years after he stepped down in 1984, and the Soviet Union seemed as powerful as ever; therefore it appeared unlikely that it would break up, let alone be ended. However, within a few years of that prophetic utterance it had all happened. The Soviet Empire broke up. Many of the Soviet states within it, such as Kazakhstan, Uzbekistan, Azerbaijan, even Georgia and Armenia became free (in fact there are more states than I have mentioned which have also become free). The grip of Marxism on Russia was loosened; the Wall dividing Berlin was destroyed and East and West Germany were reunited; the Iron Curtain fell; and the whole of Eastern Europe and the Baltic States were freed. Many of those states today are part of the European Union.

Incredibly, the old national flag of Russia with its white, red and blue bands replaced the Soviet Union's red flag with its yellow hammer and sickle. No one who has lived through that era of the domination of International Marxism which was centred in the Kremlin could ever have believed that this would happen. Even the double-headed eagle with the crown above the two heads, which represented old Russia under the Czars, appeared on the wall of the cabinet room of the new Russian government. Half the evangelical world believed that Marxism, centred in the Kremlin, was the predicted Anti-Christ which would take the whole world. Yet the Lord smashed it and broke it up.

Even more remarkable, in the nineteen-nineties, the Patriarch of the Russian Orthodox Church was allowed to conduct a solemn service of repentance for the murder of the Czar, the Czarina, and the Czarevich (Crown Prince). It began in the Cathedral and then proceeded in a sombre march around the Kremlin with candles and portraits of the murdered Royal family. Amazingly, the President of Russia, Boris Yeltsin, was present along with other leaders. No one who has lived through this era would have ever believed that this could happen or was even possible! It is astonishing to recognise that seventy years after the Marxist Constitution was signed in the Kremlin Palace it was torn up and discarded in the same Kremlin Palace.

This prophetic utterance was like light shining on what appeared to be an impossibility. For those who were watching, as well as praying, the Lord gave the right weapons to pray for the break-up of the Soviet Marxist Empire, for the releasing and for the upbuilding of the Church of God in Russia, in the former Soviet States, and in the erstwhile Communist States of the Baltic and of Eastern Europe. For some Christians it gave a clear understanding of the course that their work should take.

THE INTERNATIONAL INTERCESSOR LEADERS' CONFERENCE— NOVEMBER 1998

Here is another illustration. In one of the biennial International Intercessors leaders' conferences, which was held in Caliraya, Laguna, the Philippines, in November 1998, a prophetic utterance was given. I quote only a portion of that word.

"My anger is stirred up," says the Lord, "against those nations for they are dividing My land and seeking to destroy My heritage. My furious anger is like a boiling cauldron against those powerful states that have produced such strategies and who, by pressure and manipulation, are seeking to implement them. Now I will become their enemy, says the Lord, and I will judge them with natural disasters, by physical catastrophes, by fire, by flood, by earthquake and by eruptions. I will touch the seas, the atmosphere, the earth and all that is within them. Moreover, I will touch them where it will hurt them the most, for I will touch their power and the foundations of their affluence and prosperity. I will smash their prosperous economies, says the Lord. And I will overturn, and overturn, and overturn that they may know that I am the LORD. They sit like potentates, so safe, so secure, believing in their own cleverness and wisdom and power but I, the Lord, will cause them to stumble. I will lead them into confusion and disorder. I will blind them and delude them so that they will make mistakes, because they have not regarded Me nor honoured Me. Instead, they have devalued Me, deriding My Word and ignoring My covenants. For too long I have been quiet," says the Lord, "but now will I arise in overflowing anger and fury. In dividing My land and seeking to demoralise and destroy My people Israel, they have thrown down the gauntlet. I, the Lord of Hosts, the Almighty One, will take them on."

When this prophetic utterance came to the intercessor leaders, it was at a time of great economic prosperity, a boom in the housing market, and seeming solid financial stability. To all of us it seemed as if the prophecy was far removed from reality. Nonetheless, in 2008, ten years later, it all began to be fulfilled. Since then it has grown in power, with deep recession, high unemployment, and economic and financial instability. At the same time we have seen earthquakes, tsunamis, volcanic eruptions, floods of what the media has called, "Biblical proportions," terrible fires, and the like.

At least forty-two national intercession movements were represented at this conference, and it gave us all the opportunity to pray for the future of the nations. It also gave some light as to the strategic position and importance which Israel occupies in the purpose and economy of God. It helped us to recognise that we could not hold a balanced and sound eschatological view without understanding Israel. We also understood from this prophetic utterance the danger which the Islamic Revolution and Revival present, and the part Israel will play, by the hand of God, in its destruction.

It would always be good if we were to remember the words that the apostle Paul wrote concerning prophetic utterance: *Do not quench the Spirit; do not despise prophetic utterances. But examine everything carefully; hold fast to that which is good; abstain from every form of evil* (I Thessalonians 5:19-22 NASB).

THE OTHER FOUR GIFTS

The four gifts—healing, the effecting of miracles, various kinds of tongues, and the interpretation of tongues—may at times have a very important part to play in corporate prayer; although this manifestation of the Spirit may have more to do with other meetings of the people of God. For instance, a tongue and its interpretation in a time of corporate prayer may be a prophetic utterance, or a word of knowledge, or a word of wisdom. The Lord may be emphasizing a matter in this more distinctive manner. The gifts of healing and the effecting of miracles may also flow out of a time of corporate prayer.

The Lord Using His Word to Direct Us

Many times the manifestation of the Spirit is expressed by the use of the Word of God. In a time of corporate prayer, the Holy Spirit brings to some child of God a Scripture which he or she reads out, and it unlocks for all of us the mind and will of the Lord. Such contributions of Scripture under the government of the Spirit, may become a word of knowledge, or a word of wisdom, or a word of prophecy, and should be taken up and acted upon by the others in that prayer time. Often it has been my experience that the Lord has used some member of the body to show us the way ahead; at times the Lord has led us into the fulfilment of His will through such contributions. Someone had a word of Scripture on their heart, read it, and left others to judge it. When it was taken up by all, we so often came into the fulfilment of His mind and heart. The use of the Word of God in corporate prayer is of the highest value.

Prayer Which is Inaudible and Inexpressible

The apostle Paul writes of a ministry of prayer which is inaudible. This ministry of the Holy Spirit in our spirit is deeper than words, deeper than even a tongue, and deeper than utterance. It is an intercession that cannot be expressed in any audible language or manner. The Holy Spirit is interceding in us *for the saints* and it is *according to the will of God*. This ministry of travail is an agonizing of the Holy Spirit in our spirit; it is trapped unexpressed within the child of God and will always have a result.

And in like manner the Spirit also helpeth our infirmity: for we know not how to pray as we ought; but the Spirit himself maketh intercession for us with groanings which cannot be uttered; and he that searcheth the hearts knoweth what is the mind of the Spirit, because He maketh intercession for the saints according to the will of God (Romans 8:26-27). This is also a manifestation of the Spirit. The deepest mystery is that the expression in audible and understandable words in prayer is the least part of it! It is like the tip of an iceberg; the majority of it is hidden under the surface. This kind of intercession is in our spirit, and it is the Holy Spirit at work within us.

It is only found in those who are totally devoted to the Lord and committed to Him. Such children of God have a ministry in their spirit, which only the Lord can read, receive and understand. It is an unceasing ministry of intercession. It is a fulfilment of the word: *Pray without ceasing* (I Thessalonians 5:17).

CORPORATE PRAYER IS A TWO-WAY EXCHANGE

The time of corporate prayer is not only a time when we pour out all our needs, our burdens, and our petitions to the Lord; it is also a time when He speaks to us, revealing His mind and will. The incredible mindset that has developed amongst many Christians is that in a prayer time we have to do all the talking; we do not even expect the Lord to speak to us. Indeed, if the Lord was to answer our earnest and beseeching appeal and speak, many of us would drop dead with shock! We do not expect a corporate time of prayer to be a place where the Lord speaks to us; it is a time only for our speaking to the Lord.

The Lord Jesus went to the heart of the matter when He said: *My sheep hear my voice, and I know them, and they follow me* (John 10:27). In other words, He desires, not only to hear our voice expressing our needs and concerns, but wants us to hear His voice and follow Him. It is noteworthy that He speaks of *following Him*. We need direction from the Lord if we are truly to follow Him and do His will. How many times I have watched and heard the shepherd leading his flock. He talks to them in a language which is neither, Hebrew, Greek, or English, or any other human language, but the sheep understand him. It is the goats which present the problem; they willfully do not hear and disobey the shepherd. They want to follow their own will, their own mind, and their own satisfaction. It is a necessity however to hear the Lord if we will follow Him. There is no alternative to hearing His voice!

Many years ago I was plagued by a sister who always tried to get through to me on the telephone. She lived more than a hundred miles away. At Halford House we all knew that the moment we took up the phone and heard her voice, it would be at least forty-five to fifty minutes; and in that time we would not get a word in edgeways. Therefore, Margaret Trickey, who looked after the house, and others, tried to shield me from her. However, there were times late in the evening when I was working on a Bible study or Bible research relating to the study and was the only person in the place, and the phone would ring and it would be this sister. She always exploded with: "Praise the Lord or hallelujah; at last I have got through to you. God has given you such a gift of counsel and wisdom, and I need to avail myself of it." Before I could even say a word, she started to pour out whatever concern was on her heart.

It was always an overflowing of words. It seemed she hardly took a breath, and I found that it was impossible to say anything—not a single word. All through her speaking, every now and again, she told me how gifted I was with wisdom from the Lord, and then went on expressing her concern. This happened so often that actually I used to put the phone down and carry on with my study or research; now and again just taking it up and saying "yes." After about forty-five or fifty minutes she would say, "Praise the Lord, you have given me the counsel to do exactly what I thought I should do. Thank you again for being so available to the Lord." And with that she would ring off. I never had the chance to give her any counsel, or express any wisdom that she thought the Lord might have given me. If I had shouted at the top of my voice to her, I do not think she would have heard, because she was so full of the concern that was on her mind.

This is exactly like some of our prayer times. The dear Lord is bombarded with our concerns, with our burdens, and with our petitions, and has no chance whatsoever to utter His voice! There is not even an expectation that He would speak. Yet in the prayer time the Lord is often praised as a wonderful counsellor, and He is told that all the treasures of wisdom and knowledge are hidden in Him and that the Holy Spirit is able to make that wisdom a practical reality to us. If He were to speak, however, as I have already written, many of us in the prayer time would either faint or have a heart attack!

The lesson we need to learn from this illustration is simple and clear. We should expect the Lord to reveal His mind concerning the burdens or petitions that we are making. Corporate prayer is a two-way exchange.

PRACTICAL POINTS

Firstly: Always be available to the Holy Spirit. Many times He is unable to manifest Himself because we are unavailable. Often we think that it is enough that we are there to pray! When we come into a time of corporate prayer, we should bow our head and deliberately make ourselves available for His use in whatever way He chooses. Some Christians get very nervous about the Holy Spirit manifesting Himself, but that is no excuse for our unavailability. It may be that He will put a Scripture on your heart that will be a word of knowledge, or a word of wisdom, or even a prophetic utterance giving light on a situation or problem. However, we have to be available to him.

Secondly: Expect the Holy Spirit to prompt you and enable you to contribute. He fully understands your fear of making a mistake, or that you feel you are giving to yourself a greater prominence than you should have. However, let the Holy Spirit decide that! True humility is to be ready for the Lord to speak through you!

Thirdly: Learn from any mistake you make; remember all of us will make mistakes. We learn more from our mistakes as we grow up than in any other way. It is what we do with our mistakes that counts. It is a false humility to go into a deep depression over the mistakes we make and proceed to beat ourselves. In a time of corporate prayer the problem is that everyone knows when we make a mistake and our pride and self-estimate receives a hard blow. If, however, we learn from our mistakes, we grow in the grace and in the knowledge of the Lord.

One remembers the story of a brother who said, "Thus saith the Lord; do not fear My children, for I am with you. As Joshua led the children of Israel through the Red Sea, so will I protect and lead you. Do not fear." Then the brother said, "The Lord saith; I have made a mistake! It was Moses who led them through the Red Sea, not Joshua!" This was a mistake made in front of everyone and obviously was not a manifestation of the Spirit! One hopes that the brother learnt from his mistake!

Fourthly: Be yourself in the Lord. Do not use an artificial or a theatrical voice when the Holy Spirit manifests Himself in you. Use your normal voice and behave in your normal manner. Only remember to speak up so that everyone can hear you. What is the difference between the normal voice you use in prayer and the expression of a gift? Why do we feel that we have to become like Shakespearean actors and actresses when we use a gift? In fact many are disconcerted by such abnormality and become so distracted that they lose the leading of the Holy Spirit. When a person either shouts a gift at the top of their voice, or shrieks a tongue or prophecy, it is more an evidence of the flesh than a manifestation of the Holy Spirit!

Fifthly: Faith is always the basis for the manifestation of the Spirit and not emotion. We need to be careful that we do not exercise a spiritual gift on the basis of emotion or feeling. Some Christians seem to have the idea that the only time you can ever use such a gift is when you are engulfed with a wave of emotion and feeling. The basis for prophetic utterance in the pagan or occult world is always that a spirit possesses you, and suspends your normal judgment. You are not even aware of what you are saying or the actions you are taking. With mediums in the occult everywhere, wizards and witches in Africa and Asia, this is normally the case. When the Holy Spirit manifests Himself through a believer, that believer is always in possession of their normal judgment. They may not understand all that the Lord is saying through them, and may need to enquire of the Lord as to what it means, but their mind is not suspended. Remember the words of the apostle Paul: *The spirits of the prophets are subject to the prophets; for God is not a God of confusion, but of peace* (I Corinthians 14:32-33).

Sixthly: Spiritual gifts should never be used to manipulate or to impose one's opinion on a time of corporate prayer. That is always the flesh operating. It is interesting in this connection to remember the embargo placed by the Lord on the holy anointing oil touching the flesh (see Exodus 30:31-33). When a child of God consistently abuses corporate prayer, seeking in one way or another to manipulate the time and to impose their opinion on it, the responsible brothers for that time should speak with that person and seek to correct that one.

Lastly: As I have already written, the time of corporate prayer is like a thermometer registering the health, or otherwise, of a fellowship or an assembly. It is in fact the body of the Messiah in action. The apostle Paul writing to the Ephesians said: *We are to grow up in all aspects into him, who is the head, even Christ, from whom the whole body, being fitted and held together by what every joint supplies, according to the proper working of each individual part, causes the growth of the body for the building up of itself in love* (Ephesians 4:15-16 NASB). Please note carefully three matters: *that which every joint supplies; according to the proper working of each individual part; causes the growth of the body for the building up of itself in love.* We cannot grow up in all aspects into Him who is the Head, nor can we know the healthy and normal functioning of the body nor the body being fitted and held together, except through that which every joint supplies. Those joints are us, and everything depends on whether we are contributing what we are receiving from the Lord!

The growth of the body and the building up of itself in love is according to the proper working of each individual part. We are the individual parts of the body, and its growth and building up is dependent upon our involvement in it. Corporate prayer is all of this in action.

7
THE PLACE OF THE WORD OF GOD
IN CORPORATE PRAYER

Ephesians 6:17-18—And take the helmet of salvation, and the sword of the Spirit, which is the word of God: with all prayer and supplication praying at all seasons in the Spirit, and watching thereunto in all perseverance and supplication for all the saints.

Hebrews 4:12—For the word of God is living, and active, and sharper than any two-edged sword, and piercing even to the dividing of soul and spirit, of both joints and marrow, and quick to discern the thoughts and intents of the heart.

Revelation 1:16—And he had in his right hand seven stars: and out of his mouth proceeded a sharp two-edged sword: and his countenance was as the sun shineth in his strength.

II Corinthians 10:3-5—For though we walk in the flesh, we do not war according to the flesh (for the weapons of our warfare are not of the flesh, but mighty before God to the casting down of strongholds), casting down imaginations, and every high thing that is exalted against the knowledge of God, and bringing every thought into captivity to the obedience of Christ.

Psalm 18:29-30, 34, 37-39—For by thee I run upon a troop; and by my God do I leap over a wall. As for God, his way is perfect ... He is a shield unto all them that take refuge in Him...He teacheth my hands to war; so that mine arms do bend a bow of brass...I will pursue mine enemies, and overtake them; neither will I turn again till they are consumed. I will smite them through, so that they shall not be able to rise: they shall fall under my feet. For thou hast girded me with strength unto the battle: thou hast subdued under me those that rose up against me.

Psalm 144:1-2—Blessed be the Lord my rock, who teacheth my hands to war, and my fingers to fight: my lovingkindness, and my fortress, my high tower, and my deliverer; my shield, and he in whom I take refuge; who subdueth my people under me.

I Timothy 1:18—This charge I commit unto thee, my child Timothy, according to the prophecies which led the way to thee, that by them thou mayest war the good warfare.

THE SPIRITUAL WAR WE ARE BORN INTO AS BELIEVERS

From the moment we are born of the Spirit we enter a spiritual war zone. It does not take us long to learn that we have powerful spiritual enemies. Those enemies are out to compromise us, to entrap us, and if possible even to destroy us. They will do everything within their ability to frustrate and terminate the work of God in us. The powers of darkness never cease seeking to stop our growth in the grace and the experiential knowledge of the Lord Jesus.

Notwithstanding the conflict around us, the Lord Jesus has won the battle! He is enthroned at the right hand of the Father beyond the power of Satan and his hosts to dethrone Him. They are unable to frustrate the purpose of God for Him; His destiny is assured! Indeed, the Father has declared: *Sit thou at my right hand until I make thine enemies thy footstool* (Psalm 110:1). Satan is incapable of undoing the finished work of the Messiah or His triumph. He is beyond the power of the Archenemy of God to harm, to impair, or to damage.

Since the powers of darkness cannot dethrone the Lord Jesus, they centre their energy and activity on the redeemed in the earth. When the Messiah appeared to Saul of Tarsus, whilst Saul was yet unsaved, he heard the Lord speaking in Hebrew and saying: *Saul, Saul, why are you persecuting Me?* The Lord Jesus further emphasised this when Saul said: *Who art thou, Lord?* And Jesus said: *I am Jesus whom you are persecuting* (see Acts 26:14-15 NASB). Saul could have said: "I am not persecuting You; I am persecuting Your followers!" It is here that we make a significant and revealing discovery. Satan can only touch the Lord Jesus by touching those who belong to Him and who are alive on this fallen earth.

This is the reason for the huge battle we are in. The spirit of Antichrist, which has been in the world from the beginning, will do everything within its power to destroy the Church of God and the testimony of Jesus, and those who have been delivered from the domain of darkness and transferred into the Kingdom of His beloved Son (see Colossians 1:13). Those believers are a continual witness to the Lord Jesus and to the effectiveness of the work which He has accomplished on Calvary. It enrages Satan, and with the other enemies of God he will leave no stone unturned to compromise, to spoil, and to rob the children of God of the practical outworking of their salvation. Those enemies will seek to make them deaf and blind to the Lord Jesus, to impoverish them and to make them a contradiction of all that He is! The hatred of the powers of darkness for everything and everyone related to the Lord Jesus cannot be measured.

Everywhere we turn in the New Testament we find references to this conflict which we endure as true and faithful believers. In his letter to his spiritual son, Timothy, the apostle Paul wrote: *This charge I commit unto thee, my child Timothy, according to the prophecies which led the way to thee, that by them thou mayest war the good warfare* (I Timothy 1:18). Or again: *Suffer hardship with me, as a good soldier of Christ Jesus* (II Timothy 2:3). In the letter to the Church in Ephesus Paul writes: *Put on the whole armor of God, that ye may be able to stand against the wiles of the devil.* You do not wear armour as an evening dress, but only for war! He then further writes: *Wherefore take up the whole armor of God, that ye may be able to withstand in the evil day, and, having done all, to stand* (Ephesians 6: 11, 13). These words are the language of warfare. He is emphasizing that we who belong to the Lord are in a battle which at times can be unbelievably fierce.

THE WILES OF THE DEVIL

Paul urges us to stand against the *wiles of the Devil*. The Greek word translated by the English word *wiles* means "a scheme" or "a cunning device," and has the idea of craftiness, trickery or deceit. Since Satan cannot dethrone the Lord Jesus or frustrate the Father's purpose for Him, he throws everything he has into this war. He is out to compromise and destroy the work of the Lord and the body of our Lord Jesus, and to do that by every means available to him! In his tactics and the cunning schemes he devises, he will use every form of deceitfulness and trickery. Indeed, the apostle Paul describes the spirits which are with Satan as *seducing spirits*, and their teaching as *doctrines of demons* (see I Timothy 4:1). We should note the use of the word *seducing* because it perfectly describes Satan's tactics.

THE SWORD OF THE SPIRIT WHICH IS THE WORD OF GOD

It is noteworthy that the apostle writes: *Take the helmet of salvation, and the sword of the Spirit, which is the word of God* (Ephesians 6:17). These days in industrialised nations swords are usually hung up as a decoration; they have no actual present day use. However, in past days swords were an essential weapon. The Spirit of God reveals to us that the sword He uses is the Word of God.

The writer of the Hebrew letter underlines this when he states: *For the word of God is living and active, and sharper than any two edged sword, and piercing even to the dividing of soul and spirit, of both joints and marrow, and quick to discern the thoughts and intents of the heart* (Hebrews 4:12). It is also highly significant that when the apostle John saw the risen glorified Messiah in the midst of the seven Churches he wrote: *And he had in his right hand seven stars: and out of his mouth proceeded a sharp two-edged sword: and his countenance was as the sun shineth in his strength* (Revelation 1:16). The two-edged sword was a much more deadly and effective weapon than the normal sword; it could seriously cut up an adversary. Indeed, it was meant to finish him off! The Messiah not only had the two-edged sword, but it "proceeded" out of His mouth. This is a vivid picture of the power of God's Word; there was positive action as a result of it. It is, of course, the Holy Spirit who makes the Word of God such a living and powerful reality.

Many years ago a brother obtained an old book of Charles Haddon Spurgeon, which he had purchased in a junk shop. He brought it to Halford House and asked whether we wanted it for the library; and we accepted it gladly. To my amazement, inside the book I found an envelope with a personal letter from Spurgeon to a Baptist pastor, dated from the middle of the nineteenth century. In the letter he wrote about a controversy concerning liberal Bible theology which was, at that time, raging in Baptist circles. He urged the pastor to "stand up and be counted," and wrote, "If you feel unable to take the Sword of the Spirit (the Bible) and use it, at least let it rattle in your scabbard!" In corporate prayer we need much more than the Sword of the Spirit rattling in our scabbard; we need to learn how to use it!

THE WEAPONS OF OUR WARFARE

We should note the striking manner in which Paul writes of the warfare that we are in: *For though we walk in the flesh, we do not war according to the flesh (for the weapons of our warfare are not of the flesh, but mighty before God to the casting down of strongholds)* (II Corinthians 10:3-4). The weapons of our warfare are not in the realm of flesh and blood. It is an enormous mistake, often with very sad consequences, when we pit flesh and blood against flesh and blood. In other words we use intelligence against intelligence, philosophy against philosophy, ideology against ideology, and argument against argument. Then the weapons of our warfare are of the flesh, and our warring is according to the flesh. These weapons, with which the Holy Spirit equips us, only operate in the Presence of God. The way the apostle states it is very significant: *Mighty before God*. They can only function through His enabling power; they are inoperative when He is not present and in charge.

Charles Haddon Spurgeon once said that he could not understand why Christians spent so much valuable time defending the Word of God. He said, "The Bible does not need defending. Let the lion out of the cage and he will defend himself." In other words, preach the Word of God in power, and the results will be its defence.

Strongholds or fortresses are normally strong points in the defence of any realm. If those fortresses fall the whole region could be overrun. Paul, by the Holy Spirit, speaks of satanic strongholds or fortresses. Through the weapons provided by the Holy Spirit and operated through His power, those strongholds can be cast down; and a whole area can be opened up to the Gospel and to the saving power of the Lord Jesus. This is a tremendous lesson for those of us who are engaged in corporate prayer. The destruction of such strong points of satanic power in the line of his defence can mean a mighty breakthrough for the work of the Lord.

Similarly, this passage speaks of the casting down of *imaginations*. They are cast down through the weapons with which the Holy Spirit arms us. The Greek word translated by the English word *imaginations* (AV and ASV) means "speculations" or "philosophical reasonings." This is no small matter. For example, Darwinism is built on speculation. It also speaks of casting down *every high thing that is exalted against the knowledge of God*. There are today in this post Christian era of many former Christian nations so many "high things" that contradict the knowledge of God. These "high things" are humanistic reasonings against the revealed Word of God. For example, there is the new idea of morality, the destruction of the unborn child, the new liberal educational system, humanism itself, and much more. The apostle also speaks of *bringing every thought into captivity to the obedience of Christ*. So many philosophical and ideological systems began with a thought—for example, Marxism and Maoism. They all began with thoughts in the head of Karl Marx and Mao Tsedong. Nazism began as a thought in the head of Adolf Hitler. There is no end to such examples. The apostle Paul was not dealing with small matters when he wrote of casting down strongholds or fortresses, of casting down speculations, of casting down high things exalted against the knowledge of God, and of bringing every thought captive to Christ. These are great matters for which the Holy Spirit alone can arm us with weapons for victory!

THE NECESSITY OF SPIRITUAL EDUCATION AND TRAINING BY THE LORD

To use the spiritual weapons of our warfare requires education and training by the Lord. To handle a sword requires skill and aptitude, and much schooling in its use. Such a person also needs to be agile and healthy; we need real physical training. It is the same with other weapons; we need to be taught and trained how to operate them. As we need training, exercise and education in the physical, so it is with the spiritual.

King David is a very good illustration of such training. In Psalm 18 he records that by the Lord he could run through a troop and leap over a wall. The troop was surely not just a few, but quite a number of people, and the wall was not just knee height, but probably at least his height. He had exercised himself to run and to jump! Indeed, he goes on to say that it was the Lord who trained his hands for battle, and in such a way that his arms could bend a bow of bronze. This kind of training resulted in his being able to pursue his enemies without tiring and to overtake them. That was no "sack race;" his physical training produced great results. He speaks of not turning back until all his enemies were consumed, of shattering them so that they were not able to rise and remained under his feet. All this has its spiritual counterpart if the Lord is to train us for spiritual warfare.

David gave all the glory to the Lord when he said that it was the Lord: *Who girded him with strength for battle and subdued all those who rose up against him* (see Psalm 18:29-39). Or again when he says: *Blessed be the Lord my rock, who teacheth my hands to war, and my fingers to fight* (Psalm 144:1). This is a wonderful example of the need for spiritual education, exercise and training by the Lord. We cannot simply wander through the battlefield in a kind of daydream, expecting the Lord to protect us. We have to learn how to war the warfare, how to fight the good fight of faith, how to use the sword of the Spirit, and how to be properly and adequately clad for battle. We must also know the spiritual weapons needed in this warfare, and which operate so powerfully in the Presence of the Lord.

The apostle Paul in his letter to Timothy wrote: Take your part in suffering hardship as a good soldier of Christ Jesus. No soldier on service entangleth himself in the affairs of this life; that he may please him who enrolled him as a soldier (II Timothy 2:3-4 mg). We are all called to be soldiers of the Lord Jesus! We should remember, however, that His army is a volunteer army and not a conscripted one! For those who respond to His call, the training is hard and full of discipline, and is lifelong. Paul warns Timothy not to allow the world and its ways to compromise him, but to be devoted to the Lord and fully committed to him.

THY WORD IS TRUTH

From all that we have written so far in this chapter, we should have recognised that we are involved in warfare, whether we like it or not. In this there can be no spiritual pacifism! We are in a battle and we should not be surprised at the proximity of the enemy. The apostle Paul wrote: *For our wrestling is not against flesh and blood, but against the principalities, against the powers, against the world rulers of this darkness, against the spiritual hosts of wickedness in the heavenly places* (Ephesians 6:12). Wrestling is a contact sport, as we have already written. It is not a pleasant tennis match where we are divided from our adversary by a waist

123

high net. In wrestling you may find your opponent with his arms around you, seeking to lift you up, and throw you. He may even sit on you! This does not necessarily mean that you have lost the fight. In fact you may still win it.

God has provided us with the weapons which spell victory, despite the fierceness of the battle. In the midst of the conflict it is essential for us always to remember that the Lord Jesus has won and is enthroned. He can provide us, by the Holy Spirit, with the weapons which are necessary to enforce His victory and triumph!

What are these weapons of our warfare? Of what do they consist? They consist entirely of the truth of God. It is the only weapon which God has given to the Church and to believers. The Lord Jesus in His High Priestly prayer said: *Thy word is truth* (John 17:17). The Word of God, in its entirety, is truth. The **sword** of the Spirit, which is the Word of God, is the truth in practice. In corporate prayer, the use of this sword of the Spirit is essential if the will of God is to be fulfilled.

The truth of God, revealed in His Word, is the only weapon which paralyses the enemy. The Lord Jesus spoke of Satan as not standing in the truth for the simple reason that there is no truth in him! The Messiah called him a liar and the father of lies (see John 8:44). The only way that Satan and his host can be shattered is by the truth of God. He will laugh at anything else! In times of corporate prayer we can express great zeal and emotion; we can shout at the top of our voices; we can express great indignation and anger; and it will have no effect on Satan. He is not hurt or set back by any such outburst against him on our part. Similarly, we can preach our sermonettes or our paraphrases of whole portions of the Word of God, but it will still not hurt the enemy. Satan knows when the Scriptures we quote are given to us by the Spirit or merely a "knee jerk" reaction from our head knowledge of the Bible.

The moment, however, when with our lips we express the truth of God given to us by the Holy Spirit as weapons, Satan is not merely discomforted; he flees. It is the supreme weapon with which all the forces of evil and darkness can be overcome and defeated. If we abide in the Word of God and use it, the grip of Satan on situations and problems has to be released.

The Greek word translated by the English word *truth* means not only "sound doctrine" but "reality." When the Lord Jesus said *I am the truth*, He did not mean that He was merely the doctrine, but that He was the reality (John 14:6). It is this Eternal Reality that makes the forces of evil powerless; it confuses and defeats them. If the truth of God, as found in His Word, is placed in our hands by the Spirit of God and used, every device of Satan is rendered totally ineffective. Even the strong points of Satan can be demolished by the truth in corporate prayer.

Weapons are not produced in the first place as ornaments but to be used for defence and battle action; they are designed to protect us and to win battles. From all of this we begin to realize how we need to know our Bibles, to study them, and to memorise Scriptures. It is more than academic head knowledge that we need. The Word of God needs to be implanted in us. Mark the words of James: *Wherefore putting away all filthiness and overflowing of wickedness, receive with meekness the implanted word, which is able to save your souls* (James 1:21). The apostle Paul also emphasizes this when he writes: *Let the word of Christ dwell in you richly* (Colossians 3:16a). When the Word of God becomes flesh and blood in us, then we shall learn how effectively to use the sword of the Spirit and the other weapons of our warfare.

ETERNAL FACTS TO BE USED AS WEAPONS

The Word of God is not philosophy, speculation, or make-believe. It does not contain a large amount of exaggeration or many myths and inaccuracies. The Word of God is revealed truth; it is the revelation of eternal facts by the Spirit of God. Here are some of the eternal facts which we ought to start using as the sword of the Spirit and the weapons of our warfare.

I AM THAT I AM

The name by which God revealed Himself to Moses was *I AM THAT I AM*. He told Moses to go to Pharaoh and say, *I AM has sent me*. Here we begin at the greatest and most fundamental fact of all, "God is"—not God was, nor only God will be—but God *is*. This is the greatest weapon we can use in the battle against the enemy. If only we understood fully what this means! God never called Himself: "I have been that I have been," or "I shall be that I shall be," or "I was that I was." He called Himself *I AM THAT I AM*. *God is I AM*, and every single creature that lives and moves and has its being lives because of Him. There is nothing outside of His rule and authority. This is no small weapon to use, especially when the fact dawns upon us that even the Devil exists by the grace of God!

Everywhere you look from Genesis to Revelation you will find this great foundational and eternal fact. It is the truth which totally paralyses Satan. All sovereign authority and power belongs supremely to God. It does not belong to Satan nor to the powers of darkness. Furthermore, if *God is*, there is no problem that He cannot solve, no advance that He cannot make, and no obstacle that He cannot overcome. With Him nothing is too hard, or too difficult, or impossible!

126

Salvation alone is found in Him; as also is healing and deliverance, and wholeness. When He said to Moses, My Name is *I AM*, He was saying to Moses that He would be everything that Moses could possibly need. We should remember that Moses had been reduced by the Lord from being Pharaoh's grandson to being a nomadic shepherd in the desert. It was as if the Lord was giving to Moses a blank cheque, and all he had to do was fill in the need. Do you need salvation? I am your salvation. Do you need grace? I am your grace. Do you need power? I am your power. Do you need wisdom? I am your wisdom. Do you need life? I am your life. Do you need healing? I am your healing. What do you need? I am your all sufficiency!

The powers of darkness cannot bear this when they hear it expressed by the mouth of believers, even the youngest of believers. It paralyses them. It spells for us, however, personal and corporate victory.

The Person of the Lord Jesus

The Word became flesh and dwelt among us. That is another fundamental fact. He who always existed in the Godhead became flesh and dwelt among us. God was manifest in the flesh. The Divines of previous centuries called this truth "the Eternal Sonship of Christ." That is why John the apostle said: *Who is he that overcometh the world, but he that believeth that Jesus is the Son of God* (1 John 5:5)? This is the secret to overcoming the world; it is so simple that we miss it! It is the confession that Jesus is the Messiah, the Son of the Living God. Upon that solid Rock, the Messiah builds His Church, and the gates of hell cannot prevail against it, much as they try.

The Lord Jesus declared that all authority and power was given into His hands, both in Heaven and on this fallen earth; He commanded us therefore to go and *make disciples of all the nations*, and added: *And lo, I am with you always, even unto the end of the world* (see Matthew 28:18-20). Simply stated, the Lord Jesus said that the gates of Hell could not prevail against **His** building, and in obeying His command to go, He promised to be with us to the end of the age. Here is an immutable fact which cannot change. These declarations of the Lord Jesus can be expressed by our lips in corporate prayer, and Satan can do nothing whatsoever about it. The expression of the truth paralyses him. This is why one simple but profound declaration "Jesus is Lord" totally depresses and demoralizes satanic forces and brings about their defeat.

In the Lord Jesus, God gives us everything—His salvation, His power, His grace, His wisdom, His life, and His all. He is the Father's unspeakable gift to us, and with Him God gives everything else. It is this confession with our lips that anesthetizes Satan and his host. Satan knows that the simplest child of God can do all things in Christ who strengthens that one. Whilst any child of God abides in Christ and Christ in that one, the powers of darkness are neutralized. Here is a fact that outlasts all time and is not changed by the fierceness of the battle and the conflict we are enduring. It is the expression of this fact with our lips that can change defeat into victory. Satan cannot handle such an expression of faith!

The Finished Work of Christ

Here is another eternal fact. The work the Lord Jesus completed on the cross was foreordained from before the foundation of the world, before even time began. When He died on Calvary, He finished the work of our salvation for which He expressly came. He laid the legal foundation upon which God the Father can save us, keep us, provide for us, protect us, and bless us. Upon this basis He can turn a sinner into a saint; He can conform us to the likeness of the Messiah, no matter how twisted, or perverse, or evil a person might have been. Upon that alone we experience His everlasting mercy and steadfast love.

It is also the foundation upon which He can fulfil His Eternal Purpose for man and for the universe. Through that finished work, the Lord Jesus has beaten and utterly defeated the powers of darkness. Prior to Calvary Jesus had declared, *Now shall the prince of this world be cast out* (John 12:31b). Satan was demoted by the work of the Lord Jesus on Calvary, and there is nothing he can do about it. The apostle John wrote: *To this end was the Son of God manifested, that He might destroy the works of the devil* (1John 3:8b). The works of Satan, which are so numerous and powerful, have all been destroyed through the finished work of the Messiah. The writer of the Hebrew letter further emphasizes this fact when he wrote: *That through death He might bring to nought him that had the power of death, that is, the devil* (Hebrews 2:14b). Satan has been zeroed by the work of the Lord Jesus. The apostle Paul writes: *And He disarmed the principalities and powers, and put them to open shame, leading them captive in the triumph of Christ* (Colossians 2:15 Conybeare and Howson). The Lord Jesus has stripped naked and disarmed those spiritual principalities and powers, leading them captive in the train of His triumph.

This is not a fairy tale; it is not "make-believe;" and it is not some vague possibility. It is a fact and a reality; the Lord Jesus has brought to nought the authority, the power and the works of Satan and his host. We, however, are very conscious of the might and power of the satanic host. They seem to us to be very real and actual. Yet the Lord Jesus has disarmed them, brought their power to zero and destroyed their effectiveness! It is this fact we have to proclaim for victory over them!

The whole satanic hierarchy quakes when a child of God, however simple that one may be, expresses this reality in words. It is the absolute truth. The powers of darkness are very clever in their propaganda; they make a great noise through which they cower many believers. They make believers think that they are all powerful and fully in charge. It is not the truth; they have been brought to nought, to zero, and disarmed. The key to victory and to overcoming is found in Revelation 12:11: *And they overcame him because of the blood of the Lamb, and because of the word of their testimony; and they loved not their life even unto death.* Through the finished work of the Lord Jesus and the blood of the Lamb which represents that work, through the word of their testimony—the simple, real, and true expression of that fact—and because they had laid down their self-life, they gained the victory and overcame the Devil.

THE PRESENT POSITION OF CHRIST

The present position of the Lord Jesus is a tremendous weapon. It is another eternal fact. At this point in time Jesus is enthroned at the right hand of God the Father. He has been made King of kings and Lord of lords, and Ruler of the kings of the earth. All the rulers, the presidents, the kings of the earth, even dictators, and autocrats reign by the grace of God and only by the permission of our Lord Jesus—both the good and the bad. The Lord Jesus raises them up and brings them down. All authority and power in Heaven and on this fallen earth is in the hands of our Lord Jesus. There is, therefore, no situation either international, or national, or local which is too difficult or too complex for the Messiah to solve!

The Lord Jesus has also been made Head over all things to the Church which is His body. Considering the battle, which the Church is enduring, this fact of the present position of the Messiah is all important. Has He truly been made Head over all things to the Church? If this is truth, then it is no small weapon in our hands. After all, the Lord Jesus emphatically stated that against the Church He is building, the gates of hell cannot prevail! That is solid ground upon which to stand in prayer and intercession for the building of His Church.

He is also the King of Israel. The Lord Jesus, the Messiah, has never abdicated from the throne of David. Indeed, Isaiah prophesies: *Of the increase of his government and of peace there shall be no end, upon the throne of David, and upon his kingdom, to establish it, and to uphold it with justice and righteousness from henceforth even forever* (Isaiah 9:7). Israel believes that she is a Republic, when in fact she is a Kingdom! At some point soon the King of Israel will return to Jerusalem. This is truth and is a powerful weapon in the hands of those who pray and intercede for Israel. It would be inconceivable that the King of Israel does not watch over the destiny of Israel, and would not fulfil His purpose for her.

The present position of the Lord Jesus is truth and not a myth. If that is so, then we have incredibly powerful weapons to which the Holy Spirit can direct us. The powers of darkness and of evil have a vested interest in making us believe that they are "the be all and end all" of everything in this world. In fact they have not only been dislodged, they are disarmed and all their works have been brought to nought. It is the present powerful position of the Messiah enthroned at the Father's right hand which we need to proclaim and declare in corporate prayer.

THE IMMUTABILITY OF HIS COUNSEL

We must not only learn to use the Word of God as the revelation of eternal facts, but we must learn to stand on the immutability of His counsel. The word *immutable* simply means "unchangeable," "not subject to variation," or "no possibility of deviation." With the Lord there is no *shadow cast by turning*. He never deviates from His Eternal Purpose. In the Word of God His counsel which is immutable is revealed. That immutability is for our encouragement, comfort, and strength. No matter how great the battle which rages around us, His counsel stands fast, and however much evidence there is to the contrary, He will perform all His pleasure (see Isaiah 46:10). When the battle is at its height, there is much smoke which can blur the sharpness and clarity of our sight. We then lose sight of the immutability of His counsel and lose our way. It is the work of the Holy Spirit, the Comforter, to bring us back to clear vision, and to the right way.

One of the great South African missionaries to Southern Congo used to visit us from time to time at Halford House. Willie F. B. Burton was a remarkable servant of the Lord. He was trained by Smith Wigglesworth, and in his young days accompanied him on many of his missions. He pioneered an incredible work amongst the cannibals. He had experienced the healing of well over a thousand cases of people with terminal illness. Most of these cases were associated with his pioneering work amongst the cannibals. He rightly saw it as a sign that followed the preaching of the Gospel (see Mark 16:20), and those healings opened up whole tribes to the Lord.

Once he said to me: "I have spent my whole life reducing language to the least number of syllables which is possible. I was always preaching to people who were illiterate, and therefore I had to be as simple as possible. However, there are two words that I could never reduce to simplicity. One was "reconciliation" and the other was "immutability." After Willie Burton went to be with the Lord, I pondered much over his ministry and work, and suddenly I realized that he had seen something about the immutability of God's counsel which had become the spring board of his life and work. Simply, it was that God could not lie, and that His Word was immutable. Willie Burton lived on the faithfulness of God to His Counsel and Word, and proved it in his experience.

In corporate prayer, the statements, the declarations, the revelation of God's will and His promises are immutable. Upon this eternal fact we can stand in prayer and spiritual warfare. Out of the immutability of His counsel the Holy Spirit will arm us with many weapons.

THE REVEALED WILL OF GOD

Within the Word of God the Lord reveals His will and purpose; for example, we discover His will for the Church of God, His will for Israel and the Jewish people, His will for the nations, and His will for the work of the Gospel. We also discover His will for every human being whom He saves.

Indeed we find that the Eternal Purpose of God is a theme which begins in Genesis and is developed throughout the sixty-six books of the Bible. It ends in the book of Revelation, with the New Jerusalem coming down out of Heaven, having the glory of God. In fact, we could call the Bible "a tale of two cities." Principally, as far as God is concerned, there are only two cities; one is called Babel—its Greek form, Babylon—and the other is Jerusalem. The first city Babel, or Babylon, represents fallen man—his pride, his energy, his ingenuity. The other city, Jerusalem, represents His salvation, His redemption; simply put, it represents God Himself. Every human being is found in one or the other. Blessed are those who are born in the first and by a new birth are reregistered in the second (see Psalm 87).

Babel or Babylon is first introduced in Genesis 11 and is developed throughout the Word of God; it ends in Revelation with its final destruction. In Genesis 12 God appears to Abram, an inhabitant of Ur in the Babel complex of cities and commands him to leave and go to another land which He would give him. The writer of the Hebrew letter describes what happened to Abraham in the words: *By faith Abraham, when he was called, obeyed to go out unto a place which he was to receive for an inheritance; and he went out, not knowing whither he went... For he looked for the city which hath the foundations, whose builder and maker is God* (Hebrews 11:8-10). That city was the Jerusalem that is above. Nevertheless from that point onwards the earthly Jerusalem has represented God—His purpose, His Throne, His Kingdom, His Word, and His salvation. The earthly Jerusalem will never fade or fall until it is eclipsed by the heavenly Jerusalem!

Within all of this is a large amount of immutable truth. It should surely be the basis for much corporate prayer; for to pray within the revealed will of God makes the answer certain. The apostle John writes: *And this is the boldness which we have toward him, that, if we ask anything according to his will, he heareth us: and if we know that he heareth us whatsoever we ask, we know that we have the petitions which we have asked of him* (1John 5:14-15).

There are times when we can use the revealed will of God in the warfare which we are in. It does not matter how fierce the conflict rages around us, we can stand upon the will of God in any given situation. God spoke through Isaiah, the prophet, and declared: *Remember the former things of old: for I am God, and there is none else; I am God, and there is none like me; declaring the end from the beginning, and from ancient times things that are not yet done; saying, My counsel shall stand, and I will do all my pleasure.* (Isaiah 46:9-10). Note carefully, *declaring the end from the beginning, and from ancient times things that are not yet done.* Within this declaration we discover the weapons of our warfare, and the sword of the Spirit!

Daniel is a classic example which illustrates this. Jerusalem had been destroyed, the cities of Israel were in ruins, and the large majority of the people were exiled. In the midst of this dark situation, with seemingly no hope, Daniel discovered by the Spirit of God that seventy years was ordained for the captivity of Jerusalem. By that time he occupied a high and important position in the government of the Persian Empire. Calculating those years, he suddenly realized that there were only a few years left! Only the Holy Spirit could have revealed to Daniel that the captivity of Jerusalem began not with the siege of Nebuchadnezzar, but twenty years earlier with the reign of one of the last kings of Judah (see Daniel 9:1-3). In fact the exile lasted for fifty years, and the captivity of Jerusalem for seventy years.

With this understanding of the will of God for His people, Daniel set himself to intercede with fervent and passionate prayer and with fasting. He stood on the prophetic utterance of King Solomon, when the king dedicated the Temple (see II Chronicles 6:36-39). He opened his window and prayed towards Jerusalem. One would have thought that making the discovery he had made, he would relax and thank the Lord that it was going to happen anyway. Instead with enormous feeling he confessed the sin of himself and his people. This prayer was so precious and valuable in the eyes of the Lord that Satan arranged for Daniel to be thrown into the lions' den, but the Lord gave Daniel faith and shut the mouth of the lions. The enemies of God's purpose were in fact eaten by the lions, and Daniel lived to administer and guard the return of the people of God to Jerusalem. The Lord had in fact brought Daniel to the highest position in the empire next to the

Sultan, for this very reason! This teaches us how to use the will of God in intercession and prayer.

THE PROMISES OF GOD

In corporate prayer we must learn how to stand upon the promises of God. The apostle Paul writes: *For as many as are the promises of God, in Him they are yes; therefore also through Him is our Amen, to the glory of God through us* (II Corinthians 1:20 NASB). Within these promises of God all these eternal facts are found, and the promises express them in simple, direct, and clear language. The Holy Spirit can lead us to them and enable us to stand on them for their fulfillment. Most of us who are walking with the Lord must have had the experience of the Holy Spirit suddenly illuminating one of these promises in the midst of turmoil. When we stand on that promise, it opens the door to victory.

In Hebrews there is a beautiful comment on the promises of God: *For he is faithful that promised* (Hebrews 10:23b). The faithfulness of the Lord Jesus stands behind all the promises. The apostle Peter writes: *Whereby he hath granted unto us his precious and exceeding great promises; that through these ye may become partakers of the divine nature* (II Peter 1:4). Every time a promise is given to you, and you stand upon it and see it fulfilled, there is something more of the Lord in you.

AUNTY ELLA AND THE SEWING MACHINE

I learnt this lesson not from some great preacher, but through an old sister whom I knew as Aunty Ella. Most people in the Church thought she was a little crazy. She had been an opera singer and used to give my sister singing lessons. I would go to pick up my sister and go home with her. I was only thirteen years of age at that time, having only been saved for less than a year.

136

When I arrived at Aunty Ella's home, I knocked on the door and she told me that my sister had already gone, and said, "Why don't you come in and have a cup of tea."

As we went into her rooms, she said, "I am sorry for the mess, but I am not very practical, and I am trying to sew these curtains." She had been using her sewing machine. We just started talking about the Lord, which was something she loved to do. At that point something went wrong with the sewing machine. She tried it but it was jammed. She did a number of things but nothing worked. Then she asked me if I knew anything about sewing machines. I replied that I knew nothing whatsoever! Nevertheless, she said, "Well, have a go at it," which I did with no success. It seemed to me to be absolutely jammed.

Then she said something I have never forgotten: "Now we must ask our heavenly Father." With that she knelt down in front of the sewing machine, and pointing to the floor she said to me, "Kneel." I will never forget her prayer! Her hand went up and she said, "Oh heavenly Father, Lance and I have been having such a lovely time of fellowship about your beloved Son. As you know, I am not a very practical lady. Something has gone wrong with my sewing machine and I tried to put it right. But I am an old lady and I do not understand anything about sewing machines. And Lance, dear boy, has tried to put it right but he too, knows nothing about them! Heavenly Father, you say in your word in II Corinthians 1:20: *How many so ever be the promises of God, in him is the yea: wherefore also through him is the Amen, unto the glory of God through us.* We want to bring to you a promise from Hebrews 1:14 that the angels are, *ministering spirits, sent forth to do service for the sake of them that shall inherit salvation.* Heavenly Father, will you please send an angel to put this sewing machine right?" With that she bowed her head. I had my eyes wide open, and I touched her on the arm and said, "Aunty, try it." "Shush," she said, "give the angel time!" She knelt there with her head bowed for a minute or two; then all of a sudden she got up, drew her chair under her and went straight on with her sewing. She said, "Oh, heavenly Father, You never fail; thank You so much."

Now, of course, I was only thirteen and some people would say it was coincidence. For myself, it taught me one of the greatest lessons of my life. I had heard all sorts of people, well known people, great ministers in the pulpit. They never really meant too much to me other than they gave marvellous messages. I never really expected two-thirds of what they said to work, and I do not think anyone else did either. I was stunned by what had happened. Could an old sister, who was thought by many to be a little crazy, have taken one of the promises of God, stood on it, and seen it fulfilled? It changed my life, because it changed my attitude to the Word of God and to His promises. If He could do it for Aunty Ella, surely He could do it also for me!

I always told Aunty Ella that she taught me one simple and all important truth; that you can take a promise of God's Word on the basis of what He Himself has said and put it to the test.

In corporate prayer we need to be alive and alert to the Holy Spirit, so that at any point He can lead us to a promise. Such promises, given to a single child of God to begin with, can then be stood upon corporately. It will always lead to fulfillment and victory.

A BATTLE OVER VISAS

In a time of corporate prayer we were dealing with a highly complex matter. The problem and the situation would not move. However much we prayed concerning it, nothing materialised. It was an obstacle to the work of the Lord. The difficulty was centred in the granting of visas. Anyone who was known to be a Christian worker was more than likely to be refused a visa. We came at it from a number of different angles but nothing happened.

Then the Lord gave one of the young brothers a promise: *The Lord will guard your going out and your coming in from this time forth and forever* (Psalm 121:8 NASB). It was confirmed independently by two other believers. The Lord also gave another promise to someone else in that time of prayer: *These things saith he that is holy, he that is true, he that hath the key of David, he that openeth and none shall shut, and that shutteth and none openeth* (Revelation 3:7). Upon these two promises we all stood. It was amazing to see the result. Not only individual brothers or sisters received visas, but even whole families.

THE SPIRIT DIRECTS THE WAY TO USE THE WORD OF GOD

The all-important matter in corporate prayer is to experience the practical direction of the Holy Spirit. How are we to use the sword of the Spirit and the weapons of our warfare? It is not enough to know the Word of God, or even to memorise it, important as those matters are. By the Spirit alone can we effectively use the truth revealed in His Word. The essential and strategic matter is to know His direction. He has to reveal to us the will of God, as it relates to any situation on any level. He has to bring us to the particular aspect of the truth that will become the sword of the Spirit and the weapons that we should use, or to the promises of God that have particular relevance to the problems we face.

PASTOR FJORD CHRISTENSEN AND THE SISTER CRIPPLED WITH ARTHRITIS

Here is an illustration of the manner in which the Holy Spirit can bring a statement in God's Word and explain a situation we might face in corporate prayer. A dear Danish brother, a young man, had been with one of the great Danish servants of the Lord, Pastor Fjord Christensen. They had been called out into the country to pray for a woman who was bedridden with arthritis. She was a believer as was her husband. In the time of prayer, the young man in particular prayed with great zeal and fervour, but did not get very far. The older man, Fjord Christensen, just said, "Amen" at different points, but kept very quiet. The young brother noticed that he was looking in his Bible. All of a sudden he stopped the prayer and said to the sister: "Could you tell me, are you short-tempered?" She was startled and said, "Oh no, no, of course not." "Oh," said Fjord Christensen, and they continued to pray. A little later he stopped the prayer again and said: "Excuse me asking again, but are you quite sure that you are not irritable?" "Oh no, never! I never get irritated." So they continued to pray. Suddenly Fjord Christensen said, "Are you absolutely certain that you are not short-tempered?" She was just about to say no, when her husband, with tears in his eyes, said, "Oh, but you are, you are! It is your worst failing."

"Ah," said Fjord Christensen, "I thought so." The sister burst into tears and confessed to the Lord how short-tempered she was with her husband and everything else. When it was all confessed and she had truly repented, Fjord Christensen said, "Now we can ask the Lord to heal you." And he read her this Scripture in Proverbs 14:30: *A tranquil heart is the life of the flesh; but envy is the rottenness of the bones.* The Danish translation says, "But short-temperedness is the rottenness of the bones." While they had been praying, this verse had come to Fjord Christensen, and that is why he had broken in three times. When they laid hands on that sister, she stood up, and she went out of the house with them to say goodbye. She lived a normal life until her death, and she never had arthritis again.

This illustrates what is meant by the sword of the Spirit which is the Word of God, or the weapons of our warfare mighty before God. Many times they could have gone round in circles, praying for her healing and never touching the root of it. I am not saying of course that every case of arthritis is due to irritability or short-temperedness. The lesson we need to learn is that the Holy Spirit can take the Word of God and apply it to particular situations. Battles are won or lost in the measure in which we respond to the leadership of the Holy Spirit.

PRACTICAL POINTS

First of all, always bring your Bible to a time of prayer. It is amazing when people come to a corporate prayer time without a Bible. It is like going to battle without a gun or any weapons and equipment. Never be without your Bible.

Secondly: Use the Word of God in the prayer time as led and directed by the Holy Spirit. We can only learn by experience how to use the Word.

Thirdly: Be alive and sensitive to the Spirit; **watch** and pray. Follow Him the whole time. Do not doze or be lost in your own thoughts, but keep alert. Sometimes one sees a brother or sister looking vacantly because they are lost in their own thoughts. This kind of condition results in unrelated prayer; it is not related to anything that has gone before or will come after it. We have been dozing and suddenly woken up!

141

Fourthly: Avoid sermonettes, Bible paraphrases, Bible outlines, or preaching at God. That is not using the sword of the Spirit. Some Christians have the idea that if they can give a Bible outline Satan is frightened. He is not frightened at all. He knows these outlines which have been in the Bible for anything up to three thousand years. He knows the Bible very well. One could say that he is an avid Bible student! He is only frightened when the Holy Spirit helps you to take the Word of God and to use it powerfully concerning the matter in hand.

Fifthly: When the Lord gives you a verse or a passage of His word during corporate prayer, read it out distinctly when you contribute it. Do not feel that you have to follow such a contribution immediately with prayer. Often it is good to let others judge it first. Always read the relevant verse or verses, but not the whole chapter! Sometimes believers have some particular verse which is given to them, and they read a whole chapter and the direction of the Holy Spirit is lost.

Sixthly: Once we have discovered the weapon, we need to use it! Sometimes it does not take so long for the matter to be settled; other times it will take much longer. The government of the Spirit will decide how long we will have to use that weapon before we see the fulfillment. Remember: *Be not sluggish, but imitators of them who through faith and **patience** inherit the promises* (see Hebrews 6:12 author's emphasis).

Seventhly: In the use of any of the weapons which the Holy Spirit has given us, we need at all times to stand upon the finished work of the Lord Jesus. We have no other basis or foundation upon which we must stand and operate. It is the truth of God which is given to us as the sword of the Spirit and the weapons of our warfare. At all times, however, when we use these weapons, we must be covered. This is the meaning of putting on the whole armour of God. The Messiah Himself is that armour.

Lastly: A truth or a promise given by the Spirit needs to be stood upon, not only by the person who received it, but by all of us. Corporate prayer is an expression of the body of Christ; no one is given anything that is personal. If God gives someone a promise it is for all of us to use it.

8
EXECUTING THE WILL OF GOD IN PRAYER

Psalm 149:1, 6-9—Praise ye the Lord. Sing unto the Lord a new song, and his praise in the assembly of the saints...Let the high praises of God be in their mouth, and a two-edged sword in their hand; to execute vengeance upon the nations, and punishments upon the peoples; to bind their kings with chains, and their nobles with fetters of iron; to execute upon them the judgment written.

Psalm 118:10-17—All nations compassed me about: in the name of the Lord I will cut them off. They compassed me about; yea, they compassed me about: in the name of the Lord I will cut them off. They compassed me about like bees; they are quenched as the fires of thorns: in the name of the Lord I will cut them off. Thou didst thrust sore at me that I might fall: but the Lord helped me. The Lord is my strength and song; and he is become my salvation. The voice of rejoicing and salvation is in the tents of the righteous: the right hand of the Lord doeth valiantly. The right hand of the Lord is exalted: the right hand of the Lord doeth valiantly. I shall not die, but live, and declare the works of the Lord.

Matthew 16:18-19—And I also say unto thee, that thou art Peter, and upon this rock I will build my church; and the gates of Hades shall not prevail against it. I will give unto thee the keys of the kingdom of heaven: and whatsoever thou shalt bind on earth shall be bound in heaven; and whatsoever thou shalt loose on earth shall be loosed in heaven.

Matthew 18:18-20—Verily I say unto you, What things soever ye shall bind on earth shall be bound in heaven; and what things soever ye shall loose on earth shall be loosed in heaven. Again I say unto you, that if two of you shall agree on earth as touching anything that they shall ask, it shall be done for them of my Father who is in heaven. For where two or three are gathered together in my name, there am I in the midst of them.

Ephesians 1:20, 22-23a—Which he wrought in Christ, when he raised him from the dead, and made him to sit at his right hand in the heavenly places, far above all rule, and authority, and power, and dominion, and every name that is named...And He put all things in subjection under His feet, and gave him to be head over all things to the church, which is his body.

Ephesians 2:6—But God... raised us up with him, and made us to sit with him in the heavenly places, in Christ Jesus.

EXECUTIVE PRAYER AND ACTION

The subject of this chapter is how to execute the will of God in prayer. What is meant by executive prayer? Our beloved brother, Watchman Nee, called this "authoritative prayer." By executive prayer we mean the kind of corporate prayer which causes the will and purpose of God to be realised. It is executed in the secret place of prayer and then becomes publicly manifested by the Lord.

The word *executive* means "a person or body with the power to execute specific policies." It can be a government body or a business organization. The word *execute* means "to carry into effect," or "to follow through with an agreed policy" until its fulfillment. An executive is someone with the authority to complete and finish an assignment which has been previously decided upon by a higher body.

Incredibly, by the grace of God alone, we who have been saved and born of the Spirit are executives of the Kingdom of God. All of us have been made *kings and priests unto God*. We have been authorised in the Name of the Messiah Jesus, who is the Head of the Church, to carry out the policy of His Kingdom, and to carry into effect the decrees of the throne of God. The Messiah Jesus has made us all executives in the sense that we do not carry out our own policy or will but rather His. Indeed, we can only carry into effect the will and the policy of the throne of God and of the Lamb.

The Lord Jesus gave us a pattern prayer in which He laid down the basic principles of prayer: *Our Father who art in heaven, Hallowed be thy name. Thy kingdom come. Thy will be done, as in heaven, so on earth"* (Matthew 6:9-10). He did not teach us to pray in a kind of wishful manner: "May thy kingdom come, and may thy will be done." There is an authority in His words: *Thy kingdom come. Thy will be done, as in heaven, so on earth.* Is it only in the millennium or in the Eternal Day of the Lord that His will is to be done as it is in heaven, so on earth? It is true that only when the Lord Jesus returns will His purpose be finally and universally fulfilled. Surely, however, as the Church of God, the body of our Lord Jesus, we are meant to execute now the policy of His throne and rule the many problems and situations that we face, and carry into effect His will for us in these days before He returns!

There are so many examples of executive action within the Bible. Take Moses as one such illustration. The Lord commanded Moses and said: *Lift thou up thy rod, and stretch out thy hand over the sea, and divide it* (Exodus 14:16a). It should be noted that the Lord Himself told Moses "to divide it!" That is remarkable. It is almost laughable when you think about it! Moses knew only too well that he could not divide the Red Sea.

The point is, however, that if Moses had refused to lift up his rod, stretch out his hand over the Red Sea and say the authoritative word "be divided," it would have remained unchanged and impossible; the children of Israel would never have crossed over on foot. The purpose of God was that Moses had to speak the Lord's word to the sea! **Then God's sovereign**

power would go into effect. Moses had to express what the decree of God was. Until we declare the decree of Heaven with our lips in any matter before us, God will not act! This is so important that I will repeat it; our human lips have to utter on earth the decree that has already been passed in heaven before God will do it.

Another illustration was the crossing of the River Jordan. The Lord had told them that wherever they put the soles of their feet it would be theirs. They were told to go into the River Jordan and stand there; and that is exactly what they did. When they got their feet wet, the river stood up in a heap quite a few miles upstream at a place called Adam. It was miraculous. There it stood in a heap at Adam while they went across. It was the will of heaven that the people of God should cross into the Promised Land. It was as if Heaven said, "This Jordan is bound." But it was not bound; not until the children of God placed their feet on the actual soil, on the river bed and said: "It is bound! In the Name of our God, it is bound." Then Heaven said, "Right; it is done!" And it was done!

The Lord Jesus stated this simply and clearly when He said that if we are to enter the strong man's house and spoil his goods, we must first bind him (see Mark 3:27). It is the missing link in so many of the problems we face in evangelism, in the work of the Lord, and in the building up of the Church. The "strong man" remains in charge and immovable. Until first we go behind the scenes and bind the strong man, we cannot bring anything out of his house. The moment he is bound in the name of the Lord, you can spoil his house and his goods.

We Have Been Made a Kingship Unto God

Executive action is a matter of kingship. If we have been made "kings" it means that we are authorized executives under the King of kings. In the last book of the Bible, the Apocalypse, in the midst of fierce warfare, conflict, and the contradiction of the enthronement of our Lord Jesus, John the apostle writes: *He made us to be a kingdom, to be priests unto his God and Father* (Revelation 1:6a). And again: *Madest them to be unto our God a kingdom and priests; and they reign upon the earth* (Revelation 5:10). The Greek word translated in English in both these references as "kingdom" is followed by a number of other versions that translate it "kings." Some of the differences in translation are due to the use of different ancient texts. The problem, however, is also that the Greek word *basileia* does not merely mean the "territory or the realm" which is ruled over, but also properly "royalty" or "rule" or "dominion" or the exercise of "kingly power."

Brother Theodore Austin-Sparks used to say that this word is best understood as "kingship." God has made us a kingship, to be priests unto Him. The apostle Paul wrote that God has: *Raised us up with him, and made us to sit with him in the heavenly places, in Christ Jesus* (Ephesians 2:6). Are we to sit with Him in the heavenlies, looking comfortable and pretty and see nothing done, or are we a kingship and priests with a work to accomplish? Previously, Paul had written about the exceeding greatness of His power: *Which he wrought in Christ, when He raised him from the dead, and made him to sit at his right hand in the heavenly places, far above all rule, and authority, and power, and dominion, and every name that is named ...* He then continued: *He put all things in subjection under his feet, and gave him to be head over all things to the church, which is his body* (Ephesians 1:20-21a, 22-23a). The God of grace has given to those whom He redeems an incredible position of power under the Headship of the Lord Jesus. They are to carry into effect the decrees and the will of the Throne of God! They have been made a kingship and executives.

149

EXECUTIVE ACTION IN CORPORATE PRAYER

There can be no executive action taken outside of corporate prayer. To think that executive action can be taken by one person alone is a fallacy. It has led many believers into serious danger. Executive action is a corporate matter. It has to be the body of our Lord Jesus, which in His Name takes such action. When executive action is taken personally, that believer is uncovered and becomes a prey for the powers of darkness. Often we have hardly begun a time of corporate prayer when some Christian, very often a sister, will bind the Devil! It is a dangerous mistake to make; nor does it generally have any effect on Satan. He is not bound; indeed, he finds it rather amusing. Nevertheless, he will often hit back—and not gently! Binding and loosing is a corporate and not a personal matter.

The Lord Jesus said to Peter: *And I also say unto thee, that thou art Peter, and upon this rock I will build my church; and the gates of Hades shall not prevail against it. I will give unto thee the keys of the kingdom of heaven: and whatsoever thou shalt bind on earth shall be bound in heaven; and whatsoever thou shalt loose on earth shall be loosed in heaven* (Matthew 16:18-19). In chapter five we have already drawn attention to this declaration of our Lord Jesus. However it is so important to the matter which we are considering that it can bear reemphasis.

When the Lord Jesus said, "I will give unto you, Peter, the keys of the Kingdom of Heaven," He was in fact speaking to Peter as representing the whole body of Christ. In other words, the Messiah was giving to the Church, which He is building, authority to bind and to loose. It is very important that we understand that it is in the neuter; it is whatsoever, and not whosoever. It is also as important to recognise that the verbs "binding" and "loosing" in the Greek are perfect passive participles. The Lord Jesus was not giving to the Church the authority and the ability to loose or to bind **as the Church sees fit**. For our understanding of this vital matter it would be better translated: *Whatsoever things you bind on earth **shall have been bound in heaven**, and whatsoever thou shalt loose on earth **shall have been loosed in heaven***. In other words, we can only bind what heaven has already decreed to be bound and to loose whatever heaven has already decreed to be loosed. This is executing the will of God.

It is interesting to note that the Lord Jesus said: *Verily I say unto you, what things soever ye shall bind on earth shall be bound in heaven; and what things soever ye shall loose on earth shall be loosed in heaven. Again I say unto you, that if two of you shall agree on earth as touching anything that they shall ask, it shall be done for them of my Father who is in heaven. For where two or three are gathered together in my name, there am I in the midst of them* (Matthew 18:18-20). We have here in these verbs—binding and loosing—the same perfect passive participles. We should note that the Lord Jesus continued and spoke of Himself as being in the midst of two or three gathered in His Name. His Presence in their midst would produce their harmony, their coordination, and their being "agreed." This surely has also some real and important connection with binding and loosing. There is no way that executive action can be taken in the Name of the Lord without the oneness of the responsible and leading brothers in a time of corporate prayer. Once again we recognise that this action is not personal but corporate.

KEYS SYMBOLISE AUTHORITY

Throughout the Bible, keys symbolise authority. The apostle John heard the Lord declaring: *Fear not; I am the first and the last, and the Living one; and I was dead, and behold, I am alive forevermore, and I have **the keys** of death and hell* (Revelation

1:17b-18 AV). He also recorded the declaration of the Lord Jesus: *These things saith he that is holy, he that is true, he that hath **the key** of David, he that openeth and none shall shut, and that shutteth and none openeth* (Revelation 3:7b author's emphasis). The Lord Jesus also said to Peter: *I will give unto thee **the keys** of the kingdom of heaven: and whatsoever thou shalt bind on earth shall be bound in heaven; and whatsoever thou shalt loose on earth shall be loosed in heaven* (Matthew 16:19). The person who has the keys has the authority to lock or to unlock. It is a foolish person who gives his keys to someone he does not know; normally one gives the keys to someone whom one trusts. In so doing, one invests that person with authority.

Keys are simple and often small pieces of metal cut in diverse ways. When one is in possession of the keys, everything is straightforward. One unlocks the front door without even thinking; one can even be speaking with a friend whilst one is unlocking it. It is the same with a car; when a person unlocks the car, it is normally a very simple operation. It is even the same with a safe; there may be a large amount of value in it, but the key is very small, and the opening or locking of the safe is effortless. When you lose those keys, what is normally uncomplicated and easy becomes a difficult and often complex problem and can take many hours to solve.

My point is this: much of the Church has lost or mislaid the keys of the Kingdom. Problems that once were trouble-free have now become complex, involved, and immensely difficult. Situations which, in times of corporate prayer, could have been decisively settled by executive action have now become a permanent and insoluble obstacle. The use of those keys, which belong firstly to the Lord Jesus and have then been entrusted to

His body, is the answer and the solution to the situations and problems we face.

If we believe that the words of the apostle Paul to the Church in Ephesus were inspired by the Holy Spirit, then we understand that we are not wrestling with flesh and blood but with the principalities, and the powers, the world rulers of this darkness, and hosts of wicked spirits in the heavenlies. Can we believe that the Head of the Church, enthroned at the right hand of God, has thrown us to these spiritual forces without covering and without weapons? Has He left us to the cunning tactics and schemes of the powers of darkness to come through as best we can? Of course not! He has disarmed those principalities and powers, destroyed their works, brought their power to nought, clothed us with the armour we need, and given us the required weapons. He has also entrusted us with His keys and with His authority!

Having the keys of the Kingdom is of little point if we do not use them! We are meant not only to enquire of the Lord and earnestly to seek Him, to pour out our heart in intercession, but at times to use the keys of the Kingdom. It appears that the building work of Christ and His clear statement about the forces of evil not prevailing against it is related to our use of the keys of the Kingdom. In other words, the Lord was stating that if we use the keys of the Kingdom of Heaven, the building work will progress and nothing that Hell can do will prevail! If, however, we do not use the keys of the Kingdom of Heaven, the whole building operation will be paralysed and the forces of darkness and death will prevail.

This is borne out in the history of the Church. Every time in which there has been an immense amount of activity in the building of the House of God; we discover that there were saved men and women who were able to use the keys of the Kingdom. Each God-sent, Holy Spirit revival has been accompanied by executive action on the part of believers.

THE REASON THE LORD REQUIRES THE USE OF THE KEYS OF THE KINGDOM

We might well ask why the Lord requires us to use the keys of the Kingdom since He is both sovereign and almighty. If He has supreme authority and power, and if it has all been placed in the hands of the Lord Jesus, surely He can fulfil His purpose and His will without us. In fact, without us He would do much better! God the Father and His Messiah Jesus are, after all, the best ones to use the keys of the Kingdom. Then there can be no mistakes or failures!

It seems that there is only one answer to this question. God is training us, educating us, and disciplining us for His service. That service is not only earthly and for time, but also for eternity. In using the keys of the Kingdom in executing the will of God in corporate prayer, we learn lessons for time and eternity. We learn to discern the will of God and to obey it; we learn to depend upon the government and the wisdom of God; we learn to distinguish the voice of the Lord from all other voices including the voice of our own soul. In fact, God is educating us and training us for eternal vocation.

DIVINE AUTHORITY DELEGATED TO BELIEVERS

As we have written, keys represent the authority of the Lord Jesus, and that authority has been delegated and entrusted to believers. The authority given to us in the Name of Jesus is another way of expressing this vital truth. In the Name of Jesus we are to meet, to act, and to pray. His Name represents the authority the Father has given to us. When a woman marries a man, she takes his name, and his name is her authority. We, who have been saved by the grace of God, have been joined to the Lord Jesus and bear His Name. We have been commanded always to pray in that Name, whether personally or corporately. It is our authority. Likewise, we are members of the body of our Lord Jesus; He is our Head. In the same manner in which the name of one's head is also the name of one's body, we are to live and to do everything in the Name of the Lord Jesus. The Word of God tells us that if we ask the Father anything in His Name He will give it to us.

Concerning our meeting together in the Name of Jesus for worship, for fellowship, or for prayer, none of us will have any problem. It is the question of whether in His Name we have the authority to execute His will which raises difficulty for some. Nevertheless, there are thousands of matters in which His will needs to be done. It is the lack of executive authority in action which allows obstacles, problems, and satanic strong points to remain untouched, impassable and immovable. If we have followed the Scriptures which we have highlighted in this book, then it seems clear that we are called to take action in the Name of the Lord. It is both the calling of the Church and of the workers in the work of the Gospel, and in the work of the Lord. We need to use the keys of the Kingdom of Heaven, entrusted to us in His Name, to lock up and to unlock, to bind and to loose.

A MIDDLE EAST NUCLEAR CATASTROPHE AVERTED

In the Middle East, in the Yom Kippur War of 1973, a number of local believers met in Jerusalem for prayer. The war had reached a point where Israel was prevailing. It had not been so at the beginning. Three thousand young men had died in the defence of Israel. Now the tide was turning, but with this came great danger. The Soviet Union was a solid supporter of both Syria and

155

Egypt. She had equipped their forces with weapons and had trained their soldiers and airmen. They were her protégés.

One of the members of our group had grown up in the shadow of the Dutch Royal family. At one point the Dutch Ambassador to Israel asked to see him. He brought a message from the Queen of the Netherlands about troubling information which had come to them. The Soviet Union was planning to use a nuclear device on Tel Aviv and fire it from Alexandria, in Egypt. Already some Soviet warships had sailed across the Black Sea and the Eastern Mediterranean, and the equipment for launching the device, and the nuclear device itself, was in place. The soldiers manning this equipment were Soviet men dressed in Egyptian uniforms. The strategy was that before Israel progressed any further the device would be fired on Tel Aviv; and when the damage was done, the World Powers would be called upon to hold a peace conference to settle the Middle East problem. The damage to Israel would have been immense; many thousands of Israelis would have been killed, and most of Tel Aviv destroyed. The peace conference, of course, would not have favoured Israel.

This news stunned our prayer group. There were two or three members of the group who had been with Rees Howells throughout the years of the Second World War; there was also Colonel Orde Dobbie and his wife Flo Dobbie, there was Jan Willem van der Hoeven, and his Arab wife, Widad van der Hoeven, and Elizabeth, Baroness van Hemstra, a Lady in Waiting to the Dutch Queen, amongst others.

One of those who had been with Rees Howells had been suddenly woken up in the middle of the previous night with the words which she believed were from the Lord: "Gladys, get up and pray, My adversary is seeking to bring in Armageddon before its appointed time." After we had received the news about the Soviet's plan, Gladys Roberts told us of her experience. Interestingly, the Lord had also woken up Samuel Howells, the son of Rees Howells, in Derwen Fawr, in Wales, thousands of miles away, with the same message He had given to Gladys. We had at first wondered whether the news we had received was based on a rumour. Now we became convinced that it was from the Lord.

We went to prayer immediately and sought the Lord with earnest appeal and supplication. After a while, suddenly into my heart came a verse of Scripture from the Lord: *For nothing is hid, that shall not be made manifest; nor anything secret, that shall not be known and come to light* (Luke 8:17). I shared it and we began to ask that the Lord would make this secret and wicked strategy known to the Western powers. We prayed for some hours on the matter, because we had become convinced that a plan to defeat Israel was in motion. It was that evening that a brother came in and said: "Have you heard the news? President Nixon has called a Stage One Military Alert for all American forces." Apparently, American intelligence had picked up the fact that battalions of Soviet troops were being readied to fly from the South of the Soviet Union to the Middle East, and that they were taking with them nuclear gear to wear. Almost immediately, the Russians reloaded their device and the other equipment onto their warships and sailed back across the Eastern Mediterranean, to the Crimea. A Middle East nuclear catastrophe had been averted. This illustrates the kind of authority and power which God has placed in the hands of His children.

THE GATES OF HELL

It is highly significant that the Lord spoke of the gates of Hell, when He said: *Upon this rock I will build my church; and the gates*

157

of Hades shall not prevail against it. I will give unto thee the keys of the kingdom of heaven: and whatsoever thou shalt bind on earth shall be bound in heaven; and whatsoever thou shall loose on earth shall be loosed in heaven (Matthew 16:18-19). In my estimation the attempts to make this statement clearer to a new generation have been a mistake. To translate "the gates of Hell" as "the powers of darkness" or "forces of evil" or "gates of death" does not convey the real meaning of the words of the Lord Jesus. Literally, of course, it is the "gates of Hades," but what does that mean to most people? It is true that Hades is the gathering point of the unsaved dead, and therefore could be described as the gates of death, of darkness and of evil. However, the older translation in English—"the gates of Hell"—is much nearer to the real idea which the Lord Jesus was seeking to convey. Hell aptly describes the whole satanic hierarchy. It conveys the idea, not merely of death, but of the power and network which is behind death. The gates of the gathering point of the departed unsaved dead does not send shivers down the spine or adequately convey the powerful and dynamic threat of satanic strategy—"Hell" does!

There can be no doubt at all that Satan and the powers of darkness always use death and the fear of death as their weapon. The Lord Jesus spoke of the gates of Hell seeking to prevail against the building of His Church. He declared dogmatically that they would not prevail against His building work. The testimony within Church history witnesses to this fact. Every time the gates of Hell have nearly prevailed, the Lord Jesus, by the Holy Spirit has launched a new initiative, and His building work has continued.

There is, however, another way to look at the same truth which the Lord Jesus was seeking to reveal to us. We tend to think rightly that the gates of Hell cannot prevail against the building work of the Lord Jesus; however, we think only of an *offensive* strategy. The satanic host is seeking to halt the building work of the Lord Jesus and to destroy it. There is, on the other hand, the *defensive* strategy of the gates of Hell. Where does the Lord find the living stones for the building of His house? They are on the other side of the gates of Hell in the domain of darkness and bondage. *For he rescued us from the domain of darkness, and transferred us to the kingdom of His beloved Son* (Colossians 1:13 NASB). There are times when the building work of the Lord Jesus will break through the gates of hell and release the captives. This has happened many times in the history of the Church. There have been great awakenings in which millions have come to the Lord. Thus we have two opposite ideas in this one statement—the *offensive* strategy of the gates of Hell being thwarted; and the *defensive* strategy of those same gates being broken!

When the gates of Hell are translated as the powers of darkness or of the forces of evil, and not as the gates, we lose a vital facet of the truth. Gates can be locked up or unlocked! There are times when we need in corporate prayer to pray for the unlocking of the gates of hell to let the captives out. There are other times when we need in prayer to lock the gates so that the powers of evil cannot fulfil their strategy to destroy the building work of the Lord Jesus.

GATES SYMBOLISE POWER

In the Word of God, gates were extremely important. Every town or city had walls and gates for protection. Those gates were locked at a certain point near sundown, and unlocked at sunrise. They symbolise protective power. They were strategic because they were the only way in and the only way out. There was no point in great fortifications and walls if the gates could not be closed and kept closed.

I remember my great uncle, who lived nearly all his life in the city of Peking (today's Beijing), telling me about going out to play golf in a club in the countryside outside of Peking. While he was gone, an old warlord came up against the warlord who was in charge of Peking, and they had a big fight. This was quite normal! So the warlord in charge of Peking closed the gates, and for three months nothing could come in and nothing could go out. My great uncle lived inside the golf club for three months, but it was a very sophisticated golf club so he liked it. Can you imagine such a thing as a warlord saying, "Shut the gates," and the gates were shut. And that was the end of the matter.

Gates symbolise power. Thus the gates of Hell represent the powerful strategies of the satanic hierarchy—the principalities, the powers, the world rulers of this darkness, and hosts of wicked spirits in the heavenlies. When we feel that we have reached the point in corporate prayer where executive action can be taken, we need to lock up those gates or unlock them.

GATES SYMBOLISE COUNSEL

In the Word of God we read about the Elders sitting in the gates. The careless reader can be forgiven for thinking that this is a Middle Eastern custom. These old Elders apparently do nothing but play backgammon or smoke their nargila, or sheesha, whilst the poor serfs, and especially the women, do all the work. It is however not the Biblical meaning. The Elders sat in the gates and held court. Anyone who had a complaint or a problem could go to the gates and seek the counsel and advice of the Elders and obtain a judicial ruling. When the Elders sat in the gate, they were acting as judges.

Thus gates symbolise counsel. The gates of Hell symbolise the counsel, the will, and the strategy of the powers of darkness. It is essential in corporate prayer when we sense that the Lord has led us to a point where we can take executive action that we actually take it. The counsel of Hell, its will, and its strategy must be locked up in the Name of the Lord Jesus. The reality is that through the finished work of our Lord Jesus, the counsel and will of Hell has been disarmed; its power has been brought to zero and its works destroyed. This fact has to be proclaimed, and is the way in which we use the keys in executive action.

USING THE KEYS

What do we mean by using the keys? This is all important. One may be in possession of keys but not use them. That means one cannot unlock the front door when one comes in and one cannot lock it when one goes out; one cannot use the car because one does not use the keys one has! We may have the keys, but we do not use them. It means that there cannot be any normality in our living. This is precisely what has happened in much of the Church in the Western nations. The life and function of the Church is not normal; it is seriously impaired, and in many cases non-existent.

We find great help in the illustrations in the Old Testament. For example we read the testimony of the psalmist: *All nations compassed me about: in the name of the Lord I will cut them off. They compassed me about; yea, they compassed me about: in the name of the Lord I will cut them off. They compassed me about like bees; they are quenched as the fires of thorns: in the name of the Lord I will cut them off. Thou didst thrust sore at me that I might fall; but the Lord helped me. The Lord is my strength and song; and he is become my salvation. The voice of rejoicing and salvation is in the tents of the righteous: the right hand of the Lord doeth valiantly. The right hand of the Lord is exalted: the right hand of the Lord doeth valiantly. I shall not die, but live, and declare the works of the Lord* (Psalm 118:10-17). The psalmist was speaking of a situation that he and the people of God were facing. He writes of nations compassing him about like a swarm of bees. These nations were the enemies of God's purpose, and they wanted to destroy the work of God. A swarm of bees is no small problem! He then gives voice to his faith. Three times he states: *In the name of the Lord I will cut them off.* This is executing the will of God by faith, using the keys which God has given us!

The psalmist is warring the warfare; in prayer he is expressing God's will. The enemies of God are not accepting his challenge: *Thou didst thrust sore at me that I might fall; but the Lord helped me. The Lord is my strength and song; and he is become my salvation.* He then declares again three times: *The right hand of the Lord doeth valiantly. The right hand of the Lord is exalted: the right hand of the Lord doeth valiantly.* The three declarations by the psalmist are matched by the three declarations of Heaven at work! It is remarkable that we have here in this Psalm a clear illustration of executing the will of God. The psalmist declared three times in the situation which the people of God were facing: *In the name of the Lord I will cut them off.* It is then that the Lord acts. It is noteworthy that it is the right hand of the Lord which is exalted and which works valiantly. It is the Lord Jesus who is exalted and is enthroned at the right hand of God. Once we, as the people of God in corporate prayer, have come to a knowledge of the will of God, we can express it by faith. We are using the keys which God has entrusted to us. Then all the power of God and the grace of God are manifested in whatever situation we find ourselves. The Lord of Hosts, the Commander of the armies of Heaven, is with us, and the God of Jacob is our refuge (see Psalm 46).

For our understanding we have further help given us by the psalmist in Psalm 149: *Praise ye the Lord. Sing unto the Lord a new song, And his praise in the assembly of the saints...Let the high praises of God be in their mouth, and a two-edged sword in their hand; to execute vengeance upon the nations, and punishments upon the peoples; to bind their kings with chains, and their nobles with fetters of iron; to execute upon them the judgment written* (Psalm 149:1, 6-9). We should note the statement: To execute upon them the judgment written. In other words, we can only execute what is the will of God. All the nations and the peoples—their kings and nobles—are described as enemies of God and of His people.

The apostle Paul defines these enemies when he wrote *of: the principalities, the powers, the world rulers of this darkness, and spiritual hosts of wickedness in the heavenlies.* The only way in which we can face these spiritual forces is in the armour of God which He has provided. We have to learn how to stand in that armour, and withstand in the evil day, and having done all, to stand; we have to learn to use the sword of the Spirit which is the Word of God.

It is necessary to know the will of God concerning the spiritual enemies who come against us and express His will with our mouths in prayer. The psalmist writes of the high praises of God in their mouth and a two-edged sword in their hand. It is an extraordinary combination. This combination is the expression with our mouth of worship and praise—that is an expression of absolute faith and trust in God's will. Then in our hand is the Word of God, which is the sword of the Spirit, revealing that will. This is how we use the keys!

THE FOUR ASPECTS OF USING THE KEYS

Using the keys, which God has entrusted to us, consists of four aspects:

Declaring the Will of God

The first is declaring the will of God. Once we know what His will is from the Spirit of God concerning any situation or problem we face we need to express it in words. For example, when we come to a clear conclusion together that God is going to solve a problem or to dislodge an obstacle, or take care of some situation, we need to declare aloud that conclusion. That is using the keys! We are unlocking a matter or locking it up. We are binding something which Heaven has decreed shall be bound, or loosing something which Heaven has decreed to be loosed.

AN EXAMPLE OF ONE WHO DECLARED THE WILL OF GOD

In the biography of Fraser of Lisuland, entitled "Behind the Ranges," we have a marvellous illustration of declaring the will of God. After many years in China, he finally came to the Lisu people in South-West China, an animist tribe. They worshipped spirits and many of them were demon possessed. From the beginning of his missionary life he had felt called to the Lisu people. He was the only Christian in that whole area, ranging over many hundreds of miles. He sought to do everything he could in order to bring the Gospel to them. Not only was he unsuccessful, but in the end he found himself unable to pray. He said that it was as if an iron hand physically took hold of his throat and made it impossible for him in prayer to express anything. This happened over much time, and he wrote home to the prayer groups that supported him: "Please pray for me; I cannot get through at all even in prayer. The powers of darkness here are so tremendous." In those days letters from China to the West took months to arrive.

One day, whilst reading the Word of God, he read in Psalm 47: *Shout unto God with the voice of triumph...He is a great king over all the earth. He subdueth peoples under us, and nations under our feet...God reigneth over the nations...He is greatly exalted* (verses 1b, 2b, 3, 8a, 9b). The Lord spoke to him in his heart and said: "Shout to the Lord with the voice of triumph." Fraser decided to express his faith and his obedience in climbing the highest peak in Lisuland. When he reached the peak, he turned to the South and shouted: "Jesus Christ is Lord of Lisuland." Then turning to the North he shouted the same thing; and to the east, and to the West. Coming down from the peak he discovered that the power of the enemy had been broken, and he was able to pray without any resistance for the first time in many months.

All the prayer in the world did not do that! It was Fraser executing the will of God. He declared the facts. He expressed the truth that God reigns over Lisuland; that the Lord Jesus is Lord over the Lisu people. In that moment the keys were used and the powers of darkness in Lisuland were locked up, and the power of the Holy Spirit was released. Captives of Satan were unbound and the gates of Hell could not hold onto them. Those gates could not prevail against the Lord Jesus obtaining many more members of the body of Christ.

Within weeks, the first family of the Lisu turned to the Lord Jesus; and then another family, and another family, and many more. In the annals of the work of God in China, there is none more glorious than the work of God among the Lisu people.

In the 1980's, after all the suffering of the Lisu people and those who had laid down their lives to bring the Gospel to them, including Fraser of Lisuland, the translation of the Bible in its entirety, was published in Lisu.

All this came out of executive action in prayer. If Fraser of Lisuland had never climbed that mountain and never declared the truth, no breakthrough would ever have come. What did he declare? He declared that God reigns over Lisuland; that Jesus, the Messiah is Lord over the Lisu people; that it was the will of God for the people's bondage to be broken, and that multitudes of the Lisu should experience the saving grace and power of Christ. All of the circumstances were against him, and all the evidence seemed contrary to the Word of God; but Fraser declared the fact and from that point it began to happen.

We must learn to declare the truth of God, to declare the will of God, and the facts revealed to us by the Holy Spirit. This is the first aspect of using the keys.

Possess the Situation in the Name of the Lord

The second aspect of using the keys is to possess the situation in the Name of the Lord. Take it for the Lord and His purpose. This may involve us in binding and loosing, but we must clear the ground of lies, of phantoms, of spirits, and of everything that is contrary to the will of God. Many a time, what has once been a true work of God has deteriorated into something of the flesh. The fashion of the world, the philosophy of the world, the wisdom of the world has permeated that work. What was once organic has now become an organised system. Whatever problems or circumstances we face, we have to possess that situation for the Lord; we have to take it for the will of God to be realised. Then the power of God and the grace of God will clear the ground and make a way for the Lord to act.

The Praise and Worship of the Lord

The third aspect in using the keys is to learn to worship and praise the Lord. Often this aspect is overlooked, but executing the will of God in whatever circumstances we face involves the worship of the Lord. The psalmist has put this beautifully when he writes *of the high praises of God in our mouth and a two-edged sword in our hand.* In other words, using the sword of the Spirit involves praise and worship.

In using the keys we not only declare the will of God, and the facts that the Holy Spirit has revealed to us about any circumstance or problem; we not only possess the situation in His Name and take it for the Lord, but we also start to worship the Lord and praise Him for the victory as if the whole matter is solved. Actually, it is already decreed in Heaven, but the decree is yet to be carried out on the earth.

We have a marvellous example of this in King Jehoshaphat as recorded in II Chronicles 20. At one point in his reign, Jerusalem was surrounded by a great evil confederacy of enemy tribes and nations. Everything seemed hopeless for the people of God were blockaded. King Jehoshaphat went into the house of the Lord and described to Him the impossible situation the nation was facing. Then the people of God gathered together and enquired of the Lord. He spoke to them through a prophet; it was a manifestation of the Spirit. The prophet said: *Listen all you people of Judah and of Jerusalem, and King Jehoshaphat; do not fear, neither be in dismay by reason of this great multitude; for the battle is not yours but God's. You shall not need to fight in this battle, set yourselves, stand still, and see the salvation of the Lord. Tomorrow go out against them* (see vv. 15-17).

How did King Jehoshaphat finally use the keys? How was the will of God fulfilled? It had been revealed to them that they did not need to fight in this battle, but they were to take their position, to stand still and see the salvation of the Lord. Early the next morning, Jehoshaphat had a conference with the other leaders. The question was how to express their absolute trust in the Lord, and express it in the most concrete manner. They decided to put the Levitical Temple choir in the front of the army! They were not to sing some great militant hymn about the destruction of their enemies or the downfall of this confederacy, but they were to sing: "For the mercy of the Lord endures forever." It was like a Sunday school picnic. One side of the choir sang, "For the mercy, the steadfast love of the Lord endures forever," then the other side sang, "For the mercy, the steadfast love of the Lord endures forever." When they began to sing, everyone in the confederacy began to kill one another. That was how the people of God used the keys! When the choir finally finished their singing, not a single enemy had survived. It took them three whole days to collect all the spoil and bring it back to Jerusalem. It was a miraculous triumph.

So often, when we have been brought to a position of faith, we need to praise and worship the Lord. In such a manner we lock or unlock the situation. It is executing the will of God in practice.

Faith Needs to be Practically Expressed in Action

The fourth aspect: Faith is never true and living faith, if it is not concretely expressed. For example, Rahab put a scarlet thread in her window. That was the way she concretely expressed her faith that her home, which was in the wall, would not be destroyed when the walls of Jericho came down. In fact, it was the only part of the wall that was not destroyed. Abraham offered up Isaac as a living sacrifice, and it was the concrete expression of his faith that God would even raise Isaac from the dead. Noah built an ark hundreds of miles from the sea. It was a living and concrete expression of his faith in the Word of God. These are just a few examples of many more that we could mention.

In using the keys, we often have to take some further concrete action. For example, if we are seeking a person's healing, and the Lord has revealed that He will heal that one, we should go to that person and in the Name of the Lord lay our hands on him or her. Indeed, whenever the Lord shows us that He means to answer our prayer, we must express our trust in Him in a tangible and practical manner.

THE MIRACULOUS MEETING OF A FINANCIAL NEED

On one occasion at Halford House, the builder, Bill Richards, came into my study and said, "Has the money come?" When he first began to work for us, I had said to him that we were young people who believed in God and trusted Him for everything. I said to him: "We do not have any money, but if you do the job properly we will ask the Lord for the money, and He will provide it. If you agree to this, it means that God is employing you." And he said, "Yeah!" Years later Bill told me: "I never believed a word you said; I thought that was the way Christians talk. They have the money in the bank, and when they need to pay a builder or some other worker, they say 'the Lord has provided' and take the money out of the bank." When we first talked about his working for us, he said, "I am an atheist, I do not believe in God; but I respect those who do."

We had paid him many different sums of money for the work he did over a few years, and he had got used to our Christian phraseology. So this was why he said, "Has the money come?"

I said, "No it hasn't; have you done the job properly? Maybe you have to put in a screw here or a nail there."

"Oh," he said, "I will go and check everything, but I think the work has been done well and properly."

"When do you need the money?" I said.

He replied, "By two o'clock so I can get it into the bank by three."

I then heard myself saying, "If you have done everything properly, the Lord will provide the money by two o'clock." Bill went away very happy, because he thought I had forgotten to go down to the bank to take the money out for him.

I said to Margaret, who looked after the house, "We do not have this money, and we have already had the second post, and there were only bills in it! Let us have an early lunch and ask everyone in the house and garden to gather for prayer in the library upstairs." We had our lunch, and we were thirteen people who knelt in prayer in the library. Bill came in through the back door and looked in the kitchen, but no one was there. He crossed the main room on the ground floor and looked in my study, and there was no one there.

Then he thought he heard voices upstairs and reckoned that we were in the library. He went by the front door, climbed the stairs, and quietly opened the library door. There he saw thirteen people on their knees in a circle, and he heard Albert Luck (Eric Luck's father) praying, "Lord, we ain't got this money, and we need it by two o'clock; it is now past one o'clock. Would you please give it now?" Bill closed the library door, and we all heard him groan like an elephant giving birth, and saying, "Oh Gawd, they ain't got the money; they are actually praying for it." We heard him stumbling down the stairs like a drunk.

There on the mat behind the front door, which he had passed only a couple of minutes earlier, he found a pile of bank notes. He scooped them up, ran up the stairs, opened the door, and said,

"You can all stop praying; the money has come!" It was exactly the sum we needed, to the penny.

This is an illustration of expressing our faith in a tangible manner. I had said to Bill: "The Lord will provide the money by two o'clock." It was the key which unlocked the supply.

ANOTHER MIRACLE OF FINANCIAL SUPPLY

This is another amazing example of the Lord meeting a material need. For many years, the fellowship at Halford House had desired that the market garden attached to the property would come back to it. It was originally the garden of the old manor house built in 1710. It was now managed as a garden centre by Dan Archer. Dan Archer was the character upon which the famous BBC series "The Archers" was built. He was an old Derbyshire man, with an extraordinary character.

One day Dan Archer lumbered down to the gate between the Halford House garden and the garden centre. For some reason I happened to be alone and near the gate when he came through it. He said, "You are just the person I want to see, Lance. I am now too old to continue managing this nursery. I have decided to retire to Derbyshire, and I wondered whether you would like to buy the grounds."

Holding my breath I said, "How much do you want?"

"I want enough to buy a bungalow in Derbyshire," he said.

"How much would that be?" I replied.

"Twenty-six thousand pounds," he said. This was a very low sum at that time for a large piece of ground in the centre of

Richmond, Surrey. Once this desire of Dan Archer to sell the ground was made known, there would be many buyers.

I incredibly said, "We will take it."

Then Dan said, "I will give you a week or so to go to the bank and arrange a loan."

I could hardly believe it, but I said, "We will pay you in cash!"

"Really?" he said.

"Yes," I replied. I was so shocked, that I could not speak to anyone about this, but I went straight to the study, got on my knees and said, "Dear Lord, this is ridiculous! I have just said that we will pay for the market garden with cash, and we do not have a penny." The Lord said in my heart: "You shall have it." I was alone, but I burst out in laughter, rather like Sarah did. "Forgive me Lord," I said, "but where can this money come from? I have never trusted You for such a big sum." Again the Lord said, "You shall have it."

That evening was the normal weekly prayer meeting, and I shared what had happened. I was a little nervous about sharing the news because I knew we had absolutely no money and had bills that would have to be paid. After much prayer everyone was unanimous. We must go ahead in faith! I then asked everyone present not to tell anyone about this or to discuss it over the phone, and everyone agreed.

The next morning I had a phone call; it was Daisy, Lady Ogle. "Lance," she said. "I hear that there is a garden for sale next to Halford House." I said immediately, "Lady Ogle, you should not know this. Someone has given you this information, but everyone at the prayer meeting was sworn to secrecy. Whoever it was should not have done this! Who told you?"

"Don't get upset," she said. "come down from your high horse. At five o'clock this morning in my prayer time the Lord said to me, 'Do not buy the house! Buy the garden.' I have been phoning all my friends over the South of England to find out where this garden is. No one told me, but when I phoned Elizabeth Stearns, she said, 'Oh, Lance has told you.' And I said to Elizabeth that it was not Lance but the Lord who told me. Do you have the money for this garden?"

"No," I said.

"How much is it?" she said.

"Twenty-six thousand pounds," I said.

"You shall have the cheque by tomorrow morning." And so it was! On this occasion the key was turned when I said to Dan Archer, "You shall have it in cash." Faith has to have a concrete and tangible expression.

PRACTICAL POINTS

Here are a few practical points on executing the will of God in prayer.

Firstly: We must take our place in Christ; we must put on the whole armour of God. This is necessary in all times of corporate prayer. When, however, we take executive action, it is even more essential. We must consciously, deliberately, by faith, abide in Christ; it is the position God the Father has given us. This is our only security and safety. There we must remain. In Him and on His finished work we must stand, withstand and having done all, stand. Remember, always, we can only execute the will of God by standing in Christ. Be careful of the enemy's tactic to draw us out and uncover us. It is a very real danger. Satan's whole objective is to entice us out of our position in Christ, and thus neutralize us. He has an enormous fear of our taking executive action. The victory is ours as we stand in Christ.

Secondly: We must have a knowledge of God's will in the matter before us. There is no possibility of taking executive action until we are clear as to what the will of the *Lord is in the situation or problem we face. Paul writes: Look therefore carefully how ye walk, not as unwise, but as wise; redeeming the time, because the days are evil. Wherefore be ye not foolish, but understand what the will of the Lord is* (Ephesians 5:15-17).

Thirdly: We must open our hearts to the fullness of the Holy Spirit. We need to be filled with Him so that we are full of faith, full of power, full of grace, and full of wisdom. Again the apostle Paul commands us not to be drunk with wine, but be being filled with the Holy Spirit (see Ephesians 5:18). Why is there so little executive action taken in corporate prayer? The answer is simple. We are not being filled with the Holy Spirit. Where there is no fullness of the Holy Spirit, believers cannot rise to executive action.

Fourthly: We cannot take executive action until the Holy Spirit harmonises and coordinates us. We have to become of one mind on the matter; then we can execute the will of God in corporate prayer. This unanimity is essential. We must be patient with one another until we reach it.

Fifthly: Never enter into conversation with the Devil, calling him names, deriding him, or devaluing him. Remember that even the Archangel Michael did not dare to bring a railing accusation against him; but said: "The Lord rebuke thee, Satan." Do not think that you can call the Devil names and escape any action by him.

I remember years ago, there was a particularly bad situation over a sister who was greatly distressed by demonic activity. One young brother in the prayer time, who did not have much fear of the Lord in him, was carried away by fleshly emotion. He began to call the Devil all kinds of names: "You slimy serpent, you liar," then a whole lot of other names. Those of us who knew the Lord a little more deeply trembled for that brother. We appealed in our hearts that the Lord would cover him. That night, however, darkness fell on him and he never recovered until some eight years later when the Lord graciously restored him. In those previous years he was in darkness. Never have a conversation with the Devil!

Sixthly: See that you are right with the Lord before the prayer time begins or we waste valuable time. So often those who are main contributors become targets of the powers of darkness. Satan is the continual accuser of the brethren. We need to know how to use the shield of faith against the fiery darts of the Evil One. Remember: *If we confess our sins, he is faithful and righteous to forgive us our sins, and to cleanse us from all unrighteousness* (1 John 1:9 cp Ephesians 6:16). Sometimes it is not sin that blocks our participation in corporate prayer; it is just a sense of defilement. All of us pick up much "dirt" during a normal day. We need the blood of the Lamb, which cleanses us not only from sin, but from defilement.

Seventhly: If you are a sister, take real note of I Corinthians 11:5, 10, where it speaks of having your head covered. Far be it from me to tell you what to do, but remember "the fear of the Lord is the beginning of wisdom." There is a small statement in

175

verse 10 which lifts this whole question onto another level: *Because of the angels*. It should be enough to make any sister sit up and take note. It is often said that this matter is an Old Testament custom and has no relevance for these days. If that is the case, what else has no relevance for today both in the Old Testament and in the New Testament? Should we begin to trash whole areas of the Bible because we do not understand what is said? In my estimation this matter has very serious relevance when we take executive action. The powers of darkness are watching for any single weakness, or failing through which they can take advantage. This of course is true of both men and women. When we execute the will of God in corporate prayer, we need to be more than usually careful because principalities, powers, world rulers of darkness, hosts of wicked spirits are all involved.

Lastly: We execute the will of God by declaring positive facts—ignoring Satan and praising God. Sometimes the way to victory in executing the will of God is simply to praise the Lord as if Satan is not even in sight. This is what King Jehoshaphat ordered when he made the Temple Levitical Choir the vanguard of the army. They ignored that huge evil confederacy, all their enemies who were out to destroy them, and simply praised the Lord. They sang, "The mercy, the steadfast overcoming love of the Lord endures forever." And when they worshipped the Lord, He acted for them

9
HINDRANCES TO PRAYER

In chapter three we dealt with bad habits which destroy corporate prayer and intercession. Whilst in no way lessening the problem of bad habits, in this chapter we shall deal with even more serious hindrances. So often our prayer time is hindered, and that is a grave problem. Sometimes a heaviness or lifelessness comes down upon the whole prayer time; and as a result there is no anointing and no leading of the Spirit. Although we are saved by the grace of God and born of His Spirit, we are still human beings. The powers of darkness know only too well that we are human, and they take advantage of it. Through our failings they seek to manipulate us, and thus hinder effective prayer and intercession. In the vital matter of executive action in prayer, these hindrances can totally obstruct it. Let us then consider some of those hindrances.

UNFORGIVENESS

A severe hindrance to effectual prayer is unforgiveness. Whoever we are, whatever our background, however wonderfully we have been saved, if we have unforgiveness in our heart our prayer is valueless. It renders our words meaningless. The Lord Jesus underlined this hindrance to prayer by saying: *For if ye forgive men their trespasses, your heavenly Father will also forgive you. But if ye forgive not men their trespasses, neither will your Father forgive your trespasses* (see Matthew 6:14-15). In other words there is a total blockage to our prayer.

It is noteworthy that the Messiah in the pattern prayer which He gave us never emphasised the tremendous statements He made in it; except this one: *And forgive us our debts, as we also have forgiven our debtors* (Matthew 6:12). Upon this statement He made this solemn comment: *But if ye forgive not **men** their trespasses, neither will your Father forgive your trespasses* (v. 15). In other words, the Lord was speaking of mankind. He was not speaking only of our brothers and sisters in Christ. In His use of the word "men" we have three realms—the world, the Church, and the family. Some Christians believe that it matters not if they have an unforgiving spirit to unsaved people in the world who have done them injury or unsaved relatives. In their estimation, the words of our Lord Jesus only refer to those who are saved. However, the Lord Jesus used a generic term when He spoke of "men."

This means simply that if we have a bitter and unforgiving spirit towards people in the world or our unsaved relatives, as well as those who are our brothers and sisters in Christ, the Lord will also not forgive us. Many Christians have been deeply wounded by unsaved people in the world. When it has been a grave injury, either physical, or mental, or financial, it is understandable that people find it very hard to forgive. Likewise, it is for many Christians extremely hard to forgive when they have been injured by parents or unsaved relatives. It is not any easier to forgive when Christians deeply wound one another by word or action. Nevertheless, the Word of our Lord Jesus stands—if we forgive not we shall not be forgiven. The wound festers if left untreated and unhealed, and it has many bad consequences. It becomes a root of bitterness which can destroy the spiritual well-being of a child of God, and the well-being of many others. The only solution is to forgive others as one has been forgiven by God.

How was one forgiven by God? It was abounding grace that forgave every one of us! We need such grace to forgive others.

There are many examples of those who forgave, beginning with the Lord Jesus Himself, who said: "Father, forgive them for they know not what they do." There have been amazing testimonies of believers, who by the grace of God forgave those who injured them. Corrie Ten Boom is one powerful example. She lost her aged father and her sister in a Nazi concentration camp. It was not easy for her to forgive, but she overcame and forgave. Everyone who met Corrie spoke of the overflowing love and grace that she expressed. There have been others who lost their whole families in the Holocaust, and who in the same manner overcame and found their hearts filled with the love of God, even for their former enemies.

An unforgiving spirit destroys, but a forgiving spirit brings one into a deeper union with the Lord. Every time children of God overcome what has been done to them and forgive, they become more like their Lord. A hard and unforgiving spirit damages not only the life of that believer, but becomes a severe hindrance to personal prayer as well as corporate prayer.

Unconfessed Sin

Another huge hindrance to corporate prayer is unconfessed sin. The Psalmist says: *If I regard iniquity in my heart, the Lord will not hear* (Psalm 66:18). The salvation we have experienced is so comprehensive—all our sins have been blotted out; our transgressions have been removed as far as the East is from the West; our sin which was as scarlet has become as white as snow. Only the Lord could do this! The apostle John writes: *If we confess our sins, he is faithful and righteous to forgive us our sins, and to cleanse us from all unrighteousness* (I John 1:9). It is **unconfessed**

sin that constitutes a huge hindrance in corporate prayer. When it is confessed, the blood of the Lord Jesus cleanses us from all sin.

When there is sin in the camp, hidden and unconfessed, it hinders prayer and makes impossible any executing of the will of God. Achan disobeyed the command the Lord had given to the children of Israel. He had commanded them not to take anything in Jericho that belonged to their enemies, and Achan took much silver and gold and a number of valuable treasures and buried them in his tent. His sin caused Israel its first great defeat at Ai. Unconfessed and unrenounced sin impedes the advance and victory of God's people. We should note that although Achan's sin was unknown to the children of Israel, it still brought defeat to the whole nation.

Sin unknown to others and unconfessed has an impact on a prayer time. It is obviously a great hindrance to corporate prayer.

UNBELIEF

Unbelief or disbelief is another serious hindrance to corporate prayer. The apostle John wrote: *For whatsoever is begotten of God overcometh the world: and this is the victory that hath overcome the world, even our faith. And who is he that overcometh the world, but he that believeth that Jesus is the Son of God?* (I John 5:4-5). From this statement we understand that there can be no overcoming of the world apart from faith. John further emphasises this when he states that only what is born of God can overcome the world. Only through God-given and living faith in Jesus the Son of God can those who are born again realise the victory. We should carefully note that John wrote: *This is the victory that **hath** overcome the world.* It is a living and practical faith in Jesus the Son of God that alone spells victory! He has won the victory and there is nothing Satan can do about it. John is writing about living and working faith in the Lord Jesus as the victor and the overcomer of the world. In other words, "Without faith it is impossible to be well-pleasing unto Him; for he that cometh to God must believe that he is, and that he is a rewarder of them that seek after him (Hebrews 11:6).

It is possible to believe in one's head academically that Jesus is the Son of God, the victor and the overcomer, and in one's heart harbour unbelief. For this reason the writer of the Hebrew letter wrote: *Take heed,* **brethren***, lest haply there shall be in any one of you an evil heart of unbelief, in falling away from the living God* (Hebrews 3:12 author's emphasis). We should note that he was writing to believers. With the head we can believe that Jesus is the Son of God, but with the heart we believe that He is restricted and limited in what He can do. He can only do what our brain allows Him to do! This is an evil heart of unbelief or disbelief in a believer. It is another powerful hindrance in corporate prayer.

We are all human and our minds are often beset with doubts. Our enemy sees to that! However it does not matter, if only in our heart there is a living and practical faith in the Son of God. We should note the words of the Lord Jesus in this connection: *Have faith in God. Verily I say unto you, Whosoever shall say unto this mountain, Be thou taken up and cast into the sea; and* **shall not doubt in his heart***, but shall believe that what he saith cometh to pass; he shall have it. Therefore I say unto you, All things whatsoever ye pray and ask for, believe that ye receive them, and ye shall have them* (Mark 11:22-24 author's emphasis). In my experience, when one has had to face large and considerably complex situations, many doubts have beset one's mind. In the heart, however, there has been a living faith that the Lord would fulfil it; and He has! Supremely it is the heart which concerns the Lord.

For example, we can be facing an extremely complex problem, and we simply disbelieve. We do not believe the Lord could change that person or that set of circumstances. We cannot rise to it, and we find ourselves unable to believe that with the Lord anything is possible. Or again we are praying for someone's healing, and because we have been in touch with one or two who have not been healed, we begin to become cynical. In some way, what we believe in the head academically has not been transferred to the heart.

We should remember that at one time Peter was in prison and the Church prayed fervently for his release. An angel went and brought Peter miraculously out of the prison; but James was arrested and beheaded. One can imagine that the Church was greatly confused. In the Upper Room they had been praying fervently and taking hold of the Lord for them both, but Peter was miraculously freed and James was beheaded. Why did the Lord answer the prayer for Peter and not for James? The answer is that it was the will of God in action. Peter was released and James was martyred. It is a great mistake to believe that Peter had an angel and James had none. Peter only needed one angel; James probably had a whole band of angels who helped him through his martyrdom (see Acts 12).

Only the Spirit of God can root out of us an evil heart of unbelief. After the glorious transfiguration of the Lord Jesus, He and His disciples were walking down the mountainside when a distraught father approached them and spoke to Jesus. He was beside himself with grief for his epileptic son. He described his son's condition and what so often happened to him, and said: *But if thou canst do anything, have compassion on us, and help us. And Jesus said unto him, If thou canst! All things are possible to him that believeth. Straightway the father of the child cried out, and said: I believe; help thou mine unbelief* (see Mark 9: 22b-24). Some ancient authorities add that the father cried out with tears, *I believe; help thou mine unbelief.*

This unbelief can be in any one of us. The father was so honest and real, that in spite of His unbelief, the Lord Jesus healed the boy. We need to be as honest about any unbelief or disbelief and seek the Lord that He would deliver us from it. Never forget that the Lord is so compassionate and understanding that he knows our frame and remembers that we are dust. Many times He exclaimed concerning His own, *Oh ye of little faith.* Where there is honesty the Lord will meet us in this matter!

A FEELING OF INADEQUACY

Another hindrance in corporate prayer is the feeling of inadequacy. A child of God, surrounded by experienced intercessors and prayer warriors, can almost feel a spiritual claustrophobia. Such a believer feels totally inadequate and intimidated by the spiritual giants present. The only way to survive in such a time is to keep one's mouth closed! If, however, a child of God faces this kind of fear and becomes tongue tied and silent, he or she will never grow. We have to exercise our spiritual muscles and learn by experience.

This feeling is not only limited to those who are young in the Lord, in their teens or twenties; it is often found in those who are mature, who are in their thirties and above. The feeling of inadequacy can be found in a person of any age. It is a totally destructive attitude, because in Christ a believer is not inadequate! A child of God should be able to say: *I can do all things in him that strengtheneth me* (Philippians 4:13).

183

Sometimes the root of this sense of inadequacy is found in our pride. We are afraid that if we participate and contribute, others may see our insufficiency and incompetence or watch us making our mistakes. We as Christians would never recognize this as pride but as modesty and reticence. True humility, however, would bring us to the recognition that we need the Lord to deliver us and then to teach us and train us to participate. On so many occasions we learn through our contribution in prayer, even when we make a mistake.

For those who are young in age, in their teens or twenties, we should remember the words of the apostle Paul to Timothy: *Let no one look down on your youthfulness, but rather in speech, conduct, love, faith and purity, show yourself an example of those who believe* (I Timothy 4:12 ASB). Many years before Timothy, Jeremiah had that same experience. He felt totally inadequate and said: *Alas, Lord God! Behold, I do not know how to speak, because I am a youth. But the Lord said to me: Do not say, 'I am a youth,' because everywhere I send you, you shall go, and all that I command you, you shall speak* (Jeremiah 1:6-7 NASB). If both Timothy and Jeremiah had remained in their sense of inadequacy, not daring to speak or to act, they would never have fulfilled their ministry. By the grace and power of God they overcame that sense, grew in the Lord, and fulfilled their calling.

THE SENSE OF DEFILEMENT

Another hindrance to corporate prayer is the sense of defilement that all of us experience. We know that we have been washed in the blood of the Lamb. About that fact we have no doubt. The Lamb of God has borne away our sins. Nonetheless, all of us pick up defilement during our normal day. It is almost impossible not to be defiled by that which we see and hear in this world—on television, in magazines and newspapers, even in advertisements; in our work place or in business life, in all the places in which we rub shoulders with this world. In all of this we see and hear things which trigger fleshly desires and lusts, and we feel defiled by them. Are we to be as monks and nuns, cloistered in monasteries and convents, totally separated from the world outside? The Lord, however, told us to go into all the world and preach the Gospel. It is not possible to obey His command and not pick up defilement from that world.

The Lord Jesus on the night in which He celebrated the Passover with His disciples before His death, took a bowl of water and a towel, and washed their feet. Peter remonstrated with Jesus and would not allow Him to wash his feet. The Lord Jesus therefore said that if He did not wash Peter's feet, Peter would have no part with Him. Peter replied, *If that is so, wash me completely from my head to my feet!* Then the Lord Jesus said: *He who has bathed needs only to wash his feet, but is completely clean.* (see John 13:1-10 NASB).

The Lord Jesus was referring to the normal everyday custom in times past in the land of Israel and the Middle East. The first thing one did when visitors came into one's home was to wash their feet. In those days there was no public transport by train, bus, or car. People either walked or rode on a donkey or a horse. It was refreshing after a journey in the Middle East heat to have your feet washed. The spiritual meaning of this is simple. We may have had our sins dealt with by the finished work of the Lamb, but we pick up defilement through the course of any day. The blood of the Lamb is sufficient for that also.

This matter of defilement, which we pick up in the world, is a real hindrance to a time of corporate prayer. If we all feel "dirty" as we enter prayer, it will obviously effect our participation and contribution. We need: *The washing of regeneration and renewing of the Holy Spirit* (Titus 3:5b). It is noteworthy that the Greek word translated by the English *washing* is "Laver." This is a reference to the Laver in the Tabernacle and Temple. The Altar of Burnt Offering symbolises the complete sacrifice of the Messiah for our sin. The Laver speaks of a new birth and within that birth the washing from all defilement. Paul conveys this same idea when he writes: *That he might sanctify it, having cleansed it by the washing of water with the word* (Ephesians 5:26). Again the washing is a reference to the Laver. We ought to note the words: *Washing of water with the word*. When we read the Word of God and meditate on it, it cleanses our mind and being. This is another reason why we should memorise Scripture; for then in a time of temptation the Spirit of God can bring back into our memory some Word of His and it will cleanse us.

In every time of corporate prayer we need always to bow our heads and praise the Lord for this washing from all defilement. Then we shall not be hindered.

HUSBAND AND WIFE RELATIONSHIPS

It is interesting that the apostle Peter puts his finger on another hindrance in corporate prayer. It is the matter of the relationship of husbands and wives, one to another. This may not normally be thought to have anything to do with prayer. He wrote: *Ye husbands in like manner, dwell with your wives according to knowledge, giving honor unto the woman, as unto the weaker vessel, as being also joint heirs of the grace of life; to the end that your prayers be not hindered* (I Peter 3:7). Is it possible that a bad relationship between a believing husband and a believing wife could hinder prayer? The answer is simple; it could, and in so many cases it happens. The continuous disharmony between a couple—their arguing and rowing and dissension—hinders personal, family, and corporate prayer.

There is no inequality between men and women, as if one has greater value and use than the other in the sight of God. At the beginning of the Bible it is recorded: *And God created man in his own image, in the image of God created he him; male and female created he them* (Genesis 1:27). They were created to be joint-heirs of the grace of life. Nonetheless, husbands are urged to dwell with their wives *according to knowledge, giving honor unto the woman, as unto the weaker vessel*. There is no question about the authority and inspiration of the Word of God, as always it proves to be absolutely correct. However, some ladies appear to be anything but weaker vessels! Some of them are physically, mentally, and spiritually incredibly tough. Indeed, within the Word of God we have some amazing examples: Jael, Deborah, Jezebel, Anna the prophetess, Lydia, and a number more. From unsaved society we could mention many more such tough ladies!

When the Word of God speaks of women as the *weaker vessel*, it means that they are built on a different principle than the man. They are of equal value to men and equal in the work that they perform, joint heirs of physical life, and complementary to each other. Nonetheless, they are entirely different in the principle upon which they are built, both mentally and physically. Women are different than men, and rightly so. Apart from any other consideration the fact remains that a woman gives birth to a new human being, and it takes nine months from the conception to the birth. Men do not have that experience. Of course, both men and women are joint-heirs of that life, but there is a real difference between the function of the man and of the woman.

It is interesting to note what the Word states concerning the place and function of women. They are to: *Rule the household* (see I Timothy 5:14). Men ought to recognize that their wives are to take responsibility for the home and household. The Greek word translated by the English as *rule* is a strong word. It means that the wife is to be the guide of the house, to rule it and head up the practical work of the household. Proverbs 31:10-31 is read aloud at every Jewish wedding. If one reads carefully these verses, the woman described within them is not at all like the normal idea of a wife that is prevalent among some. She is incredible and certainly not a chattel. This woman weaves carpets and carpets her home, makes clothes, buys and sells fields, plants vineyards, and sells whatever she weaves.

A husband is to dwell with his wife according to knowledge. The NASB translates this as: *Live with your wives in an understanding way, as with a weaker vessel*. Much of the disharmony between husbands and wives arises from a misunderstanding of the different roles they are to play. The husband is to be the "head" and to make the final decisions. That is his God-given role. When there is an understanding of the role of the husband and the role of the wife in their relationship, much of the friction disappears. Friction, dissension, even fighting is solved when the self-life of both of them is laid down! When husband and wife pray together every day, this can also release tension and cement the relationship.

Whatever we understand about the relationship of husbands and wives, when there is friction, discord, strife and antagonism, it is a genuine hindrance to prayer.

DISHARMONY

Disharmony and discord are another hindrance to corporate prayer. It does not take the enemy long to be able to cause discord amongst believers. One marvels at the matters on which believers fall out. It reminds me of the story of an enormous controversy in the Middle Ages which swept through the synagogues in Russia. It was centred on the question as to how many angels could stand on a pin head! It was so fierce that it split person from person, and even synagogue from synagogue.

Only let your manner of life be worthy of the gospel of Christ: that, whether I come and see you or be absent, I may hear of your state, that ye stand fast in one spirit, with one soul striving for the faith of the gospel (Philippians 1:27). It is noteworthy that the apostle writes of these children of God standing in one spirit, with one soul. If we are born of the spirit of God, we do not have to fight to be of *one* spirit; we **are** *one* spirit. There is only *one* Holy Spirit. No matter what our race, tribe, colour, temperament, background or language, we can all stand in *one Spirit*. We have all been baptised into one body by the one Spirit.

It is standing with one soul striving for the faith of the Gospel which presents the difficulty. To stand with one soul is a miracle of the first order, and only the Lord can work it. Disharmony between our souls is a natural phenomenon. It is the easiest thing in the world to strive with one another, rather than to be with one soul striving for the faith of the Gospel. If we take the history of the Church, or of the work of God, it is filled with evidence of faction, disharmony, and division. All this arises from our soul where our will, reason, and emotion is centred. To bring us to stand with one soul is no small work for the Holy Spirit. It is, however, a vital necessity.

The number of prayer meetings that have died from this disharmony and discord is innumerable. Even in one small local prayer meeting discord can arise, which can develop into division, and finally kills all prayer. Only by *holding fast the head* can the body function and grow with the growth of God. The answer to this condition is to give up all right to oneself, to take up the cross, and to follow the Lord Jesus. To lose one's self-life is to find one's true self in the resurrection life and power of the Lord Jesus. It is then possible to stand with one soul striving for the faith of the Gospel.

TWO GREATLY USED MISSIONARIES

A little piece of grit in a machine can finally bring about much damage. It is amazing how small the matters are, which cause disharmony and discord in prayer times. One of my dear and close friends, who worked for many years in India, used to give missionaries a time of rest in her beautiful home in the Nilgri hills. There were two remarkable and outstanding servants of God who used to avail themselves of this offer. Both of them had been greatly used by the Lord in the work He had given them to do. In the prayer times that my friend led in her home, she had to be very careful where she sat these two sisters! If they were anywhere near each other, there would be trouble. One of those missionaries was very sweet, artistic, and sensitive. Her prayer was always "on the ball." She had a flowery but powerful way of praying. The other missionary was direct, precise, and to the point. Indeed she was often thought to be more like a man than a woman. One of my other friends, a well-known servant of the Lord, used to say that he would give anything to see what this other missionary saw in the Name of Jesus. Her prayer was so authoritative, powerful, and to the point.

These two dear missionaries could not abide each other. When the first prayed in her normal manner, the other would explode, and say under her breath, but clearly heard by all: "Get to the point, woman!" Or, "Silly woman, does she think she will be heard for her beautiful oratory?!" These two sisters had led works in which thousands had found the Lord, but when it came to corporate prayer they were totally disabled. As far as I know they never overcame their problems.

Would to God that every hindrance to corporate prayer was removed, however small or however great they may be. We are in an enormous battle, and sometimes the conflict overwhelms us. We need the grace and the power of God to face these hindrances and be finished with them. The possibility of defeat by the enemies of God, and the consequences that would follow such a defeat, are too alarming to contemplate.

10
THE MYSTERY OF INTERCESSION

Isaiah 62:1-7 – For Zion's sake will I not hold my peace, and for Jerusalem's sake I will not rest, until her righteousness go forth as brightness, and her salvation as a lamp that burneth. And the nations shall see thy righteousness, and all kings thy glory, and thou shalt be called by a new name, which the mouth of the Lord shall name. Thou shalt also be a crown of beauty in the hand of the Lord, and a royal diadem in the hand of thy God. Thou shalt no more be termed Forsaken; neither shall thy land any more be termed Desolate: but thou shalt be called Hephzibah [My delight is in her], and thy land Beulah; for the Lord delighteth in thee, and thy land shall be married. For as a young man marrieth a virgin, so shall thy sons marry thee; and as the bridegroom rejoiceth over the bride, so shall thy God rejoice over thee. I have set watchman upon thy walls, O Jerusalem; they shall never hold their peace day nor night: ye that are the Lord's remembrancers, take ye no rest, and give him no rest, till he establish, and till he make Jerusalem a praise in the earth.

Daniel 9:1-5 – In the first year of Darius the son of Ahasuerus, of the seed of the Medes, who was made king over the realm of the Chaldeans, in the first year of his reign I, Daniel, understood by the books the number of the years whereof the word of the Lord came to Jeremiah the prophet, for the accomplishment of the desolations of Jerusalem, even seventy years. And I set my face unto the Lord God, to seek by prayer and supplications, with fasting and sackcloth and ashes. And I prayed unto the Lord my God, and made confession, and said, Oh, Lord, the great and dreadful God, who keepeth covenant and lovingkindness with them that love him and keep his commandments, we have sinned, and have dealt perversely, and have done wickedly, and have rebelled, even turning aside from thy precepts and from thine ordinances.

No child of God can become an intercessor without facing **the mystery** of intercession. If true intercession begins with an understanding of the will of God, why do we need to intercede? Surely if it is His will, it will come to pass anyway. Why should the Lord want to involve us in its fulfilment? We can state with certainty that the Lord Jesus will not fulfil His will without our involvement. **Therefore the only satisfactory answer to these questions is amazing: He requires us to be in fellowship with Him!** Intercession thus becomes a school in which the Messiah teaches us how to discern His will, read His mind, and in simple faith obey Him. It becomes a practical expression of fellowship with Him. He is also training us for eternal government and to reign with Him forever. In other words, He is schooling us for eternal service!

THE BURDEN OF THE LORD JESUS—THE INTERCESSOR

We face the essential mystery of intercession when we read the words of the Lord spoken through the prophet Isaiah, as recorded in Isaiah 62. He declared: *For Zion's sake will I not hold my peace, and for Jerusalem's sake I will not rest, until her righteousness go forth as brightness, and her salvation as a lamp that burneth* (v. 1). It is of great importance that we should understand who is speaking. Is it the intercession of Isaiah or the intercession of the Lord Jesus? Clearly it is the Messiah who is speaking; Isaiah was not setting watchmen on the walls of Jerusalem! It is the Lord Jesus who says: *I have set watchmen upon thy walls, O Jerusalem* (v. 6). It becomes even clearer from Isaiah

61:1: The Spirit of the Lord Jehovah is upon me; because the Lord hath anointed me to preach good tidings unto the meek. On a Sabbath in the synagogue at Nazareth, the Lord Jesus read these words and said: *Today hath this scripture been fulfilled in your ears* (Luke 4:21 cp. verses 18-19). Plainly, it is the Messiah Jesus who is revealing the burden of His heart in Isaiah 62.

The Lord Jesus declares that He cannot hold His peace nor rest, until Zion's righteousness go forth as brightness and as a lamp that burns, and all the nations will see it. This Zion, this Jerusalem, will be called *Hephzibah* and *Beulah.* Translated it is "My delight is in her" and "she is married." He declares: *For as a young man marrieth a virgin, so shall thy sons marry thee; and as the bridegroom rejoiceth over the bride, so shall thy God rejoice over thee* (v. 5).

This is a revelation of the will of God for those whom He redeems. It expresses the burden on the heart of the Intercessor, Jesus the Messiah. His concern is for the complete fulfilment of the Eternal Purpose of God. In one sense, and not to be discounted, it also refers to the earthly Jerusalem, to the final salvation of the Jewish people, and the completion of the circle of redemption (see Romans 11:25-29). This circle began with Abraham and the Lord's promise to him: *I will make of thee a great nation, ...and in thee shall all the families of the earth be blessed* (Genesis 12:2a-3b). In other words, it was a two-fold promise. That nation was Israel, through whom came the Messiah after the flesh, and of whom is salvation, and by whom came the Word of God from Genesis to Revelation, with the possible exception of Luke and Acts.

The Lord's purpose was also that from all the nations there would be an innumerable number of redeemed Gentiles: *In thee* *shall **all the families of the earth** be blessed*. This circle of redemption and salvation began with the Jews. The Gospel was first to the Jew and then to the Gentile; then the full number of the Gentiles who will be saved; and finally it will end with the salvation of Israel and of the Jewish people—the natural branches of the olive tree being reingrafted into their own olive tree. It is the earthly Jerusalem to which the Messiah Jesus returns. That fact alone has to be significant! What in the world is the Messiah thinking by returning to the capital city of a "historic mistake," an "accident of history?" It can only mean that God has a purpose to save Israel and the Jewish people! Since the earthly Jerusalem and the recreated State of Israel figure so much in the purpose of God, there is, as we would expect, much conflict and war over it. Israel and the Jewish people are an integral part of God's redeeming purpose, and the powers of darkness cannot rest until they annihilate them. They will fail!

It also gloriously refers to the Jerusalem which is above, which is our mother, and whose maker and builder is God. When that Jerusalem descends out of Heaven, having the glory of God, the purpose of God for this universe and for mankind will be finally fulfilled. Over this there is also a huge and almighty battle. Will the Church of God, the Bride of Christ, ever make herself ready for the Lord? It is the revealed will of God that, at least in a remnant, it will be fulfilled. That new Man, in which there is neither Jew nor Gentile, is the focal point of the spiritual war in which we find ourselves.

THE BURDEN OF THE INTERCESSOR SHARED
WITH HIS INTERCESSORS

It is amazing to discover from this prophecy that the Lord's burden is then transferred exactly to these watchmen on the walls of Jerusalem. The words He uses to express **His** burden are precisely the same words He uses to describe the burden that the watchmen should bear! He said of Himself: *For Zion's sake will I not hold my peace, and for Jerusalem's sake I will not rest, until ...* Now He says of these watchmen: ***They** shall never hold their peace day nor night: Ye that are the Lord's remembrancers, take ye no rest, and give him no rest, till ...* (author's emphasis). Here we are at the heart of genuine intercession; it began with the Lord—the Intercessor—and it is transferred to His intercessors, and shared with them.

We should note the words: *Ye that are the Lord's **remembrancers**.* It is with this translation of the Hebrew in the American Standard Version, the English Revised Version, Young's Literal Translation, and the Jewish Publication Society that we come face to face with the mystery of intercession. Why do we need to remind the Lord of His will or of His purpose or of His Word? It is extraordinary that we should be the Lord's "remembrancers," as if He has forgotten His counsel, which He has not! Nonetheless we are to be as "secretaries," reminding Him of His appointments. The only explanation has to be that He desires us to be co-workers together with Him, and is training us for much greater service in eternity.

THE PRACTICAL COMMITMENT OF HIS INTERCESSORS

In disclosing the burden of His heart in Isaiah 62, the Lord Jesus ended with the notable words: *Go through, go through the gates, prepare ye the way of the people; cast up, cast up the highway; gather out the stones; lift up an ensign for the peoples* (Isaiah 62:10). These words are striking! The watchmen on the walls of Jerusalem, called and appointed by the Lord, through their travailing and costly intercession, are actually participating in the fulfilment of the will of God.

We have in these commands of the Messiah an extraordinary commentary on genuine intercession. The first command is to *go through, go through the gates*. In other words, real intercession is a total commitment to the purpose of God. Those gates are the gates of Jerusalem. Even the earthly Jerusalem is a symbol of the Eternal Purpose of God, and His will to fulfil that purpose. Patently, the New Jerusalem which comes down from Heaven expresses the final realisation of God's goal. Genuine intercession, even when it is related to lesser matters, is always linked to the accomplishment of God's final aim. The intercessor may not even be aware of that! The fact of the matter is simple. Our intercession is not just viewing or studying the gates of Jerusalem from afar; it is a "going through the gates." To "go through" those gates means that one has committed oneself to the Lord and to His purpose.

The second command of the Lord Jesus is, *prepare ye the way of the people*. There are many human beings trapped behind the gates of Hell. It is the purpose of the Lord to break open those gates of Hell and to let the captives out. Within this command is the call to costly intercession on behalf of those who are bound, blind, deaf, and dead to the Lord Jesus. Within those human beings are the "living stones" with which the Lord will build His Church. Those who at present are not the people of God will gloriously become the people of God!

The next two commands, *cast up, cast up the highway; gather out the stones*, is the expansion of this truth. This highway is more than a "way." Normally, it denotes some major thoroughfare from a far greater distance. These watchmen on the walls of Jerusalem are not only praying for the people near at hand but for those who are at a great distance. The stones which need to be removed from such a way are those enormous and mountainous obstacles that can only be tackled in intercession and by living faith. When the Holy Spirit places in the hands of the intercessors the right weapons, then satanic strongholds, speculative theories, high things exalted against the knowledge of God are cast down, and thoughts are led captive to Him. These are the huge boulders that can stop this highway from being built. We should note the double imperative: "go through, go through," and "cast up, cast up," is the Hebrew way of underlining and emphasising a matter. It is an emphatic command to the watchmen to be totally and practically involved.

The last command, *lift up an ensign for the peoples* is full of spiritual significance. Wherever the ensign flies, there is the King or Commander. Through intercession we run up the ensign, and we make it known to the powers of darkness that the Messiah Jesus, the King of kings, is present. We declare that Jesus is Lord; that in intercession we are about His business. We have the armour of God, the weapons of God, the sword of the Spirit, and the immutable counsel of God! Satan cannot undo the finished work of the Lord Jesus, or dethrone Him. The ensign simply proclaims the absolute victory of Christ.

TRAVAILING INTERCESSION FOR INDIA

There were two dear and precious sisters whom I came to know—Daisy Lady Ogle and Miss Sinclair. They well illustrate the power of corporate intercession. They became good friends of mine. They were called by the Lord to give themselves in travailing intercession for India. At the time, there were multitudinous Christian denominations in India, some good and some bad. The Lord revealed to these sisters that in India there was no man whom He could use during those days. He burdened them to give themselves to intercession, that the Lord would raise up a powerful and prophetic voice in India. They spent some years in such intercession.

On one particular day they went to hear an Indian preacher. He was a Sikh who had been wonderfully saved. When he testified to his family about his saving experience, he was thrown out of his family and home. Whilst he was preaching, the Spirit of God said to Lady Ogle: "This is the man for whom you have prayed." It was Bahkt Singh. Then the Lord said to her and Miss Sinclair: "Now pray for this man, for I will greatly use him in India."

Thus it came to pass. Through this one precious servant of God, tens of thousands of Indians came to know the Lord from all over India. The Convocations which he held in different cities were crowded to overflowing with thousands of Indians. The impact of the ministry of this one man reached throughout India and Bangladesh, and to the ends of the world. This is an illustration of the Holy Spirit revealing God's will to His intercessors, and through their intercession fulfilling His purpose. We should note that this was corporate intercession, but generally and normally, it was only the two sisters who interceded. Sometimes visiting friends joined them.

TRAVAILING INTERCESSION FOR CHINA

Margaret Barber is also another illustration of the power of intercession. She was sure that the Lord had called her to China, and she went through the normal missionary preparation. She went out with a Mission and was stationed in Foochow in Fukien. She was teaching in a mission school and was a very good teacher with unusual talent; the pupils in the school became greatly attached to her. There developed over a few years jealousies in some of the other missionary teachers. Out of these jealousies a whole number of charges were made against Margaret Barber. The charges were fierce, including immodest behaviour with the pupils, and even immoral relationships. She was finally forced to resign and returned home to Great Britain, with her calling to China seemingly destroyed.

Whilst in Britain she went to some meetings at which a godly Bishop was speaking. She was so helped by his ministry that she asked if she could see him. When finally she saw him, she poured out her whole story.

He listened to it all and said, "Did you, in fact, sin in any way? Was there any truth in the charges?"

She replied that there was no truth whatsoever in the accusations, and that she had not sinned in those ways.

Then the Bishop asked her: "Do you believe that the Lord called you to China?"

"Yes, He has," replied Miss Barber.

He responded, "Then to China you must return!"

Miss Barber exclaimed, "But I have no mission to go with!"

"Mission or no mission," he said, "with the Lord alone you go back to China."

Margaret Barber took her niece and returned to China. She returned to the walled city of Foochow in the Province of Fukien, but realised it would be unwise to live within the city walls because of the mission from which she had been forced to resign.

She found therefore a home in Pagoda Anchorage outside the city walls. It was, in fact, where all the Tea Clippers anchored and were loaded. In a fierce gale she watched with horror as a ship was wrecked. It seemed to her that it was a picture of the events which caused her resignation. She felt that her life and ministry had been shipwrecked. Out of this experience she wrote a poem entitled, "Wrecked."

"Wrecked outright on Jesus' breast:"
Only "wrecked" souls thus can sing;
Little boats that hug the shore,
Fearing what the storm may bring,
Never find on Jesus' breast,
All that "wrecked" souls mean by rest.

"Wrecked outright!" So we lament;
But when storms have done their worst,
Then the soul, surviving all,
In Eternal arms is nursed;
There to find that nought can move
One, embosomed in such love.

"Wrecked outright!" No more to own
E'en a craft to sail the sea;
Still a voyager, yet now
Anchored to infinity;
Nothing left to do but fling
Care aside, and simply cling.

"Wrecked outright!" Twas purest gain,
Henceforth other craft can see
That the storm may be a boon,
That, however rough the sea,

God Himself doth watchful stand,
For the "wreck" is in His hand.

This remarkable poem, born in pain and human rejection, reveals Margaret Barber's deep trust in the Lord. She was not merely wrecked, but "wrecked outright on **Jesus' breast**." Whatever had befallen her, she found in Him her overcoming! She became through her painful experience "anchored to infinity."

Margaret Barber felt that due to what had happened to her and her ministry, the Lord was calling her to intercession. She and her niece therefore travailed in intercessory prayer for China. It was the experience of being wrecked and damaged by fellow missionaries and other believers which led both her and her niece into that ministry of intercession. She was totally shut up to it by circumstances beyond her recall.

They prayed that God would raise up in China a man who was Chinese, whom the Lord could use mightily. Their travailing ministry lasted many years. In their home in Pagoda Anchorage, in the early 1920's, she held a Bible study for young Chinese men who were students. It was at their request that she held it. In that Bible study was a young man named Watchman Nee, amongst others. Through him the Lord was to do a huge work in China and beyond. It was a ministry that was to touch the whole world. The Lord birthed in Watchman Nee one of the truly great ministries in the history of the pilgrim Church. Through his ministry so many thousands came to the Lord, and many more thousands came into a much deeper understanding of the Christian life, of the Church, and of the Eternal Purpose of God.

Brother Nee was imprisoned for over a quarter of a century, and went finally to be with his Lord, after being moved from one forced labour camp to another. Watchman Nee always said of

Margaret Barber that she was his greatest mentor, and that he had learnt most through her. The intercession of these two sisters had powerfully touched the purpose of God for China, and the world. If being "wrecked outright on Jesus breast" led to such an outcome, it was well worth it!

TRAVAILING INTERCESSION FOR THE MIDDLE EAST

Another illustration of the power of corporate intercession was that of Alexandra Liblik and Kathleen Smythe. It was my privilege to have known these two prayer warriors. They had worked for years with the Egypt General Mission in Egypt. It was the policy of the mission that their workers should retire when they reached normal retiring age. These two sisters, however, felt that God had called them to the Middle East and to Egypt in particular, and therefore felt that they should remain. They took an apartment in the high street of Port Said and continued their ministry of intercession.

I was serving in the Royal Air Force and was an aide and secretary in the Chaplains Branch. I had been seriously ill and the RAF medical specialists advised that I should have a time of convalescence. The problem was I did not know where to go. The wife of the Superintendent in the E.G.M, in Ismailiya, Susan Hamill, said to me, "I know of the best place you could go." It was the home of these two old retired E.G.M missionaries in Port Said. She said, "You must be careful because you are young, irreverent, and arrogant, and these are extremely godly sisters." It was thus that I came to know Aunty Alex and Aunty Kathleen!

Of course, for the first week I was not allowed to join in their times of prayer. I had to rest! However, I became more and more curious about what was going on with them. At breakfast they would talk about a letter which they had received from either

Algiers or Baghdad or Khartoum, or some other part of the Middle East. The letters were all about problems or situations that the saints were facing in those places. Sometimes it was a phone call, but the response was always the same. Aunty Kathleen would say with a loud voice, which I could hear in my bedroom: "Alex, prayer." With that I heard their footsteps going down the hallway to the lounge and the door shutting. I could not, for the life of me, think of what was transpiring in that lounge. Sometimes in the evening there would be another phone call and I heard Aunty Kathleen saying, "Yes, praise the Lord, we got the victory midday." Of course, they prayed about some matters for years before they saw the answer; and some others were only answered after they went to be with the Lord!

It seemed to me that these two sisters were running a "spiritual intelligence agency," a kind of "spiritual security service." I was eaten up with curiosity; but I was not allowed to be involved. Then came the day when they read a letter at breakfast from Damanhur, Egypt about an appalling situation in the Church there. It had reached the point where it looked as if a division would take place. Aunty Alex said to me: "Would you like to join us in intercession this morning?" I put on my best British manner and said noncommittally: "Oh, that would be very nice." Of course I had been dying to get into that lounge and see what was happening!

I was not really prepared for that time! When we three were there in the lounge, Aunty Kathleen read the letter in Arabic and translated it for me. Aunty Alex said, "Do you understand this terrible situation?" "Yes," I replied, "I think I do." Then she said, "Do either of you have a Word of Scripture for us from the Lord?" Aunty Kathleen said that she had, and it was from Obadiah, and she read it out. I did not even know where Obadiah was, let alone how it could have anything to do with a situation in Damanhur. All of us got on our knees. To me it was a revelation. They never prayed long prayers, but it went from one to the other, backwards and forwards. They took this verse in Obadiah, stood on it, and proclaimed it. I was dumbfounded, and unusually silent. Then Aunty Kathleen said, "Do you think we are through?" Aunty Alex replied, "No, I think we have a little way to go." So we went on. Then all of a sudden one of them began to praise the Lord, and then the other; and we finally arose from our knees.

The only way I can describe this prayer time was that it was like two helmeted naval sailors on a battle ship, manning one of the smaller guns, and firing at an enemy aircraft until finally they downed it. They had to get it in their sights before it was destroyed. It was such a shock to me that I had to go to my bedroom and lie down on my bed. I had never seen anything like it! That evening there was a phone call from Damanhur that a miracle had taken place; the two main antagonists had broken down in tears and repented. It had resulted in a mini revival. This was my introduction to genuine intercession.

I once asked Aunty Alex how many people she had led to the Lord in her long life of service in Egypt. She held up her hand with her five fingers outstretched. In my arrogant and irreverent way (at that time I was a teenager) I said, "Is it worth it?" She said, "There will come a day when a huge harvest will come out of Islam."

That day has arrived. There are more Muslims coming to the Lord than at any time, since the inception of Islam in the seventh century. It is due to people like Alexandra Liblik and Kathleen Smythe, and many others over the centuries that have fulfilled a ministry of travail for Muslims. They did not live to see on earth the fulfilment of their travail, but they died in faith, and their works do follow them!

In these instances, two believers interceded, sometimes with others joining them periodically. Corporate intercession must have a minimum of two believers; or of course many more.

DANIEL THE INTERCESSOR

Daniel is a remarkable example of a divinely appointed intercessor. He is a telling illustration of the kind of spiritual character required, the price to be paid, and the determined and single-minded purpose of heart needed.

It is interesting to note in the Old Testament, that in each of the great turning points of Divine history, we discover intercessors—Abraham, Moses, Samuel, Daniel, Nehemiah, and Ezra. Six great intercessors, who in fellowship with the Lord, were involved in the fulfilment of His will for the people of God. Abraham was the beginning of the people of God; Moses was the creation of the nation; Samuel was the introduction of the Kingdom; Daniel was the return of the Jews from exile and the rebuilding of the Land; Nehemiah was the restoration of Jerusalem; Ezra was the reinstitution of the Word of God as the sole authority for the people of God.

There was no greater intercessor than Daniel. Even though we recognise Daniel as one of the most significant prophetic voices in the Bible, in the Jewish arrangement of the Old Testament he is found in its third division, the Writings. The Rabbis recognised that Daniel was supremely an intercessor; and they considered that an intercessor took precedence over even a prophet.

Daniel's life and ministry teaches us so much about intercession. In one sense, his prayer ministry was personal and not corporate. However, it would be strange if he had not involved others in intercession; for example, Shadrach, Meshach, and Abednego. Nevertheless, we learn so much about the principles of genuine intercession from Daniel's own experience.

THE DEVELOPMENT OF DANIEL AS AN INTERCESSOR

The Lord's development of Daniel, as an intercessor, may never have been realised but for Daniel's total devotion and commitment to God. He had suffered deeply. He had been made a eunuch by the Babylonians in order that they could enter him for Government Service. Only those exiled younger people, who came from aristocratic families and were exceptional, could be entered for Babylonian Government Service. His faithfulness to the Lord was expressed in his resolute refusal to compromise. He refused even to eat anything that was not kosher; for that he could have been demoted and expelled. Instead, the Lord favoured him, and he rose from position to position, until he occupied the highest position in the Empire next to the Emperor, the Sultan himself, and thus oversaw the return of the exiled Jews to the Land. Daniel began to be honored in the Babylonian Empire, and was elevated from position to position. Then in the Persian Empire, following the Babylonian, he reached the zenith of power. It is evidence of the kind of life and character Daniel had; an example of the words: *For them that honor me I will honor* (I Samuel 2:30b). The Lord Himself planned to place one of His servants, Daniel, in a powerful position where he could facilitate and guard the fulfilment of His will. Even so, it still required the total commitment and cooperation of the vessel!

THE CRUCIAL DISCOVERY DANIEL MADE

From the beginning, Daniel was apparently an intercessor. It was, however, while he was reading Jeremiah that he made a crucial discovery, and from it he discovered that the exile would last only seventy years (see Daniel 9:2). The interesting point was that he did not date the seventy years of Jerusalem's captivity from King Zedekiah, the last king of Judah, but rather from King Jehoiakim. Only the Spirit of God could have revealed that fact to him. When he made the calculation he realised there were only a couple of years left to its completion. It was a key discovery which led to his intercession and to the intercession of other faithful believers with him.

DANIEL'S RESPONSE TO HIS DISCOVERY

The response of Daniel was significant and strategically important to the purpose of God. Having discovered that it was the will of God for the terrible captivity and desolation of Jerusalem to end within a few years, he set himself with determination to deep and travailing intercession. One would have thought that the knowledge of God's will for the ending of the captivity of Jerusalem and of the Jewish people would have caused him to relax. After all, who can stand against the will of God or assist Him in its fulfilment? It will be fulfilled despite the contradiction and power of Satan and his host—whether we pray or not!

In fact, instead of relaxing and resting in God's revealed will, Daniel gave himself single-mindedly and unwaveringly to costly prayer. He opened his window in the direction of Jerusalem and the destroyed House of God, and stood on King Solomon's prophetic words: *If they take thought in the land where they are taken captive, and repent and make supplication to You in the land of their captivity, saying, 'We have sinned, we have committed iniquity and have acted wickedly;' if they return to You with all their heart and with all their soul in the land of their captivity, where they have been taken captive, and pray toward their land which You have given to their fathers, and the city which You have chosen, and toward the house which I have built for Your name, then hear from heaven, from Your dwelling place, their prayer and supplications, and maintain their cause, and forgive Your people who have sinned against You* (II Chronicles 6:37-39 NASB). Daniel's opening of the window towards Jerusalem is significant. It was a physical act, which expressed his faith. His absolute trust in the Word of God through King Solomon was concretely expressed in the opening of his window. He was obeying God's Word: *If they pray toward the land ...and the city... and the house*, the Lord would hear and act.

In place of a carefree, lackadaisical approach to the understanding the Spirit of God had given him, Daniel interceded with fasting, sackcloth, and ashes. One could be forgiven for thinking that he had not discovered the will of God for the ending of the captivity of Jerusalem. Would to God there was this kind of prayer in the Divine judgement which is falling on the nations; for example, on the United States, on the United Kingdom, and on the nations of the European Union; and of course, on many other nations! In Daniel 9 we have a précis of Daniel's intercessory ministry. It is clear that the prophetic words of King Solomon became the fuel for his intercession. It was the Word of God which he used as the weapons of his warfare.

SATAN'S PLOT TO END DANIEL AND HIS INTERCESSION

It is not hard to belittle this kind of intercessory ministry, considering it as "going overboard" and as being "extreme." However, the powers of darkness and evil trembled at Daniel's intercession. They looked into every possibility to neutralise and destroy it and him! The plan they finally concocted is outlined in Daniel, chapter 6. If we compare Daniel 5:31 with Daniel 9:1, we discover that Daniel's vital intercession and the lions' den were at the same time. From this we understand how important Daniel's intercession was at that point in history. Satan had to destroy that intercession.

Satan's plan, executed through the commissioners and the satraps, was that King Darius should issue a Royal statute that could not be altered: *Whosoever shall ask a petition of any god or man for thirty days, save of thee, O King, he shall be cast into the den of lions* (Daniel 6:7b). Satan was thrilled that Daniel's intercession appeared to be finished, and if Daniel was so foolish as to continue interceding, the lions would put an end to him. Daniel, however, recognised the Royal statute as a plan to nullify his intercession and continued defiantly. His enemies were keenly waiting to see if he would still keep his window open toward Jerusalem. Daniel persisted in his intercession, with the window opened, and was thrown into the lions' den. Now it was Heaven's concern! The Lord sent an angel to shut the lions' mouths, and Daniel came out of the lions' den to continue his ministry of intercession! Instead of Daniel and his intercession being destroyed, it was his enemies who ended as a meal for the lions. Daniel lived to see the return carried out—the beginning of the rebuilding of the House of God, and of Jerusalem; and the beginning of the restoration of the Promised Land.

GOD'S ESTIMATE OF THE VALUE OF DANIEL'S INTERCESSION

The Lord put an unbelievably high value on Daniel's ministry of intercession. So much of God's purpose depended on it; but even Daniel could not see that. It is no wonder that when the Archangel Gabriel came to Daniel, he said: *O Daniel, I am now come forth to give thee wisdom and understanding. At the beginning of thy supplications the commandment went forth, and I am come to tell thee; for thou are greatly beloved* (Daniel 9:22b-23a). The Lord and His angels greatly loved Daniel. His ministry of intercession was not only concerned with the return of the Jewish people from the Exile, the rebuilding of the House of the Lord, and Jerusalem, and the restoration of the Land. It was supremely related to the coming of the Messiah and His work.

It was the Archangel Gabriel who explained to Daniel that his intercessory ministry was centred in the coming of the Messiah, the Prince (see Daniel 9:24-27). Daniel had already interpreted the dream of King Nebuchadnezzar. He understood that "the stone which was cut out of the mountain without hands" that broke in pieces the whole monolith was the King Messiah, Jesus. His was a Kingdom which God would set up, and would never be destroyed (see Daniel 2:44-45). In the vision which Daniel himself had of the four wild beasts *there came with the clouds of heaven one like unto a son of man, and he came even to the ancient of days … And there was given him dominion, and glory, and a kingdom, that all the peoples, nations, and languages should serve him* (see Daniel 7:13a-14a). This Son of Man was the Messiah Jesus.

After all, without the return of the Jews from the Exile to the Promised Land, there would have been no Bethlehem in which the Messiah could have been born, according to Micah's prophetic word: *But thou, Bethlehem Ephrathah, which art little to be among the thousands of Judah, out of thee shall one come forth unto me that is to be ruler in Israel; whose goings forth are from of old, from everlasting* (Micah 5:2).

There would have also been no Galilee, or Nazareth, and Capernaum in which He spent twenty-six or more years of His earthly life according to the prophecy of Isaiah: *But there shall be no gloom to her that was in anguish. In the former time he brought into contempt the land of Zebulun and the land of Naphtali; but in the latter time hath he made it glorious, by the way of the sea, beyond the Jordan, Galilee of the nations. The people that walked in darkness have seen a great light: they that dwelt in the land of the shadow of death, upon them hath the light shined* (Isaiah 9:1-2). We should note that the great Via Maris, the Way of the Sea, went a few miles South of Nazareth and just North of Capernaum.

Furthermore, there would have been no House of the Lord to which the Messiah could suddenly have come, according to Malachi 3:1: *Behold, I send my messenger, and he shall prepare the way before me: and the Lord, whom ye seek, will suddenly come to his temple; and the messenger of the covenant, whom ye desire, behold, he cometh, saith Jehovah of hosts.* Indeed the Jewish people could have been assimilated, as so many other ethnic groups have been, and would have disappeared from history.

The will of God was vastly different according to Jeremiah the prophet: *If these ordinances depart from before me, saith the Lord, then the seed of Israel also shall cease from being a nation before me forever. Thus saith the Lord: If heaven above can be measured, and the foundations of the earth searched out beneath, then will I also cast off all the seed of Israel for all that they have done, saith the Lord.* (Jeremiah 31:36-37). So much of the prophetic Word of God would have been unfulfilled unless the Jews had returned to the Promised Land and rebuilt the land and its cities.

One cannot overestimate the value of Daniel's intercessory ministry, because through it God gave him an understanding of world history and the final restoration of all things, and the fulfilment of the Eternal Purpose of God. God had specifically given wisdom to understand these matters. This is true of all genuine intercessors. Few have any idea of the manner in which their intercession is related to the overall purpose and plan of God. Through intercession deep understanding is given by the Spirit of God concerning world history, concerning particular nations, and concerning the goal of God throughout human history.

THE NECESSITY OF A CLEAR KNOWLEDGE OF GOD'S WILL

From Isaiah, chapter 62, and Daniel, 9, we learn one simple but all important lesson. Without a clear knowledge of the will of God there can be no intercession; it is a primary necessity. In fact, without the knowledge of His will for any situation—international, national, local, family, or personal—we will spend our time "beating the air."

With normal prayer we can petition God, plead with Him, and seek an answer. We are not clear as to what His will might be; it is therefore a "hit or miss" affair. We are not sure how the Lord will react and respond. He can say, "Yes" or "No" or "Wait." However, with intercession an essential and elementary requirement is to know His will. Without such knowledge we cannot proceed; it is that awareness which brings the assurance of faith that He will, in fact, perform it. We need carefully to heed the injunction of the apostle Paul: *Be ye not foolish, but understand what the will of the Lord is* (Ephesians 5:17).

With the comprehension of His will in any situation we face, the Holy Spirit will bring to our mind the Word of God upon which we can stand. It is the sword of the Spirit and the weapons of our warfare. We learn this in particular from Daniel's intercession.

TOTAL COMMITMENT TO THE LORD JESUS REQUIRED

With prayer or petition or even thanksgiving we can be uncommitted believers. We can be truly saved but self-centred, self-gratifying, and self-advancing. Intercession, however, requires our total commitment to the Lord—spirit, soul, and body. It demands the surrender of our will to His will. The Lord Jesus has to be the Lord of our whole being. To be an effective intercessor one needs to be filled with the Holy Spirit; for it is the Spirit alone who can make the Lordship of Christ a reality in the life of a believer. This is perfectly illustrated in Daniel's life and ministry.

All of this may cause many Christians to be afraid of intercession; they might feel that the cost is too high! It is, however, the responsibility of the Lord Jesus Himself to educate and to train us in intercession. He requires only one thing—an initial and total commitment. He will then begin the training, the discipline, and the education which will finally produce an intercessor. Once again we learn from Daniel; it was his total uncompromising commitment and surrender to the Lord which allowed the Holy Spirit to make him an intercessor.

There is an old Chinese proverb which we do well to take heed: "A journey of a thousand miles begins with one step." This journey will finally end in the Throne of God! Nevertheless, it begins with one step, and that step the child of God must take. Can we understand this from the words of the Lord: *Thou shalt also be* **a crown of beauty** *in the hand of the Lord, and* **a royal diadem** *in the hand of thy God* (Isaiah 62:3 author's emphasis)? It is worth mentioning that we do not wear the crown of beauty or the royal diadem, but **we are**, in the hand of God, a crown of beauty and a royal diadem. Such a crown or diadem is worn on the head as the emblem of authority and supremacy. It is God Himself who will wear this crown! Is this not putting in another way the words of our Lord Jesus: *He that overcometh, I will give to him to sit down with me in my throne, as I also overcame, and sat down with my Father in his throne* (Revelation 3:21)?

THE POWER OF CORPORATE INTERCESSION

Corporate intercession is the most powerful form of intercession, but it is rarely found. When the Lord brings together a group of believers whom He has trained and birthed as intercessors, it is remarkable. The consequences of such corporate intercession can impact and affect a nation; it can even change the course of history. One such example, as we have already mentioned, was the Moravian Church and their incredible intercessory ministry. Another was the group of one hundred and twenty Christians, led by Rees Howells in Derwen Fawr in South-West Wales. The Lord used their intercession to chart and safeguard the course of the Second World War, and also to bring about the re-creation of the State of Israel, amongst other matters.

Suffice it to state that the powers of darkness will do everything they can to destroy such corporate intercession. Even if many Christians are not aware of its importance, the satanic host well understands its vital and strategic nature. For them, those groups must be neutralised and destroyed, and they will use every weapon in their armoury to reach that aim. Satan's headquarters tremble at the possibility of corporate intercession groups, and the havoc they will wreak on the satanic network. For the fulfilment of the purpose of God these intercessors are strategic and vital. To be involved in corporate intercession requires genuine commitment to the Lord, and a genuine commitment to one another in the Lord.

In any living and faithful company of God's people there should be a nucleus of those who have laid down their lives and have presented their bodies as a living sacrifice to God. Then the great work of qualifying them to be intercessors begins. It will cost them everything. It is the education, training, and discipline of the Holy Spirit which alone can qualify a child of God to be part of corporate intercession. Once He has established that nucleus of intercessors, it is amazing to see how the Lord adds others to their number; even those who have only recently been saved. It will be through the older ones and the manner in which they intercede that the younger ones will learn. Genuine prayer and intercession is like an infectious disease! It is not taught, it is caught!

The enormous danger of a book like this is real! Many will see it as "methods" in prayer or as the "methodology" of intercession. Others will take it as a book of "patterns" for prayer—how to get corporate prayer groups "off the ground." This book was written in fact to help those corporate prayer groups which are already experiencing "prayer warfare" and intercession. It can prune out the false ideas and wrong concepts, and lead us to understand the essential and living principles out of which true intercession is produced. What, however, is really needed are people who know how to "war the warfare" and how truly to intercede. Other believers will then learn by their example.

Sometimes in the most marvellous ways the Lord will take the whole Church into a ministry of intercession, and the youngest will benefit by it, and will be part of that intercession. In this way, young believers will grow in the Lord, and almost unwittingly learn how to pray and to intercede. Nor are such times boring; they can be thrilling!

The Lord Jesus knows only too well the battle over corporate intercession. He has not left us to muddle through, but has made His grace and power available to us. If we open our hearts to the burden of intercession on His heart and allow Him to share it with us, the Holy Spirit will then conceive that burden in our spirit. It may at times involve long and costly travail, but always there will be an outcome. Even if we do not live to see the fulfilment of such travail in our lifetime, we shall see it in eternity. This journey of faith will end in the Throne of God, and in His glory. The Lord prizes the intercessor because he or she is so near to His heart. One day, when we hear the whole story, we will understand how such intercession and such fellowship with the Lord Jesus has been at the centre of the performance of His will on this fallen earth.

11
THE CALL TO INTERCESSION

I Timothy 2:1-4—I exhort therefore, first of all, that supplications, prayers, intercessions, thanksgivings, be made for all men; for kings and all that are in high place; that we may lead a tranquil and quiet life in all godliness and gravity. This is good and acceptable in the sight of God our Saviour; who would have all men to be saved, and come to the knowledge of the truth.

Ezekiel 22:30-31—And I sought for a man among them, that should build up the wall, and stand in the gap before me for the land, that I should not destroy it; but I found none. Therefore have I poured out mine indignation upon them; I have consumed them with the fire of my wrath: their own way have I brought upon their heads, saith the Lord Jehovah.

Ezekiel 18:23 NASB—'Do I have any pleasure in the death of the wicked,' declares the Lord God, 'rather than that he should turn from his ways and live?'

Ezekiel 18:32 NASB—'For I have no pleasure in the death of anyone who dies,' declares the Lord God. 'Therefore, repent and live.'

Ezekiel 33:11a NASB— Say to them, 'As I live!' declares the Lord God, 'I take no pleasure in the death of the wicked, but rather that the wicked turn from his way and live. Turn back, turn back from your evil ways!'

Judgment is one of the major themes in the Word of God. This theme of Divine Judgment begins in the book of Genesis and ends in the book of Revelation. Even a superficial reading of the Bible would bring us to that conclusion. Of course, there are other great themes. Everywhere we turn in the sixty-six books of the Bible we discover Christ as the centre and circumference of God's Eternal Purpose—the Love and Mercy of God, the Saving Grace of God, the Redeemed, the Eternal Purpose of God, the House of God, and many others.

The concept that the grace of God is not found in the Old Testament, but only in the New Testament, is false. The grace of God is found as much in the Old Testament as it is in the New. Likewise, it is often stated that God's judgment is confined to the Old Testament. The last book of the Bible, the Apocalypse, or the Revelation of Jesus Christ, confounds that theory, for it describes some of the most severe judgments in the Word of God.

The apostle John wrote: *For the law was given through Moses; grace and truth came through Jesus Christ* (John 1:17). Some preachers and teachers have stated that the thirty-nine books of the Old Covenant are all to do with law and severe judgment, and only in the twenty-seven books of the New Covenant is grace and truth found. In fact, all thirty-nine books of the Old Testament point to Jesus the Messiah, because through type and figure we discover the grace and the truth, which is found in Him and through Him alone. No one has ever been saved by the blood of bulls, of goats or of lambs, but only because the sacrifice of them prefigured the finished work of the Messiah. Through all these means the Lord Jesus was foreshown. The Messiah Jesus, as the grace and truth of God, is found everywhere in the sixty-six books of the Bible. Even the Law of Moses was *our tutor to bring us unto Christ, that we might be justified by faith* (Galatians 3:24). In other words, everything in the Old Testament pointed to the fact that all grace and truth is centred in Him. In the New Testament that which was prefigured in the Old Testament became glorious fact in the Messiah.

DIVINE JUDGMENT

Throughout the Bible the judgment of God on all iniquity, wickedness, sin, and evil is pronounced clearly and dogmatically. Wherever there is evil and sin, Divine judgment is inevitable; and that on every level—whether international, national, local, or personal. There can be no love or mercy of God without judgment on iniquity and sin. The Throne of the Almighty is not corrupt. He does not overlook evil simply because it suits Him and His policies.

When we come to the conclusion of the Bible, the Apocalypse, or the Revelation of Jesus Christ, we discover some of the gravest judgments in the Word of God poured out on this world. For this reason many Christians are reticent about reading it. Before the Kingdom of God comes in public manifestation, before a new Heaven and a new earth appears, before the New Jerusalem comes down from Heaven, before the saints of the Most High possess the Kingdom forever, the severest judgments in the Bible will fall on all the nations of the earth. The final judgment of the Great White Throne will have been given before the Eternal Purpose of God is fulfilled and completed. At the Great White Throne the whole of history will be judged, all its wrongs righted, and all that is evil and false judged and forever put away (see Revelation 20:11). From all of this we understand one simple fact that Divine judgment is an essential principle.

DOES GOD ENJOY JUDGMENT?

The idea that God enjoys judgment or that He takes great pleasure in it is entirely wrong. It is true that the Lord enjoys destroying wickedness and evil and clearing it away from the universe. After all, sin and iniquity bring misery, darkness, and corruption on everyone. It is, however, a caricature of the character of God that depicts Him as someone who enjoys judgment on mankind. His Word is abundantly clear that He does not enjoy harming or destroying human beings. Take for example what the Lord declares through the prophet Ezekiel: *Do I have any pleasure in the death of the wicked, declares the Lord God, rather than that he should turn from his ways and live?* And again: *For I have no pleasure in the death of anyone who dies, declares the Lord God. Therefore, repent and live.* Or again: *Say to them, As I live! declares the Lord God, I take no pleasure in the death of the wicked, but rather that the wicked turn from his way and live. Turn back, turn back from your evil ways!* (Ezekiel 18:23, 32; 33:11 NASB). These words spoken to the House of Israel, nevertheless, reveal a universal law of His; the Lord desires salvation and deliverance rather than judgment, destruction, and death.

THE NECESSITY OF INTERCESSION IN TIMES OF DIVINE JUDGMENT AND TURMOIL

As we move ever further into the last era of world history before the Lord returns, the judgment of the nations will be universal. The Word of God in many places speaks of the conflict and turmoil at the end of history. We are told that there will be signs in sun, and moon, and stars, and a shaking of everything that can be shaken in both the heavens and on the earth. It will not only be political, economic, financial, and social, but also spiritual. Even the physical make up of the planet will be shaken—seasons, tides, sea levels, and climate will all be touched. Concerning the end of the age, the Lord Jesus declared: *And there shall be signs in sun and moon and stars; and upon the earth distress of nations, in perplexity for the roaring of the sea and the billows; men fainting for fear, and for expectation of the things which are coming on the world: for the powers of the heavens shall be shaken. And then shall they see the Son of man coming in a cloud with power and great glory. But when these things begin to come to pass, look up, and lift up your heads; because your redemption draweth nigh* (Luke 21:25-28). It would seem that already we are moving into this era. If that is true we need to hear the call of God to intercession. As we have before stated, the Lord has no enjoyment or pleasure in judgment. He longs for the salvation of all who would call upon Him. We must learn how to intercede in the midst of all the turmoil, conflict, and war.

In these conditions, there are many areas in which intercession is vital and essential. If men's and women's hearts are fainting for fear, intercession is required for their salvation and deliverance. Those gates of Hell which hold them in bondage and fear need to be unlocked so that the captives can be liberated. The apostle Peter, quoting the prophet Joel, proclaimed: *The sun shall be turned into darkness, and the moon into blood, before the day of the Lord come, that great and notable day: and it shall be, that whosoever shall call on the name of the Lord shall be saved* (Acts 2:20-21). In other words, everything may be shaken to pieces and normal life could be shattered, but *whosoever shall call on the name of the Lord shall be saved.* There will be a harvest of precious souls to the very end. They will, however, need to know the Name of the Lord Jesus; hence the need to evangelise by one means or another. That is God's call to intercession.

THE DIVINE CALL TO INTERCESSION

Paul urged Christians with the words: *I exhort therefore, **first of all**, that supplications, prayers, intercessions, thanksgivings, be made **for all men; for kings and all that are in high place**; that we may lead a tranquil and quiet life in all godliness and gravity. **This is good and acceptable in the sight of God our Saviour**; who would have all men to be saved, and come to the knowledge of the truth* (I Timothy 2:1-4 author's emphasis). Firstly, we should note that the apostle saw the prayer of the Church to be absolutely essential—*first of all*. Secondly, such prayer is *for all men*, not only the saints. Thirdly, the Church is to pray for *kings and all that are in high place*. Lastly, we should mark well that this kind of prayer is *good and acceptable in the sight of God our Saviour*.

When Paul wrote of prayer and intercession for kings and all who are in high places, obviously he did not mean that we should only pray for kings and those in authority who were children of God. Many of the kings and those who occupied positions of authority in Paul's day were not only unsaved, many of them were unjust, corrupt, dictatorial tyrants and harboured bitter hatred for Christians and for the Gospel. Such men did everything they could to destroy the Gospel's advance.

It was not that Paul was urging us to pray for politics, but rather that we should pray for a condition where the Gospel could be preached, where the work of the Lord could advance, where the Church of God could be built up, His Eternal Purpose could be understood, and His work in our lives realised. He explains why we have to pray for political leaders and those who are in government: *That we may lead a tranquil and quiet life in all godliness and dignity* (NASB). He then continues, that God *would have all men to be saved and come to the knowledge of the truth*. It is this kind of prayer ministry that is good and acceptable in the sight of God.

Who else can stand on the earth and at the same time be in the heavenlies in Christ but the true Church of God? Joined to the Messiah Jesus enthroned at the right hand of God, they intercede that the will of God be done as in Heaven so on earth. It is the will of the Head in Heaven expressed by the body on earth! This is the Divine call to intercession.

THE NECESSITY OF INTERCESSORS THAT STAND IN THE GAP BEFORE HIM

The Lord cried out through the prophet Ezekiel: *And I sought for a man among them, that should build up the wall, and stand in the gap before me for the land, that I should not destroy it; but I found none. Therefore have I poured out mine indignation upon them; I have consumed them with the fire of my wrath; their own way have I brought upon their heads, saith the Lord Jehovah* (Ezekiel 22:30-31). We should take notice that the judgment of God fell on Israel because there was no child of God "to build up the wall and to stand in the gap." It is incredible that since there was no intercessor, the destruction of the Land came. The Lord Himself stated this fact, and nothing could be clearer than this! Judgment was decreed and there was no one who would stand in the gap and intercede.

These words of the Lord bring us face to face with the necessity of intercession. Even if judgment is inevitable because of the sin and iniquity of a nation and its land, intercession would see innumerable numbers of unsaved men and women coming to the Lord. If there are no intercessors in the gap, the judgment will come and be total.

In times of great upheaval, it has always been an opportunity for the Holy Spirit to bring the unsaved to the Lord. We should not be downcast and demoralised by the events of the last era of world history. As we have repeatedly written, everything that can be shaken will be shaken, *that those things which are not shaken may remain. Wherefore, receiving a kingdom that cannot be shaken, let us have grace, whereby we may offer service well-pleasing to God with reverence and awe* (Hebrews 12:27b-28). It is the King who is unshakable; and therefore His Throne, His Government, and His Will are also all unshakable. There is no reason whatsoever for us to be depressed unless our treasure is found on this earth. Instead, we can experience in the midst of the shaking and turmoil the grace of God through which we can serve God in a well-pleasing manner.

THE CHARACTER OF FIVE GENUINE INTERCESSORS

There are many accounts of intercessors, in the Word of God, who did stand in the gap. They heeded the call of God to intercede. We will mention only five such intercessors—Abraham, Moses, Nehemiah, Ezra, and Paul. There is also one, Jonah, who never interceded but from whose life and ministry we learn so much about the necessity of intercession. Indeed, he wrote his story in such a manner that we understand the Divine call to intercession. From all of these we learn the spiritual character which the Lord looks for in intercessors.

Abraham and the Judgment on Sodom and Gomorrah

God's judgment on Sodom and Gomorrah and the intercession of Abraham reveal what we have called a universal law of God. He always desires salvation and deliverance, rather than judgment, destruction, and death.

The iniquity and sin of Sodom and Gomorrah was so great that God decided on a total judgment. The catastrophe that overtook those two cities was utter and complete. It was in fact one of the most fertile places in the whole region; and it was for this reason that Lot had chosen it. The judgment upon it was so great that to this day it is a totally barren area within Israel.

The Lord and two angels had enjoyed a meal with Abraham and Sarah. They were about to leave, when the Lord said: *Shall I hide from Abraham that which I do; seeing that Abraham shall surely become a great and mighty nation, and all the nations of the earth shall be blessed in him?* (Genesis 18:17-18). The Lord then revealed to Abraham His will concerning Sodom and Gomorrah, the cities of the plain. He had decided on a total judgment.

The event that followed was remarkable: The Lord and Abraham began to bargain! The focal point of it was whether the Lord would judge those cities if there were fifty righteous persons within them. The Lord declared that if there were fifty, He would not consume the cities. Slowly, Abraham went down from fifty to forty-five, to forty, until he reached only ten. It transpired that there were not even ten righteous persons in the cities of the plain. It is sad that Abraham did not go down to five, but in fact there were not even five righteous persons! The judgment of God was therefore inevitable. Out of that catastrophe, only four people were saved, and one of them, Lot's wife, was turned into a pillar of salt when she looked back.

One does not wish to be irreverent, but it seems to me that when the Lord disclosed His will to Abraham, He had a twinkle in His eye. He knew from the beginning exactly how many righteous persons there were in those cities. Why then did He go through all the bargaining procedure unless He was proving what kind of spiritual character Abraham had! The Lord did not want to judge those cities, and if there had been only ten righteous people, the catastrophe would not have overtaken them. In fact, the Lord would have had mercy upon those cities if there had only been five. What this event revealed was that Abraham had the same heart attitude as the Lord Himself had. Abraham displayed the spiritual character that God required in an intercessor.

From this account we understand that the Lord does not enjoy judgment and waits for an intercessor to plead for mercy. He will do anything to avert judgment; hence the critical importance of intercession. The intercessor has to stand in the gap before the Lord.

Moses and the Rebellious Children of Israel

Moses and the sinning children of Israel is another illustration of this universal law of God. The children of Israel had been continuously murmuring and rebelling against the Lord. Their sin reached its climax when they made a molten gold calf and worshipped it. The Lord was angry and said to Moses: *I have seen this people, and, behold, it is a stiffnecked people: now therefore let me alone, that my wrath may wax hot against them, and that I may consume them: and I will make of thee a great nation* (Exodus 32:9-10). As with Abraham, so with Moses, the Lord was testing him. If there had been any self-centeredness in Moses, even a little of it, the thought that he could become the father of a new nation would have had a powerful attraction. Instead, he pleaded with the Lord: *Why doth thy wrath wax hot against thy people, that thou hast brought forth out of the land of Egypt with great power and with a mighty hand? Wherefore should the Egyptians speak, saying, For evil did he bring them forth, to slay them in the mountains, and to consume them from the face of the earth? Turn from thy fierce wrath, and repent of this evil against thy people. Remember Abraham, Isaac, and Israel, thy servants, to whom thou swarest by thine own self, and saidst unto them, I will multiply your seed as the stars of heaven, and all this land that I have spoken of will I give unto your seed, and they shall inherit it forever* (Exodus 32:11-13).

Was it truly the will of the Lord to destroy the children of Israel or was He testing Moses? We should note how Moses discerned the true will of God in his intercession. He reminds the Lord of the forefathers—Abraham, Isaac, Israel, and the Lord's covenant and promise to them. One of the points he also made in his intercession was that the children of Israel bore the testimony of the Lord before the Egyptians. If the Lord forsook them and destroyed them, the testimony they bore of deliverance from Egypt would not have had any meaning. If they were to be destroyed in the wilderness what was the point in their being delivered from Egypt? The display of Divine and saving power, and the miracles that the Egyptians had witnessed would have come to nought!

It is even more amazing that a few days later Moses intercedes again and says: *Oh, this people have sinned a great sin, and have made them gods of gold. Yet now, if thou wilt forgive their sin—; and if not, blot me, I pray thee, out of thy book which thou hast written* (Exodus 32:31-32). It must have been an enormous joy to the Lord to see in Moses His own character. Moses was prepared to be blotted out if only the Lord would forgive the children of Israel. This is genuine intercession. He was interceding for the children of Israel, and for the sinfulness and evil which warranted God's judgment on them. In his intercession he was so identified with them that he was ready to be blotted out that they might be saved. In this attitude, Moses foreshadowed the mind of

Christ, who humbled Himself to death, even to death upon a cross, that we sinners might be saved!

From the intercession of Moses we learn one supreme lesson. It is that our self-life has to be laid down if we are truly to intercede. The Lord knew exactly what He was doing when He said to Moses, "I will make of thee a great nation." If there had been an unbroken self-life, Moses could have responded very favourably to such a suggestion! The fact that Moses laid down his self-life was the ground out of which the Spirit of God produced spiritual character. That character was expressed in the manner in which he was prepared to be blotted out as long as the people of God were forgiven.

We learn one further lesson: **Apparently**, the will of the Lord was to destroy the children of Israel. However, that was not true. Moses recognised the faithfulness of God. It was the Lord who was proving Moses as to whether he was clear about the covenant He had made with Abraham, Isaac, and Jacob. Moses discerned the actual will of God, and in this he revealed how near to the heart of God he was.

The Intercession of Ezra and Nehemiah

These two great saints of God are another illustration of intercession. The city of Jerusalem lay waste. The walls were broken down, the gates had been consumed by fire, the House of the Lord was in ruins, and the condition of the people was not much better. The Word of God was widely not heeded or obeyed. Ezra and Nehemiah faced an almost impossible situation. The obstacles in front of them were mountainous and complex. Furthermore, there were those who did everything in their power to stop the rebuilding of the House of God, the rebuilding of Jerusalem and its walls, and the restoration of the Word of God in its fullness. Here we recognise the hand of the Lord through Daniel. The Lord had brought Daniel to the highest position next to the Emperor, and He enabled him to protect the rebuilding programme and the full recovery of the Word of God. He had not returned with the faithful but had remained in Persia to oversee the return of the Jews. The Lord had also brought together a number of faithful men who supported Ezra and Nehemiah— Zerubbabel the Governor, the prophets Haggai, and Zechariah, Joshua the High Priest, and others.

The intercession of Ezra and Nehemiah was absolutely essential to this work. The record of Ezra's intercession is found in Ezra 9:5-15. Here is a portion of it: *I arose up from my fasting, even with my garment and my robe rent; and I fell upon my knees, and spread out my hands unto the Lord my God; and I said, Oh my God, I am ashamed and blushed to lift up my face to thee, my God; for our iniquities are increased over our head, and our guiltiness is grown up unto the heavens. Since the days of our fathers we have been exceeding guilty unto this day; and for our iniquities have we, our kings, and our priests, been delivered into the hand of the kings of the lands, to the sword, to captivity, and to plunder, and to confusion of face, as it is this day.*

This reveals a total commitment to the Lord and a devotion to the purpose of God. The manner in which Ezra prayed is akin to Daniel. He does not intercede as if he was good and righteous and the rest of the people were sinful and unfaithful. He prays as if he himself had sinned as deeply and fully as they had. It reveals to us the essential character required of an intercessor. Ezra identifies himself with all the people who had sinned and fallen away from the Lord, and who had contradicted His Word. It was as if he was a leader amongst them in sin and backsliding. Daniel had exactly the same spirit and attitude. Here we are at the heart of genuine intercession.

We have the record of Nehemiah's intercession in Nehemiah 1:1-11. Here is a portion of it: *I sat down and wept, and mourned certain days; and I fasted and prayed before the God of heaven, and said, I beseech thee, Oh Jehovah, the God of heaven, the great and terrible God, that keepeth covenant and lovingkindness with them that love him and keep his commandments: ...I confess the sins of the children of Israel, which we have sinned against thee. Yea, I and my father's house have sinned: we have dealt very corruptly against thee, and have not kept the commandments, nor the statues, nor the ordinances.*

The intercession of Nehemiah consumed him, spirit, soul, and body. He was so committed to the Lord, that it was actually expressed in his face and body. He was cup bearer to King Artaxerxes, and the King noticed that there was something wrong with him. He asked him: *Why is your face sad, seeing you are not sick? This is nothing but sorrow of heart* (see v. 2). Out of this conversation came the King's decree concerning the rebuilding of Jerusalem and its walls. We see from Nehemiah's intercession that he understood the will of the Lord to rebuild Jerusalem. His intercession brought about the fulfilment of God's will for it. Jerusalem was completely rebuilt—the House of the Lord, the city, its walls, and its gates. From all of this we recognise two basic factors in genuine intercession. The first factor is that we have to become completely identified with the people for whom we are interceding. It is not 'they" who have sinned, but "we."

The second factor is that in travailing intercession there is much "sorrow of heart." We see this in the apostle Paul when he spoke of the unceasing pain and sorrow in his heart. Can there be real intercession without such sorrow and travail? Nehemiah said, *I sat down and wept, and mourned certain days.* It is said of Ezra: *Now while Ezra prayed and made confession, weeping and casting himself down before the house of God* (Ezra 10:1a). This kind of intercession is not empty words; it moves the whole being, and totally consumes the person. These two factors are essential in genuine intercession. Once more we recognise the character of intercessors.

The Intercession of the Apostle Paul

The apostle Paul is another illustration of genuine intercession and the spiritual character that God desires in the intercessor. We hear the words he used in his letter to the Christians in Rome: *I am telling the truth in Christ, I am not lying, my conscience bearing me witness in the Holy Spirit, that I have great sorrow and unceasing grief in my heart. For I could wish that I myself were accursed, separated from Christ for the sake of my brethren, my kinsmen according to the flesh, who are Israelites* (Romans 9:1-4a NASB). This burden that Paul continuously bore for Israel and the Jewish people is not a superficial and trite kind of prayer burden; it was something which consumed his being. We should note the manner in which he introduces it: *I am telling the truth in Christ, I am not lying, my conscience bearing me witness in the Holy Spirit.* Obviously, he wanted the believers in Rome to understand that this burden was genuine. He was not simply using words without meaning! He even went so far as to write, *I could wish that I myself were accursed, separated from Christ.* Those are unbelievable words! He was prepared to be cursed and divorced from the Messiah for the sake of the salvation of the Jewish people. This kind of costly intercession is so rare. Would to God that in Christians there could be found the same travailing spirit for Israel and the Jewish people as was found in the apostle Paul. The enormous bitterness between the Church and the Jewish people, which has resulted in so much bloodshed and sorrow, would have been removed by such intercession.

In his intercession Paul revealed the same kind of heart which the Lord had looked for in Abraham, Moses, Ezra, and Nehemiah. The apostle also revealed the same spirit as in the Lord Jesus who wept over Jerusalem: *O Jerusalem, Jerusalem, that killeth the prophets, and stoneth them that are sent unto her! how often would I have gathered thy children together, even as a hen gathereth her own brood under her wings, and ye would not! Behold, your house is left unto you desolate: and I say unto you, Ye shall not see me, until ye shall say, Blessed is he that cometh in the name of the Lord* (Luke 13:34-35 cp. Luke 19:41-44). This burden never left the apostle. He describes it as great sorrow and unceasing grief. He interceded throughout the years left to him before his martyrdom with this burden for Israel and the Jewish people that they might be saved. Through the long centuries until these times, there have always been Jews saved by the grace of God, but not in great numbers. Nevertheless, at the end of days the Lord will save multitudes of the Jewish people.

It was not only for the Jews that the apostle interceded. He had an all-consuming burden for the Church, and it is expressed in most of the letters he wrote. He desired above all to present them as a pure virgin to Christ. His intercession was that they should make themselves ready for the marriage of the Lamb (see II Corinthians 11:2 cp. Revelation 19:7-8). The heart of his intercession is seen in the words he used when writing to the Galatian church: *My little children, of whom I am again in travail until Christ be formed in you* (Galatians 4:19). He uses in Greek a very strong verb translated in English as "travail" or "labour." It is the pains of childbirth. Such travail, when it is the Holy Spirit who has conceived the burden in the intercessor, is painful and costly but will always have a successful outcome. This is the character of a true intercessor.

We should notice that the burden which Paul had for the Jewish people and for the Church of God were within the revealed will of God. His intercession was based on that. He understood that the will of God was clear and gave himself in intercession that the Lord would fulfil it.

JONAH AND THE JUDGMENT OF GOD ON NINEVEH

The account of Jonah and God's judgment upon Nineveh is different than the previous accounts. Jonah never interceded for Nineveh; he was only too glad that it would be judged! God had called Jonah to go to Nineveh and pronounce His judgment upon it for all their sin and iniquity. Nineveh, the capital of Assyria, was a very large ancient metropolis; it took three days to cross it by foot. The Assyrians were famous in the ancient world for their cruelty and brutality. The moment the Lord spoke to Jonah he fled from the Lord and bought a ticket in Joppa (modern day Jaffa), and boarded a cargo boat going to Tarshish. It was in the opposite direction to Nineveh! He wanted to put as much distance as he could between himself and the Lord. His problem was simple: although the Lord had commissioned him to proclaim judgment on Nineveh, he suspected that the Lord might change His mind and forgive them if they repented. In this he correctly understood the heart and mind of the Lord!

An enormous storm arranged by the Lord hit the ship, and all the sailors and passengers panicked. They lightened the load by throwing overboard all its cargo; it made, however, no difference. The captain then asked them to pray to their gods, for he thought there was little hope of survival. When there was no response from their idols, the sailors cast lots to discover which person had sinned and caused the storm; and the lot fell on Jonah! When they asked him what he had done to warrant such a storm, he confessed that he was running away from a God-given commission. He also told them that the only way the storm could be calmed was to cast him into the sea. The storm was so violent, and the possibility of survival so small, that with much misgiving the sailors threw him overboard.

The Lord, however, had prepared a great fish which swallowed Jonah. We then have an account of one of the most remarkable prayer meetings in history and in the Bible! The prayer meeting consisted of only two persons—Jonah and the Lord. Jonah stood on the Word of the Lord that if he prayed toward the holy Temple in Jerusalem, the Lord would hear and answer (see Jonah, chapter 2). How he knew the right direction to take within the belly of the great fish, one does not know! The Lord heard and answered his prayer, and caused the fish to vomit out Jonah upon dry land. Then the Lord said for the second time: "Go to Nineveh." This time Jonah obeyed to go with alacrity!

When Jonah arrived in Nineveh, he threw his heart into his message. He knew only too well how savage and brutal the Assyrians were. Then an astounding miracle took place; the whole of Nineveh repented, from the king to the simplest person. The king himself took off his robes and covered himself with sackcloth and sat in ashes. He proclaimed a total fast for every person in Nineveh and for all the livestock, calling on the people to repent from their evil ways and from violence. Jonah had preached many times in Israel, but he had never seen anything like this happen! And because of their repentance the Lord cancelled His judgment.

In fact, the judgment on Nineveh and the Assyrians was deferred to a century later.

Jonah was very upset and angry with the Lord, and he bitterly complained to Him. He asked the Lord to take his life because he could see no further point in living. This was not the kind of intercession which the Lord desired! In fact, Jonah never interceded for this city once in his whole time there and probably in his whole life up to that point! No wonder the Lord said to him, *Doest thou well to be angry?* Jonah never answered Him but stomped out of the city, and he sat on the east side of it in a huff and deep depression. He made for himself a booth, and waited to see if the Lord would change His mind and finally judge Nineveh.

The Lord prepared a gourd to climb up on Jonah's booth and give him shade. Jonah was very happy about that, but the Lord had also prepared a worm that caused the gourd to die; and at the same time caused a sultry east wind to blow. Jonah said, *It is better for me to die than to live.* It had almost become a refrain! Then the Lord said to Jonah, *You have been so upset and sorry about a gourd that came up in a day and died in a day; yet you cannot understand why I have had compassion on this great city where there are 120,000 toddlers and so many animals* (see Jonah 4:10-11)!

Jonah was a truly great man! Only he could have written this book and left it where everyone can judge him for his meanness, his little-mindedness, and even his racism. Jonah clearly repented of his whole attitude, because the manner in which he wrote his book reveals that he was a changed man. It reveals that the Lord transformed Jonah and produced such spiritual character that he could write this book and leave himself open to judgment, as if he was a narrow-minded, hardhearted, totally uncaring individual.

The story of Jonah reveals more clearly than anything else that the Lord will cancel judgment if there is genuine repentance. God had sent Jonah with a dogmatic and fiery message of total judgment, as if He was not a God of love and compassion. Once, however, the Ninevites truly repented and turned from their evil and their violence, He had compassion upon them. It was a great shock to Jonah to realise that God knew the streets and homes of Nineveh as much as He knew the streets and homes of Jerusalem. He even knew the number of innocent toddlers there were in that great city—one hundred and twenty thousand. It was an even greater surprise to Jonah that the Lord also knew the animals in Nineveh and cared for them!

SOME AREAS IN WHICH VITAL AND STRATEGIC INTERCESSION IS REQUIRED

It is clear from what we have considered that intercession is vital and strategic in the fulfilment of the purpose of God. As we have already stated, in critical times during history, the Lord has raised up intercessors who have stood in the gap, and seen the will of God performed.

This is a selection of some main and basic areas in which strategic intercession is required. It is of course not an exhaustive list. In the days into which we are moving, the Lord calls us to intercession. The greater the turmoil and conflict, the greater the shaking of all things in the heavens and on the earth, the more crucial and necessary intercession will be.

The Salvation of the Unsaved

The Lord has solemnly commissioned us in the words: *Go ye therefore, and make disciples of all the nations* (Matthew 28:19). We have no legitimate reason to disobey this command, even if in the last era of world history it will be exceedingly difficult due to war, turmoil, conflict, and violently anti-biblical legislation. The Lord's commission is clear and there is no excuse for disobedience! We should note the words with which the Lord summed up His command: *And lo, I am with you always, even unto the end of the world* (v. 20). In these words no ground is given for opting out in the last part of the era, however impossible the conditions might be. We should remember the words of St. Francis of Assisi, a true believer and born of the Spirit: "Preach the Gospel always; if necessary use words." In other words, when we cannot preach the Gospel, let our lives and conduct express the truth and the reality of the Gospel, and thus win unsaved men and women to the Lord.

The Lord Jesus declared: *And this gospel of the kingdom shall be preached in the whole world for a testimony unto all the nations; and then shall the end come* (Matthew 24:14). We know from the prophetic words of Joel, quoted on the day of Pentecost by the apostle Peter, that to the very end of time, *whosoever shall call on the name of the Lord shall be saved* (Joel 2:32 cp. Acts 2:21). There is a massive harvest to be reaped at the very end of time. It is clearly revealed as the will of God in the Bible.

Kings, Presidents, and Those in High Places

We have already drawn attention a number of times to the words of the apostle Paul in his letter to Timothy (see I Timothy 2:1-4). Satan and his network will make sure that those in the highest places will oppose the preaching and the advance of the Gospel. We are expressly urged to pray that governments will take the kind of action that will allow us to lead a *tranquil and quiet life*. This is *good and acceptable in the sight of God our Saviour; who would have all men to be saved, and come to the knowledge of the truth.* In other words, we need to make intercession for the governments and leaders of nations that they will create and maintain stable conditions in which the Gospel can be preached and advanced, and the Church of God can be built up. By intercession, led and empowered by the Holy Spirit, the blockages and hindrances, often governmentally inspired, can be removed. These satanic fortresses have to be cast down that the will of God be fulfilled.

There are times in history when those in authority have had the power to stop the preaching of the Gospel and to impose limitations on the building up of the Church. Although it has been extremely difficult for believers, it has not stopped the intercession required, and in the end those conditions have been changed. It is true that often under the most unhelpful circumstances and even violent persecution, unsaved people have been saved, and the Church has been built up. Indeed, at times the Church and the work of the Lord have been healthier in those conditions than in full freedom. The old adage that "the blood of the martyrs is the seed of the Church" has been many times fulfilled in the history of the Church.

Nonetheless, we are called upon to pray for all those in authority who have actual and practical power over national life and our lives so that conditions may be created and sustained, which will allow the work of the Gospel to be fulfilled. God's Word reveals that this is His will.

The Spiritual Growth of Believers

It is worth noting that our Lord Jesus commissioned us to preach the Gospel and make disciples of all the nations. He did not command us to make converts! There is a vast difference between a convert and a disciple. The purpose of God to redeem an innumerable multitude does not end with their conversion; they need to become disciples. However perilous and difficult the times, we are called to intercede for the spiritual growth of believers. The Word of God puts great emphasis on this matter. The apostle Peter, writing about the last era of world history, states: *But grow in the grace and knowledge of our Lord and Savior Jesus Christ* (II Peter 3:18). In the midst of the shaking of the universe and much conflict, this purpose of God to create disciples will advance to fulfilment.

Spiritually, we are born of the Spirit and we are born babes. We are not to remain in that condition, but we are to become children, and then grow up further to become responsible sons in the household of God. The problem we have is that the vast majority of Christians remain babes and never grow up to become spiritual adults. The necessity of spiritual growth to maturity is emphasised everywhere in the Bible. It is the revealed will of God for believers that they should come to full maturity in Christ.

The Church, the Body of Christ

This subject for intercession is vital and all important. On no other matter have the powers of darkness made such an onslaught. If they can redirect the Church and make it something different than what the Lord intended it to be, they can frustrate the whole purpose of God. The history of the Church is filled with examples of this. The call of God to intercession is that His will and purpose for the Church be performed.

We should pray for the church—for the planting of true Churches, for their building up, and for their living witness. A true Church is to hold the Testimony of Jesus; that is the essential meaning and significance of it (see Revelation 1-3). When the Testimony of Jesus is no longer held, and is lost, the Church becomes a social club, a human organisation and system! It becomes something it was never intended to be. It was

241

constituted to be the body of the Lord Jesus, who is its Head—to be the expression of His salvation, of His resurrection life and power, of His love and grace. Each of the churches at the beginning of the book of Revelation is symbolised by a lampstand. The point of the symbolism is light. The Church is to shine with the light of Christ until the end! This is a vital subject for intercession.

The need for the House of God to be built, for the Bride of Christ, the Wife of the Lamb to make herself ready for the wedding, also necessitates true intercession. It is the revealed will of God. Over this we can be sure that there will be much satanic opposition. However, if it is the Church which the Messiah is building, the gates of Hell will not prevail against His work!

The Work of the Lord

Another main area for intercession is the work of the Lord. We are not writing about our work for the Lord, but the work of the Lord! There is a vast difference between working for the Lord and being a co-worker with Him in His work. If it is His work, He will provide the wisdom, the power, and the direction we need. He will materially and financially take care of His work. The spiritual health of the work of God—its advance and expansion— is a main area for intercession. Everything obviously depends upon the spiritual character of the workers. If there is no growing Christ-likeness, no growth in spiritual character in those workers, the work of the Lord will deteriorate into a work of the flesh.

By the Holy Spirit the apostle Paul wrote: *And he gave some as apostles, and some as prophets, and some as evangelists, and some as pastors and teachers, for the equipping of the saints for the work of service, to the building up of the body of Christ; until we all attain to the unity of the faith, and of the knowledge of the Son of God, to a mature man, to the measure of the stature which belongs to the fullness of Christ* (Ephesians 4:11-13 NASB).

This is a description of the workers in the work of the Lord. They are all given by the ascended and glorified Messiah to the Church, for the equipping of the saints for the work of service, to the building up of the body of Christ. Mark carefully that these workers are specifically given to help spiritual children become mature; that they might reach the measure of the stature which belongs to the fullness of Christ. They are given to help us attain to the unity of the faith, and of the knowledge of the Son of God.

There is no way the work of the Lord can advance if there is no spiritual character or growing Christ-likeness in the workers. Here is an urgent need for intercession. If there is superficiality in the workers, the work will be superficial. If the workers are promoting false teaching, the result will be spiritual poverty and division. It can even deteriorate to "seducing spirits" and "doctrines of demons" (see I Timothy 4:1). Such deterioration in spiritual character will lead to an apostate Church and work that is not the work of God. It is revealed in the Word of God to be His will in order that His work should be spiritually healthy.

Israel and the Jewish People

Another main area for intercession is Israel and the Jewish people. We need to intercede for Israel that she will not be annihilated but may come into the salvation and the redemption of God. In the prophecies of the last era in world history the recreated State of Israel figures very greatly. If one approaches this controversial subject with an open mind, the Lord will give an understanding of the mystery of Israel (see Romans 11:25-29). It will, however, be impossible to understand what is happening at the end of time, if one has not a clear understanding of Israel's place in the will of God. In eschatology, Israel figures very greatly.

It is no wonder that Satan hates the Jewish people with an undying and intense hatred. If they have done Satan's will, if they are unsaved and in unbelief, why does Satan still abhor and loathe this people? Is it not because he recognises, what many Christians fail to see, that the recreated nation of Israel is a bell tolling out his end! The thought that they will be saved and redeemed is too much for Satan, and sadly for some believers. It is for this reason that we have to intercede for her salvation. We must stand in the gap for Israel and the Jewish people. Through flesh and blood, Satan will seek not only the liquidation of Israel, but the annihilation of the Jewish people as well. The fact is simple; the power and influence of Islam is growing with enormous force. Militant Islam unashamedly speaks of the destruction of Israel and the Jewish people as one of its supreme aims. We must stand in the Presence of God for them, and within the revealed will of God for this nation.

According to God's Word, the regathered and recreated Israel stands, even in her unbelief, as a witness to the immutability of His counsel. Until the Jewish people are saved by the grace of God, the purpose of God for the Church cannot be fulfilled. These are the natural branches that God laid aside, which will be reingrafted by Him into their own olive tree (see Romans 11:16-18). In God's Word this is revealed as His will and is another vital subject of intercession.

HIS APPOINTED INTERCESSORS ON THE WALLS OF JERUSALEM

In this chapter we have considered the essential necessity of intercession in times of Divine judgment upon the world. We are steadily moving into that era. We should remember, however, that supremely the Lord calls us to intercession for the fulfilment of His Eternal Purpose; that is the focal point of all God-given intercession. All other forms of intercession are related to it, even when we are unaware of that fact.

We have been appointed by God Himself to be watchmen on the walls of Jerusalem, with the same burden and the same zeal and determination that He has. It is both staggering and humbling that the Lord calls such frail human creatures as ourselves to join Him in the work of intercession. For the fulfilment of that calling He provides us with all the grace, the power, and the wisdom that we need.

12
THE CHALLENGE AND THE COST
OF CORPORATE INTERCESSION

Ezekiel 22:30—And I sought for a man among them, that should build up the wall, and stand in the gap before me for the land...but I found none.

Isaiah 64:7—There is none that calleth upon my name, that stirreth up himself to take hold of thee; for thou hast hid thy face from us, and hast consumed us by means of our iniquities.

Romans 12:1-2—I beseech you therefore, brethren, by the mercies of God, to present your bodies a living sacrifice, holy, acceptable to God, which is your spiritual service. And be not fashioned according to this world: but be ye transformed by the renewing of your mind, that ye may prove what is the good and acceptable and perfect will of God.

Romans 8:22-23, 26-27—For we know that the whole creation groaneth and travaileth in pain together until now. And not only so, but ourselves also, who have the first fruits of the Spirit, even we ourselves groan within ourselves, waiting for our adoption, to wit, the redemption of our body... In like manner the Spirit also helpeth our infirmity: for we know not how to pray as we ought; but the Spirit himself maketh intercession for us with groanings which cannot be uttered; and he that searcheth the hearts knoweth what is the mind of the Spirit, because he maketh intercession for the saints according to the will of God.

Galatians 4:19 – My little children, of whom I am again in travail until Christ be formed in you.

THE CHALLENGE OF THE LORD

In this book we have written much about the necessity of intercession. We have sought to point out its strategic nature in the spiritual warfare in which we find ourselves. The challenge of the Lord is simple and direct: Where are the intercessors? As we view the condition of the Church of God in our day—the conflict, the turmoil, and the shaking which is taking place in all the nations—we hear the Divine cry: *And I sought for a man among them, that should build up the wall, and stand in the gap before me for the land ... but I found none* (Ezekiel 22:30). We should allow that sorrowing voice of the Lord to pierce our hearts. In another place Isaiah cries: *There is none that calleth upon thy name, that stirreth up himself to take hold of thee; for thou hast hid thy face from us, and hast consumed us by means of our iniquities* (Isaiah 64:7). It is shocking that in a day when there are so many Christians and so much preaching in the Western world—the so-called Christian world—one can search for a long time to find a company of intercessors. It could be said that true and effective intercession is almost a lost art. It should, however, be said that in the so-called third world, often called the "mission field" by the western Church, there is much effective prayer and intercession. There is also, in many cases, a real expression of the Church as the body of Christ. May the Lord continue to do a genuine work in those areas of the world!

Could it be possible that in so much evangelical correctness, the Lord Jesus is outside, knocking on the door? In so many cases we live in a Laodicean condition. His Name is used, His Word is preached, but He is outside of it all, shut out and seeking to come in. In the final analysis the Lord is seeking fellowship. *Behold I stand at the door and knock: If any man hear my voice and open the door, I will come in to him, and will sup with him, and he with me*

(Revelation 3:20). Dining together in the ancient world, and indeed in much of the modern world, is an expression of fellowship. The Lord was seeking heart to heart fellowship with the Church at Laodicea. They had an incredibly high spiritual estimate of themselves, but the estimate of Christ concerning them was in total contradiction to theirs. The corporate self-estimate which they held was completely false and they were unaware of it. One should have expected it, since the Lord Jesus had been shut out of the organisation! How can a Church be "the Church" if the Lord Jesus, its Head and Saviour is shut outside and is plaintively asking: *If any man hear my voice and open the door, I will come in to him ...* He did not say, "If My Church hears My voice," or "If a few of you hear my voice," but He said, *If any man hear My voice.* That reveals how far the deterioration had gone in Laodicea. He had come down to individual believers in the Church.

Genuine intercession is, in essence, fellowship with the Lord. If we have understood this book, intercession can only begin in His fellowship with us and our fellowship with Him. His burden has to be transferred to us and shared with us. We have to discern His will and then act upon it in fellowship with Him. The Church in Laodicea had all the "trappings," all the correct theology and doctrine, and probably had a complete methodology for everything. There was, however, no genuine and true intercession, because there was no fellowship with the Lord. Intercession is a thermometer by which the health of any Church or work can be taken! No intercession—the Lord is outside. Real intercession—the Lord is Head and Lord in practice.

The challenge of the Lord is directed toward every believer whether man or woman, young or old. It is to take the first step and, whatever the cost, commit oneself totally to His Lordship.

Without that utter commitment there can be no intercessor and no intercession. It is as straightforward as that!

The Objective of the Gospel—A Living Sacrifice

The apostle Paul, summing up one of the clearest expositions of the Gospel in the New Testament (Romans, chapters 1-8), and the truth of Divine election as seen in Israel and the Church (Romans, chapters 9-11), declares: *I beseech you therefore, brethren, by the mercies of God, to present your bodies a living sacrifice, holy, acceptable to God, which is your spiritual service. And be not fashioned according to this world: but be ye transformed by the renewing of your mind, that ye may prove what is the good and acceptable and perfect will of God* (Romans 12:1-2).

We should mark well the little word *therefore*. Paul is summing up the previous eleven chapters. This is the objective of the Gospel, that we should be a living sacrifice. All the mercies of God shown in the Gospel and in God's election are to lead us to this goal!

It is no wonder that in our generation this truth has no widespread popularity in Christian circles. It is not generally believed that the saving grace and power of God should lead us to be a living sacrifice. There is, however, no Divine alternative! The culmination of the preaching of the Gospel should lead us to be totally surrendered to the Lord. In these days we live in a "self-centred" Christianity and not a Christ-centred Christianity. We no longer preach a Gospel that demands a practical service and worship. The result is that as converts we tend to look for a self-satisfying Gospel. It is all centred in our needs, our satisfaction, and our self-realisation and development. Discipleship, on the other hand, requires a life laid down in the worship and service of

God. Discipleship is outward looking—from Christ as the centre of one's life rather than self as the centre.

THE WOMAN WITH THE ALABASTER CRUSE

The Lord Jesus declared that the act of a certain woman would always be *spoken of for a memorial of her*. In other words, He linked it to the preaching of the Gospel throughout the whole world. He associated her act of sacrifice with the Gospel. She had come to Jesus with an alabaster cruse of spikenard which represented her precious life savings. She had broken the cruse and poured the spikenard oil over the head of Jesus. His disciples had been greatly displeased at what they called "this waste of money." They felt that at the very least it should have been sold and given to the poor.

The Lord Jesus, on the contrary, said: *Let her alone; why trouble ye her? ... She hath anointed my body beforehand for the burying. And verily I say unto you, Wheresoever the Gospel shall be preached throughout the whole world, that also which this woman hath done shall be spoken of for a memorial of her* (Mark 14:6a; 8b-9). It is highly significant that Jesus singled out this woman's act, and **linked it to the Gospel**. The breaking of the cruse of alabaster and the pouring out of the precious spikenard expressed her readiness to be a "living sacrifice." The Lord associated her total and costly sacrifice with the Gospel. It is, in fact, the same idea as we have in Paul's words, that we should *present our bodies a living sacrifice.*

IF ANY MAN COME AFTER ME

When the Lord Jesus, for the first time, spoke of His crucifixion, His burial, and His resurrection, it was a great shock to the twelve disciples. Peter would not hear of it and rebuked Jesus, saying that whilst he was alive it would never happen! The

Lord Jesus, looking into Peter's eyes, said: *Get thee behind me, Satan; for thou mindest not the things of God, but the things of men* (Mark 8:33). Then the Messiah gathered to Himself the multitude with His disciples. This action is of the utmost significance because it denotes that what He was about to state has the most serious relevance to both the Gospel and to discipleship. It was Peter's adamant assertion that he would stop the Lord going to the cross that led to the statement. The Lord equated Peter's stance with Satan! This reveals the poison of the uncrucified self-life. It cannot hear of the cross and is always the ground in us for Satan's work. Peter's spontaneous self-life made it impossible for him to mind the things of God but only the things of men!

The Lord Jesus then said: *If any man would come after me, let him deny himself, and take up his cross, and follow me. For whosoever would save his life shall lose it; and whosoever shall lose his life for my sake and the gospel's shall save it* (Mark 8:34b-35). Underline these words: *If any man would come after me, let him deny himself.* A true disciple has to deny himself and give up all right to himself. One cannot follow the Lord Jesus and experience the fullness of salvation without losing one's self-life. The Greek word here used and translated by the English word *life* is the self or soul-life. It is the Greek word *psuche* from which we derive "psychology" and "psychiatry." If you deny yourself, give up all right to yourself, the Lord becomes the defender of your rights. When we lose our self-life for His sake, we receive back our self-life under new management—His Lordship. Once again we see that the goal of the Gospel is to lose our self-life for His sake and the Gospel's.

The problem with much of modern Christianity is that it only believes half the Gospel. Here in these words of the Lord Jesus we have the other half. Without this part of the Gospel we shall never experience His resurrection power and life. We shall never overcome; and the fullness and the power of the Holy Spirit will be blocked by an unbroken, uncrucified self-life! The Gospel is not only about salvation from sin; it is also about salvation from the self-life. After all it is not only sin that is the problem in the history of mankind; it is also self-centred aggrandisement, self-glorification, self-realisation and self-worship; in a word, humanism.

YOUR SPIRITUALLY INTELLIGENT WORSHIP AND SERVICE

It is interesting to note Paul's word that presenting one's body as a living sacrifice is "spiritual service." The Greek is not so easily translatable; it is variously translated in different English versions as either "reasonable service," "rational service," "intelligent service," or "reasonable worship," and "spiritual worship," etc.

Many years ago I asked a Cambridge Don how best to translate these words, and it was an eye-opening time for me. He explained that the whole manner in which Paul expressed it was not conveyed by the English "which is your spiritual service." He said that the Greek has the idea of "reason," and even if you translated it in English as "your rational or reasonable service," or even "spiritual worship," it does not fully convey what Paul wrote. I asked whether one could translate it as "your spiritually intelligent worship." He said those words conveyed the real meaning, but one should add the words "and service." To be a living sacrifice is one's "spiritually intelligent worship and service." It is this total commitment to the Lord which will lead to a transformation by the renewing of one's mind, and to a proving of the *good and acceptable and perfect will of God.*

THE DIVINE "DILEMMA"

It is not theologically correct to speak of God facing or having a dilemma. Nonetheless, the Lord faces an enormous problem with His call to intercession. When intercession is genuine, it is the burden of the Lord Jesus which is shared by the Holy Spirit with His intercessors. The Spirit of God conceives that burden in the spirit of the believer. The burden then becomes a travailing of spirit. The apostle Paul uses this word travail when he wrote: *My little children of whom I am again in travail, until Christ be formed in you* (Galatians 4:19). The Greek word is powerful; it is the "pangs" of childbirth. This accurately describes the experience of a real intercessor. It is a burden conceived by the Holy Spirit which grows within the believer; and one cannot be relieved of this burden until it is fulfilled. It is costly and painful but ends in birth! That is exactly the course of true intercession. It begins with the Spirit of God conceiving the burden within us, then proceeds with the pangs of birth, and ends with new life!

Very often this kind of travailing intercession can hardly be expressed in words. It is like an iceberg; nine-tenths of it is not seen; it is under the surface. The words that are used audibly, express the smallest percentage of the burden. For this reason the apostle writes: *The Spirit himself maketh intercession for us, with groanings which cannot be uttered. And he that searcheth the heart knoweth what is the mind of the Spirit, because he maketh intercession for the saints according to the will of God* (Romans 8:26b-27). So deep is this form of intercession that even the groanings cannot be audibly uttered.

A certain minimal maturity is necessary before one can travail. Babes cannot travail, nor can children! A human being has to reach a certain level of maturity before they can know the "pangs" of childbirth. With this point, we have reached what I have described as the Divine dilemma. The Church of God is filled with babies! There is nothing more beautiful than a baby, but when a human being reaches the age of thirty, or forty, or more, and has remained a child, it is abnormal. The Church is filled with Christians who have been born of the Spirit and have never grown. They cannot be soldiers of the Lord Jesus Christ nor can they be intercessors. They are not spiritual adults!

There has never been a point in history where corporate intercession is more necessary and essential than the era into which we are moving. What is the Lord to do? If the babies would grow in the grace and knowledge of the Lord Jesus, all would be well. They would grow into children and from children into spiritual adolescents, and from adolescence to adulthood. Maturity begins when we move from the basis of a self-centred life to a Christ-centred life. When that happens, it is no longer what one "obtains" for oneself, but what "He" obtains in us. It is no longer "my joy" but "His joy;" not "my satisfaction" but "His satisfaction;" not "my will" but "His will." This is the beginning of spiritual maturity.

We have called this the "Divine dilemma." As has been already stated, in one sense the Almighty cannot have a dilemma. What, however, is He to do? Where are the intercessors? Upon whom can He call? Where can we find the character that Count Zinzendorf and his followers had which led to their intercession? Where can we find the character of John Wesley, when at the age of ninety-four, he was still travelling on horseback in the British weather and preaching four times a day? Where can we find the character of John Knox who, in a time of intercession for the salvation of Scotland, was so consumed with the burden that he cried out to the Lord: "Give me Scotland, else I die!" And the Lord gave him Scotland! Where can we find today this same kind of spirit which energised countless servants of God throughout the history of the Church? Instead, we have a comfortable, complacent, and laid back kind of Christianity; a Laodicean Church and situation. This is the Divine dilemma!

THE COST OF ANSWERING THE CHALLENGE

It was a time of crisis for the people of God when one man heard the voice of the Lord: *Whom shall I send, and who will go for us?* That man was Isaiah. It was to be the birth of one of the greatest prophetic ministries in the Old Testament; but it did not just happen. Isaiah said: *Here am I, send me.* And the Lord sent him (see Isaiah 6). He was utterly faithful to the end, and in his eighties he was martyred. He had fled into an ancient olive tree and hid within its huge trunk, and they sawed through it and thus murdered him.

The Divine challenge is personal. We are also at a great turning point in history, and we need to hear the voice of God: *Whom shall I send, and who will go for us?* Whether it is to preach, or to go to the ends of the earth, or to be an intercessor, it is the same. It begins with the readiness to respond to the challenge of the Lord: *Here am I, send me.*

To be an intercessor one has to be a living sacrifice. There is no alternative! This challenge comes to all of us. Without such single-minded devotion to the Lord, one cannot be used by Him in this way. To answer the challenge will cost us everything. It is for this reason that we are called to be living sacrifices. Once you present your whole being as a living sacrifice, there is no need for discussion of the cost. The cost in fact is total. Whether it is your life savings in an alabaster cruse, broken and poured out upon the Lord, or whether it is giving up all right to yourself, taking up your cross, and following Him, or whether it is the total laying down of one's self-life for Him and the Gospel, it is the same. There is no further need to argue about the cost. It has already been paid! In one act of total commitment to the Lord all the issues have been settled!

Once we are totally committed to Him, He takes full responsibility for us in every way. The Lord Jesus said: *Seek ye first his kingdom, and his righteousness; and all these things shall be added unto you* (Matthew 6:33). When we fully obey the Lord and put Him first, He takes care of us. Has anyone ever sacrificed their all for Him and not found that He adds all these things to us? In the glory yet to be, no one who has surrendered their all to Him will talk about the cost. It is swallowed up in all the fullness into which we have come. We will never be able to talk about the Lord being in debt to us, for we are forever indebted to Him.

THE CHALLENGE TO MEN TO BE INTERCESSORS

It is interesting to observe that in our situation today most intercessors are women. We thank God for them; it is hard to imagine what we would do without their intercession. Whatever though has happened to the men? It is true that Paul once said that widows should give themselves to prayer, but his words were never meant to exclude men, or to give men an excuse for not being in the forefront of intercession. Christian men ought to hear and face the challenge of the Lord; their place should be in the vanguard of intercession. After all, we should note that most of the intercessors in the Bible were men.

Where have all the men gone? It is extraordinary that in this warfare and conflict, we do not see them in the lead. If you are a man you should take up the Divine challenge and commit yourself fully to Him. There is an idea with some men that to be an intercessor or involved in intercession is not manly; it is "women's work."

This is entirely false. The fact that most of the intercessors in the Bible were men speaks for itself. We should remember the incredible story of the Second World War years in which a company of one hundred and twenty Christians, mostly young men and women, met together in intercession. That war was basically determined by such intercession. We should also remember Dennis Clark, who founded the Intercessors for Britain and was the inspiration of many other national intercession movements throughout the world. How many problems both international and national were touched by that kind of intercession! The Divine challenge is to men and it is up to them to face it and commit themselves to Him.

THE CHALLENGE TO WOMEN TO BE INTERCESSORS

We should never underrate the intercession of sisters. So often when the men have failed, the women have manfully risen to the occasion and won the battle in prayer and intercession. In the warfare and battle they have often borne the brunt of satanic onslaught. The Bible has some wonderful examples of women who have been intercessors: Queen Esther, Deborah, Hannah, Anna the prophetess, Lydia, and others. We should never devalue the enormous contribution that sisters have made in intercession, and the huge part they have played in pioneering missionary work all over the world.

At the turn of the last century an old Russian monk prophesied to a young Russian believer. That believer was Mother Barbara, who for many years until she went to be with the Lord, was Mother Superior of the Russian Convent of Saint Mary Magdalene on the Mount of Olives, Jerusalem. The monk prophesied, among other matters, that the Lord would use praying women to save Great Britain in war. The First World War was from 1914-1918, and the Second World War was from 1939-1945. Britain was saved in those two wars by praying women. Since then the Lord has been using sisters in such movements as the Lydia Prayer Movement, and the Women's Prayer and Bible Weeks, to touch many problems. May the Lord greatly increase the number of women intercessors!

THE CHALLENGE TO YOUNG PEOPLE

It is not so abnormal that most intercessors are of a mature age; after all, experience and age count. If any young people have read this book, they should understand that to be an intercessor begins with a total commitment to the Lord. However young you are, you have to take the first step in a journey that will lead you to the Throne of God. Do not allow the enemy to discourage you by making you feel insignificant and inexperienced, surrounded by great prayer warriors. Young people rarely understand how uplifting and renewing it is for the older intercessors to hear young intercessors contributing in intercession. Do not think that intercession is for the old, that it has nothing to do with youth. We should begin to intercede when we are young.

If you will surrender totally to the Lord, He will educate you, train you, and discipline you. You will make mistakes but as long as you learn through them you will grow up to be an intercessor. We should remember that Nicholas Count Zinzendorf was a young man when he stood before that oil painting of the Crucified Christ. He was transfixed by it for nearly an hour, and the words written below it pierced his heart: "This is what I have done for thee; what hast thou done for Me?" It led to Count Zinzendorf's total commitment to the Lord, and to one of the most glorious phases in the history of the Church—the Moravian Movement of the Spirit of God. The Count became a living sacrifice and influenced untold numbers of believers to follow his example. Remember this if you are young! No one can exaggerate what God can do with a young person who totally commits himself or herself to the Lord.

We do not have to wait until we have reached a certain age to be an intercessor. The youngest of us, if once we have taken that first step of total commitment, can learn how to intercede, and learn by experience to become a true intercessor. If you hear the Lord crying, *Whom shall I send, and who will go for us*, let the response of your heart be, *Here am I, send me*. Remember how Jeremiah felt when the Lord first challenged him to follow His call. Jeremiah expressed his feeling of inadequacy when he said: *Behold, I do not know how to speak, because I am a youth* (Jeremiah 1:6 NASB). Jeremiah faced the challenge with living faith and committed himself into the hands of God. He went on in a long life to fulfil one of the greatest prophetic ministries in the Word of God.

THE FELLOWSHIP OF HIS SON, JESUS CHRIST OUR LORD

There is no calling of God greater or more valuable to Him than to be an intercessor. The Lord prizes the intercessor above all other ministries. Of course, often it is combined with other gifts. For example, an apostle, like Paul, was both an apostle and an intercessor. We have prophets like Daniel, and teachers like Ezra, who were also intercessors.

Why is the intercessor so precious to the Lord? Why does the Lord prize intercession so highly? It is because at the heart of intercession is deep fellowship with the Lord. Above all other ministries or gifts, the intercessor must walk in fellowship with Him. In this book we have repeatedly written of intercession as being a question of fellowship with the Lord, and His fellowship with us. The burden He transmits to us, which is conceived in us by the Holy Spirit, stems from that fellowship.

The Greek word *koinonia* translated by the English word *fellowship* is a word full of meaning; it means "partnership," "communion," "having something in common," "communication," and "participation." This illuminates our understanding of fellowship. It is not merely "chit-chat," or "camaraderie!" Paul wrote: *God is faithful, through whom ye were called into the fellowship of his Son Jesus Christ our Lord* (I Corinthians 1:9). We have been called by God into a partnership, a communion, a sharing of the Lord Jesus. He is the Head, we are the body. Genuine intercession is a communion between the Lord and us; it is a partnership. In particular it results in His communicating the burdens on His heart. To be an intercessor is to be a participant in the fulfilment of the will of God.

The call to intercession is a call into practical fellowship with the Lord Jesus. Above and beyond all else, it is a heart matter. It is His heart and our heart in communion. It is for this reason that the intercessor is so precious to the Lord. The Lord called King David: "A man after His own heart." The many Psalms which David composed reveal the kind of heart he had. Even when he fell into deep and terrible sin, the two Psalms which he wrote after that fall—Psalm 32 and 51—still reveal the kind of heart that God seeks. When the Lord has your heart, He has you!

It is interesting and highly significant that the apostle Paul beseeches us: *To present your **bodies** a living sa*crifice (Romans 12:1). Why would Paul use the term *bodies*? Why could Paul not have used the words, *your whole spirit, soul, and body*, or *your whole beings*, or *your hearts*? Instead, he uses the most down to earth part of our being which is our physical body. Here we come to an essential meaning of intercession. The Lord, dwelling in our spirit, uses our body to go, to serve, to feel, to react, to respond, and to do His will. In all the upheavals and turmoil in the last era of world history, He does not want us to be spiritual automatons or Christian machines; but we are to have feelings, and reactions to the tragedies around us. The Lord Himself has those feelings and reactions; notwithstanding, many Christians have suppressed those emotions in themselves as being unspiritual.

We have recognised this in the story of Jonah and Nineveh. Jonah was impervious to Nineveh's coming judgment, and he was an ice box! On the gourd he had compassion but not on Assyria! He did not intercede for Nineveh because he had no feeling or emotion for the people who were to be judged. The Lord could not break through in Jonah with His burden; therefore Jonah could not intercede! The Lord wants not only our spirit, which is all important, but our soul and body. The Lord Jesus, who is the revelation of the mind and the heart of God, the expression of God's character and being, wept at the tomb of Lazarus; and He wept over Jerusalem (see John 11:35 cp. Luke 19:41). In us He will do the same!

THE THRONE AND THE GLORY OF GOD

Genuine intercessors will end in the Throne of God and in the Glory of God. To reach that goal, their spiritual education and training is lifelong and hard. It involves much discipline. The intercessor has to learn to read the mind and will of God, and then to stand in faith, whatever the battle, until it is fulfilled. He or she has to learn to distinguish the Lord's voice from all others, including the voice of his or her own soul. The intercessor has to learn how to "hear" the Lord's voice.

There is much affliction, tribulation, and trial to be borne on the way to that end. Through this the intercessor learns much. When the Throne of God is reached, His glory will make any affliction and hardship that we have endured more than worthwhile. The intercessor has learned to view everything through fellowship with the Lord. In this manner the Lord trains the intercessor for His Throne and eternal government. The intercessor has not learned through books; it is not mere head knowledge. He or she has been trained by intimate experience of the Lord through fellowship with Him. It is not that study is valueless, or useless; it is neither of those. The study of the Word of God is, in fact, all important. The apostle Paul wrote to Timothy that through God's Word: *"The man of God may be complete, furnished completely unto every good work* (II Timothy 3:17). Nonetheless, it is more often in times of crisis, emergency, and even anguish, that we come to know the Lord on a far deeper level than ever before. His word comes to dwell in us! What the Lord gives us in such times becomes foundational; it can never be taken away. We should note the words of the Preacher: *I know that, whatsoever God doeth, it shall be forever: nothing can be put to it, nor anything taken from it; and God hath done it, that men should fear before him* (Ecclesiastes 3:14).

The Lord's training of us for the Throne stems from a direct, living, and practical relationship to Him; from intimate fellowship with Him. There are many ways in which the Lord can train us, but intercession is the most intense and direct way.

AN ACT OF TOTAL COMMITMENT, THE FIRST STEP

In this book we have written much about prayer and intercession—its strategic necessity, its character and nature, its essential mystery, and the execution of the will of God. When all is said and done, practically it comes to one simple step of faith, a total commitment to the Lord, a full surrender of our will to His. Without that first step there is no possibility of becoming an intercessor. The Divine call to intercession means nothing if this first step is not taken. The Almighty can challenge us again and again to become an intercessor, but if the first act of total commitment and surrender to Him is not made, His challenge goes unheeded. In the final analysis it all comes down to a living and practical response on our part.

There is a hymn, composed by George Matheson, who was a Church of Scotland minister in the nineteenth century, which sums up the utter commitment to the Lord Jesus we have to make. George Matheson, as a young man, had been engaged to be married, when he learnt sadly that he was going blind, and that nothing medically could be done about it. When he broke the news to his fiancé, she told him that she could not go through life with a blind man and at that point she left him! In fact, later she married another man. George Matheson went blind whilst studying for the ministry. His sister had taken full care of him, but she herself then married. On the day that her marriage took place, in intense sadness he was alone.

His blindness, his sister's marriage, and the memory of his fiancé leaving him, led him into great mental anguish. He felt there was no hope of a normal life; he would be only an object of pity. At that point, when all seemed the darkest, and he was totally alone, the Lord spoke to him and gave him this hymn. George Matheson wrote it down, he says, in five minutes. The only answer to the disaster that had befallen him and the heartbreak he was feeling was that he should be completely devoted to the Lord and surrendered to Him. These words of his sum up what it means to be a living sacrifice, that first step of total commitment to the Lord Jesus.

1. O Love, that wilt not let me go,
   I rest my weary soul in Thee;
   I give Thee back the life I owe,
   That in Thine ocean depths its flow
   May richer, fuller be.

2. O Light, that followest all my way,
   I yield my flickering torch to Thee;
   My heart restores its borrowed ray,
   That in thy sunshine's blaze its day
   May brighter, fairer be.

3. O Joy, that seekest me through pain,
   I cannot close my heart to Thee;
   I trace the rainbow through the rain,
   And feel the promise is not vain,
   That morn shall tearless be.

4. O Cross, that liftest up my head,
   I dare not ask to fly from Thee;
   I lay in dust life's glory dead,
   And from the ground there blossoms red
   Life that shall endless be.

May the Lord help every reader of this book to answer the Divine challenge to prayer and intercession, and not reject it. If you are unable to find words to express your commitment to the Lord, why not use the words of the last stanza of this hymn. Such a surrender to the Messiah will make you part of His Bride, of the New Jerusalem. You will take the first step in a journey that will end in the Throne of God and the Glory of God. You will certainly never regret it!

EPILOGUE

I would like to tell you about our experience in this matter of intercession in the company that I was part of in Richmond, England. In the beginning of August, 1951, I and a few others here in this town were deeply burdened for the state of things. We felt that with all the great evangelical paraphernalia we had around us, we were not really seeing people touched for the Lord locally, nor were we seeing any real building work. To put it into words, which I could not have done then, God had no home in Richmond. He had plenty of believers and plenty of evangelical places of worship, but there seemed to be no home for the Lord.

At that time, all the talk was the Hebrides revival. There were two old ladies who had spent six months in prayer every night until, in the most sovereign way, God poured out His Spirit upon the Hebrides. And there were seven old gentlemen on the other end of the island, unbeknown to the two sisters, who had met once a week for two years for a prolonged session of prayer to pray for the same moving of the Spirit of God upon those islands. Everyone talked about it at the time, hoping that this outpouring would come south to England and we would see something happening everywhere.

At the same time, I had read Charles Finney's *Lectures On Revival*. And if you wish to be deeply disturbed, then read these lectures of Finney's and, particularly, the chapter on "Plowing Up the Fallow Ground." I found myself very, very disturbed at that time, along with seven others who were burdened. We talked about it, not knowing whether this burden was a burden of God or whether it was emotional, and subject to outside influences that were not from the Lord.

A COVENANT TO PRAY

So we covenanted together to do an extraordinary thing. We would not speak about revival, read about revival or pray about revival for one whole month; and if at the end of that one month this burden was still in us, we would know it was the Lord. Thus we covenanted to give ourselves to prayer until the Lord did something. So for the month of August, 1951, we neither spoke about revival, nor read about it, nor prayed about it.

At the end of the month, we found that the burden in us was greater than ever. It was a pain. I was only a young Christian, but I can only describe it as an incurable pain. I could not get it out of my system. It was just there, like a deep, deep anguish of spirit.

On the first day of September, 1951, we started to pray; and we prayed every evening of September, October, November, and December, up to the Christmas of 1951. Our times of prayer began just after seven o'clock and went on until ten or ten-thirty. In the middle of it, we had the severest fog that London has ever known in which three thousand people died. For ten days we could not see across the street. All transport stopped at one point and it was hopeless. But it never stopped our prayer. We walked every evening to those times of prayer. Sometimes, there were only two of us. Nevertheless, we were never less than two and we were never more than eight; but we prayed every single night. We used to pray on Saturday afternoon from two o'clock until six o'clock so that we could go to the young people's time in the evening. We also got permission to pray in the vestry of the church on Sunday evening so that we were not a faction or division, and we prayed for the service as well.

The most incredible thing was that we did not know too much about prayer. I had learned some lessons in intercession in Egypt, and I had seen a whole number of people saved that God had put on my heart. It had cost me everything to pray for those different ones. However, I knew nothing of corporate intercession.

ONE SIMPLE BURDEN FOR PRAYER

It was amazing that we had one simple burden and we never varied from that burden. It was not as if we prayed for Nepal or China or Japan or Australia or America; we prayed simply for Richmond and the Thames Valley. We prayed night after night for something like three hours— never less than three hours—and you know how hard it is to sustain prayer for half an hour. As I recall that time, I am still amazed at it. It is like a dream. But I remember that when we began, we could do nothing else but pray. At the end of those three hours it was like a tank that had drained all of its water and one could get up quite relieved. But by the next morning the tank was full again. You just felt un-comfortable and unhappy, as if you had a pain inside, and the only way to let it out was prayer.

That was my first real experience of corporate intercession, but it was the Spirit of God who was in us, keeping alive a burden. We prayed for nightclubs, for hospitals, for schools, for colleges. We prayed for all the different places. It is a very interesting thing that many of these schools that have seen blessing are the places we prayed for, night after night. Of course, we had no idea that one of the nightclubs we prayed for would be closed down by the police for immorality, and we would actually get possession of it and meet there for one whole year. That would never have entered our heads when we were praying.

Those four months of prayer for the same thing was an incredible experience. We felt as if we were in a sovereign flow of God. You know how hard it is to pray for one subject for half an hour. We prayed for virtually one subject from all angles for three hours every single day right up to Christmas of 1951. Out of that came Koinonia—that interdenominational get-together of young people in this town just to wait upon the Lord. And it was there that God met us and began to do some remarkable things out of which all this work came.

THE BURDEN LIFTED

Now my point is this: we had covenanted with the Lord that we would not stop praying until we saw two things—the unsaved in Richmond turning to the Lord, and the people of God renewed. We went on praying in 1952 for the first three weeks of January, but the interesting thing was the burden was lifted, and we could not go on anymore. We could not understand it, and we felt so terrible because we had covenanted with the Lord that we would pray until we saw this thing happen. But never in our wildest moments did we think of Koinonia as an answer to our prayers. And because the Holy Spirit was in charge, we knew that we could not 'flog a dead horse.' We found that it was no good just going on in prayer evening after evening because the whole anointing had gone from it. So we gave it over to the Lord and said, "Lord, we leave it with You. You bring it back at the right time."

In those very early days, from time to time, we had weeks of prayer which were tremendous times. We had those weeks of prayer where we really laid hold of the Lord for this area; and it was the same old burden again—that God would do something.

And always we got the same promise, that in the end, God would do it, and we found the burden lifted. It was our experience of corporate intercession.

THE SAME BURDEN TEN YEARS LATER

It is an amazing thing to me that exactly a decade later in September of 1961, we began to pray again with exactly the same burden. Leading up to that were studies on the book of Joel and the recognition that the prophecy quoted by the apostle Peter, on the day of Pentecost, had not been exhausted on the day of Pentecost, but it has included the whole of the age in which we are found, right to its end. We had studies on the book of Jonah and were shocked to discover that God was as interested in Nineveh as He was in Jerusalem, and He knew the people of Nineveh as much as He knew the people of Jerusalem. Out of this, once again, came two burdens. One was that unsaved people would be saved in our area, and the second was that God would do something new in His people all over the country.

From 1951 to 1961, God led us and we saw some very precious truths. Above all, we experienced some very great ways of the Lord, but we were a shut-up company—ostracised. No one would touch us with a barge pole. We were the off-scouring. We belonged to that most dreadful of all groups, Honor Oak; and anyone who was associated with Honor Oak was absolutely beyond the pale. "Be careful of them. They have got some sort of spiritual infection that will touch others and destroy them." As a result, for those ten years, hardly any one ran the blockade and joined us except those whom God saved among us.

I went away in August of 1961 and a dear brother said to the whole company at the time: "Do you not feel that God is calling us to prayer? And if He is calling us to prayer, are we prepared to sacrifice everything that we may intercede?" And while I was away, they decided: "Right, we will sacrifice everything. Every gathering will go by the board except the Lord's table and the Sunday evening gathering. Everything else will be prayer—Monday, Tuesday, Wednesday, Thursday, Friday and Saturday. We will meet every night for prayer, and we will take hold of the Lord, as He enables us, until something happens."

THE BURDEN EXTENDED TO THE WHOLE BRITISH ISLES

The remarkable thing is no one recognised that it was ten years to the day that we had started to pray. It was only a month afterwards that we suddenly realised we were back again on the same old thing. Only this time, instead of praying for Richmond and the Thames Valley, we were praying for the whole British Isles and beyond them. We prayed that the House of God would be built in the whole British Isles and that there would be a renewal that would sweep the people of God into a new way with the Lord.

We went through one whole year and never had a Bible study during that time. The amazing thing is that we began to see quite a number of people saved. We went into our second year and still did not have a Bible study. This was now two years without a Bible study. During those two years we had so many new ones saved, almost sort of unwittingly, someone said, "Don't you think they ought to be taught?" The only thing they were getting was prayer; and even though they were growing marvellously in prayer, there was no actual teaching. So we brought back the Thursday Bible study.

Then we had Sunday and Thursday meetings, and every other night was prayer. By then, some people thought we were crazy. They had always thought we were crazy outside the company, but even people inside the company began to think we were taking this prayer thing too far. I remember people coming to me and saying: "I think all this prayer is ridiculous; it is destroying everybody. People are absolutely worn-out. Where are we getting? We are getting nowhere." But we had a burden in our heart that something had to be done, that something had to go through. We could not let it go, and we were very conscious of it ourselves: "Are we flogging a dead horse? Here we are day in and day out, saying the same thing, taking hold of the Lord, and yet we cannot get away from it."

A WORD COMES FROM THE LORD

I remember so well that Wednesday of the third year. It was the fewest we had ever been—maybe about fifteen in all—in the prayer meeting. None of the responsible folks were there. But that Wednesday was incredible. Oh, it was an oppressive time! Now this may encourage you because, so often, we feel that when there is oppression there is something wrong, when in actual fact there may be something very right. When there is a deep oppression that comes upon a company, you may be right on the brink of very real blessing.

That night, I remember that we were deeply depressed, and I was thinking to myself: "I really think that we are flogging a dead horse. I am going to talk to the brothers as to whether we should really let this whole thing go. It is really silly, just fifteen of us." Suddenly, it was as if all of us looked into Heaven—and that is the only way to describe it. As we were looking into Heaven, the time became hilarious. We laughed. It had been such a heavy dose; then we were laughing and, sort of, almost stupid. All of a sudden, a word came from the Lord: "Within a year, the walls will come down." And it was confirmed in other ways.

THE SPIRIT WAS POURED OUT

Of course, people thought we were praying for the local. However, we were not praying only for the local; we were praying for the whole country. And the most interesting thing was that a while later we heard that down in Cornwall, the Spirit of God had been poured out on a group there. That was the beginnings in our country of what has been called the *Charismatics*. Then we heard reports of all these people speaking in tongues, and we were very suspicious of it. Everyone thought: "That is not what we were praying for." But I do remember, and I thought it was so wonderful, that when we were praying, a brother said, "Lord, we do not care what You do; we are even prepared to speak in tongues. Lord, if You could only do something with Your people everywhere."

I remember that quite clearly. But the incredible thing is that whatever our feeling was at the time, the walls came down; and by the grace of God, they have never been put up again. Until that date, we were an ostracised company. From that date onward, our ministry as a company extended to the ends of this country and, in many ways, all over the world, because God had started to do something which was irreversible. Whatever people may say about the Charismatics, it has brought innumerable thousands into a new experience of the Lord. People who were dead, dry, old bones, whom you could not have fellowship with, not for all the tea in China, suddenly, you would meet them and you could have fellowship with them. They were hungry for fellowship. They wanted fellowship; and they began to talk about being in the body of Christ. I remember one famous evangelist's wife saying to a mutual friend: "I cannot understand Lance. All this talk about the body is so niggardly. When we are in heaven and see our Lord Jesus, it will all seem so silly and small." But then we found people everywhere talking about the body, about being in the body of Christ.

In those days, if you met in a house or in a home, you were considered to be absolutely below par. There was something very, very suspicious about you. From then on, we began to discover all over the country—in farmhouses, in homes, in cottages, in big beautiful houses—people were meeting in drawing rooms and lounges to worship the Lord, to study the Word, to seek God in prayer. I am not saying there are not great weaknesses and excesses and failings, and so on, but the fact of the matter is that God was doing something which was irreversible.

I do not want any of you ever to forget that it was four years of prayer. The last year we spent every evening praising the Lord. I am not saying that it was hard to praise the Lord, but we praised the Lord that the walls were down, and it seemed so stupid. But the Lord said it, and so we said, "We are going to praise Him; we will not pray anymore. We have spent three years in prayer, now we will praise the Lord."

THE HIDDEN MINISTRY

We must be very careful that we do not lose what God has given us in this matter. Intercession is the most hidden of all ministries. By its very nature, the laying down of a life is not a thing that is trumpeted; it is within a person's being or a company's being. For the most part, it is hidden.

There are few who are prepared to enter such a ministry of intercession. I believe that with all of our failings in this part of God's family, He has taught us something about intercession which has been, if I may so say it, incredibly precious to the Lord. I believe, also, that it is something which the Devil hates, and he will work unceasingly, as we grow larger and become more popular and more in demand, to take away and to undermine such a ministry. We need to hear the cry of God: "I sought for a man to stand in the gap and to build the wall, but I found none. Therefore, have I poured out my indignation upon the land."

For this kind of intercession, which is born of the Holy Spirit, there is no alternative to being a living sacrifice. There is no other possibility. The challenge comes to us all

Other Books Printed By

Christian Testimony Ministry

278

42353810R00158

Made in the USA
Lexington, KY
17 June 2015